Ralf Buckley

Perspectives in Environmental Management

Springer-Verlag
Berlin Heidelberg New York
London Paris Tokyo
Hong Kong Barcelona
Budapest

Professor RALF BUCKLEY
Griffith University Gold Coast
Queensland 4215
Australia

ISBN 3-540-53815-1 Springer-Verlag Berlin Heidelberg New York
ISBN 0-387-53815-1 Springer-Verlag New York Berlin Heidelberg

Library of Congress Cataloging-in-Publication Data. Buckley, Ralf. Perspectives in environment management / Ralf Buckley. p. cm. Essays originally published between 1988 and 1990. Includes index. ISBN 3-540-53815-1. -- ISBN 0-387-53815-1 (U.S.) 1. Environmental protection. 2. Environmental auditing. 3. Liability for environmental damages. I. Title. TD170.B83   1991   363.7--dc20   91-17891

© Springer-Verlag Berlin Heidelberg 1991
Printed in Germany

Typesetting (media conversion): Elsner & Behrens GmbH, Oftersheim
Printing and binding: Konrad Triltsch, Graphischer Betrieb, Würzburg
32/3145-543210 – Printed on acid-free paper

Preface

This book is a collection of papers and presentations on various aspects of environmental planning and management. They were all written in 1989 and 1990, except for the first which was initially published in 1988 and provides a setting and direction for the rest. They are international in scope and application; and if some have a slightly Australian flavour, I hope this may complement the American and European emphasis of other recent texts in this field.

RALF BUCKLEY

Contents

List of Acronyms Used in the Text

ADB	Asian Development Bank
AIB	Australian Institute of Biology
ALARA	as low as reasonably achievable (principle used in environmental licencing)
ATIA	Australian Tourism Industry Association
BACT	best available control technology (used in environmental licencing)
BHP	Broken Hill Proprietary Ltd. (a large steel company)
BOD	biological oxygen demand
BPT	best practicable technology (a less stringent stipulation than BACT)
CEO	chief executive officer
CGL	comprehensive, or commercial, general liability (insurance policy type)
CVM	contingent valuation method (used in environmental accounting)
DEIS	draft environmental impact statement
DWN	developed western nations
EBCA	environmental benefit-cost analysis
ec	electrical conductivity
EC	environmental costs
EEIS	economic and environmental impact statement
EIA	environmental impact assessment (a process)
EIL	environmental impairment liability (insurance policy type)
EIOA	environmental input-output analysis (economic modelling technique)
EIS	environmental impact statement (formal document produced by EIA)
EPM	environmental planning and management
ES	environmental sensitivity
ESM	environmental sensitivity mapping

FOB	free on board (referring to valuation of export cargo or freight)
FOI	freedom of information
FRED	flexible regional environmental database
FRG	Federal Republic of Germany
GDP	gross domestic product
GIS	geographic information system
GNP	gross national product
HDS	humungous development syndrome
IAC	Industries Assistance Commission
IEPM	integrated environmental planning and management
LDC	less developed country
LWRA	land and water resources allocation
M&A	merger and acquisition
MLA	multilateral lending agency
NGO	non-governmental organisation
NOI	notice of intent
NPWS	National Parks and Wildlife Service
N-S	north-south
OHS	occupational
ORV	off-road vehicle
PACD	Plan of Action to Combat Desertification (by UNEP, q.v.)
PEA	preliminary environmental assessment
PER	public environmental report
PL	product liability (insurance policy type)
ppb	parts per billion
ppm	parts per million
RA	resource accounting
R&D	research and development
REP	regional environmental plan
REPM	regional environmental planning and management
RP	retention pond
SNA	System of National Accounts (used for calculating GNP)
SPCC	State Pollution Control Commission
TCM	total catchment management
tds	total dissolved salts, total dissolved solids (water quality parameter)

UNEP   United Nations Environment Programme
UNESCAP United Nations Economic and Social
         Commission for Asia and the Pacific
USCEQ   United States Council on Environmental Quality
USEPA   United States Environment Protection Agency
VOC   volatile organic carbon
WTAC   willingness to accept compensation
         (measure of value used in CVM, q.v.)
WTP   willingness to pay
         (measure of value used in CVM, q.v.)
4WD   four-wheel drive vehicle

Abbreviations for units used in text and tables. [...] concentration of ... (used for air and water quality parameters, e.g.); a year; Bq becquerel (unit of radioactivity); °C degree Centigrade; d day; dBA decibel A (unit of noise intensity); g gramme; GJ gigajoule (unit of energy); GW gigawatt (unit of power, e.g. electricity output); ha hectare; J joule; km kilometre; l litre; M mega-, i.e. $10^6 \times$ (e.g. 1 Ml is one million litres); m metre (m^3, cubic metre); mg milligramme, i.e. 10^{-3} gramme; mo month; s second; Sv sievert (unit of radioactive exposure); W watt.

Symbols for chemical elements and compounds used in text and tables. Ca calcium; Cd cadmium; Cl chlorine; CO_2 carbon dioxide; Cu copper; F fluorine; F^- fluoride; Mn manganese; NO_x oxides of nitrogen; O_2 molecular oxygen (as normally present in the atmosphere); Ra radium; Ra^{226} radium-226, an isotope of radium; Rn radon; Pb lead; S sulphur; SO_2 sulphur dioxide; SO_4, SO_4^{2-} sulphate; Si silicon; U uranium; U^{234} uranium-234, an isotope of uranium; U^{238} uranium-238, another isotope of uranium; Zn zinc

Chapter 1

Critical Problems

This paper, written in 1987 and first published in 1988; sets out some of the major problems which are addressed in subsequent chapters. Since then, progress has been made on all four of the main research fronts considered here: but all four are still critical, and most of this paper is still equally valid today.

Abstract

Improvement in environmental planning and management (EPM) requires increased integration in four respects: spatial, temporal, economic and administrative. These respects are not independent; and to be effective, integration must improve in all four simultaneously.

To illustrate this, four critical research fronts are examined: conceptual approaches and technical tools for land and water resources allocation (LWRA) in regional EPM; environmental audit and operational feedback; ecological-economic exchange rates, and discount rates, in environmental benefit-cost analysis (EBCA); and EPM in development aid.

Specific problems which are identified as worthy of (and in some cases already receiving) immediate research effort include: non-parametric LWRA procedures; "active" geographic information systems (GIS's) incorporating LWRA criteria; systematic multi-project environmental audit; modifications to EPM legislation to increase public accountability of development and regulatory agencies; estimation of option costs for land degradation and species extinction; rational and unambiguous determination of discount rates in EBCA; and determination of the economic costs and benefits of EPM in development aid.

> Improved EPM techniques, however, are rarely adopted without substantial electoral pressure, and this is contingent on public environmental awareness. One potential key for rapid improvement in such awareness is through "grey power": environmental education of senior citizens.

Introduction: Research Fronts

The aim of this assessment is to identify problems and research directions in environmental planning and management (EPM) which are current, critical, and basic: problems, that is, which are of immediate practical application; which represent bottlenecks to improved EPM; and which are relevant to a wide range of specific EPM issues and projects.

The present framework for EPM is largely compartmentalised into three separate areas of legislation, regulation and associated techniques. These are: land and water resources planning (LWRP); pollution control (PC); and single-project environmental impact assessment (EIA). Whilst this framework and its associated EPM techniques have done yeoman service during the past two decades, they are proving inadequate to deal with present-day problems and needs.

An improved EPM framework requires increased spatial, temporal, economic, and administrative integration of EPM techniques and procedures. To be effective, integration must take place in all four respects simultaneously. Spatial integration, for example, requires improvement in regional EPM (REPM) techniques: and several of the major REPM techniques have an economic basis, such as environmental benefit-cost analysis (EBCA), environmental input-output analysis (EIOA), and energy-economy-environment modelling (EEEM). Temporal integration requires better mechanisms for scoping, public participation, monitoring, audit and operational feedback: and these will only occur if the administrative framework for EIA is modified so that developers, regulatory authorities and the public treat major-project EPM as an ongoing process, rather than a once-off "EIS hurdle" followed by a relatively formalised and ineffective monitoring programme. Perhaps most importantly, EPM decisions are not simply the rational outcome of technical planning evaluations, but form part of a political process. Unquantifiable values, if they affect voting patterns, are as relevant as values which can be expressed in parametric terms such as currency units. In addition, in any decision made as part of a political process in a western democracy, the values held by swinging voters in marginal electorates will be given disproportionate weight.

It is also apparent that EPM processes cover a range of scales in all four of these respects, and that some techniques are more valuable in particular scale ranges. In general, technical information is likely to be most useful if geared to the same scale as used for making decisions. One of the major shortcomings of single-project EIA, for example, is that it can tend to preempt land-use and water-resources planning at a regional scale. Again, the net benefit of a particular development project at a regional scale, with or without including environmental costs and benefits, may not correspond to its net benefit at a national or local scale.

The specific problems examined here are as follows. In improving spatial integration, the key component is the allocation of land and water resources between competing uses (LWRA). The inadequacy of present LWRA procedures is at the heart of many major environmental controversies. Improved conceptual and technical tools for LWRA are therefore needed urgently. At a conceptual level, the main prospects for improving LWRA are regional-scale EBCA, and non-parametric ranking systems. At a technical level, the most promising tools are flexible regional environmental databases (FRED's) or geographic information systems (GIS's).

As regards integration in time (IEPM), the weakest link at present is the feedback link: monitoring actual impacts, comparing them to predicted impacts, and modifying operations as required to reduce impacts which prove to be more adverse than predicted. The most critical research front here is environmental impact audit, the systematic checking of actual against predicted impacts. Increased public account-ability is also required to strengthen the feedback link.

In improving the economic integration of EPM, the most fundamental problem is the determination of appropriate exchange rates between ecological and economic values. Equally critical in most applications, and equally controversial, is the choice of discount rates.

On the administrative side there are many pressing problems, but the most urgent of all seems to be the improvement of EPM in development aid.

The identification of these specific problems is in no way intended to belittle the importance of other research fronts in EPM, of which there are many. Five such fronts may perhaps be singled out for particular mention[1]. The first is the improvement of basic EIA techniques and procedures (e.g. Beanlands and Duinker 1984; Shopley and Fuggle 1984; Duinker and Baskerville 1986; Duinker and Beanlands 1986; Hollick 1986; Ross 1987; Wright and Greene 1987). The second is the development of multiple and sequential land use strategies and multi-objective planning techniques (e.g. Buckley 1985; Burton 1985; Butler 1985). The third is the entire field of environmental economics, particularly at a regional scale, and including EIOA and EEEM (e.g. James 1983; Lonergan and Cocklin 1985; Solomon 1985; Braat and van Lierop 1986; Camara et al. 1986; James and Chambers 1986; Leontief 1986; Brouwer and Nijkamp 1987; Costanza and Daly 1987; Goodland and Ledec 1987; van der Ploeg et al. 1987). The fourth is the incorporation of risk and probability aspects in EPM, and in EBCA in particular (e.g. Danby 1985; Miller 1985; Russell and Gruber 1987; Suter et al. 1987); and the fifth is the application of mediation and conflict resolution techniques in EPM (e.g. Richey et al. 1985; Davos 1986; Miller and Cuff 1986; Bowonder 1987).

Integration in Space: Land and Water Resources Allocation

One ever-present problem in any form of REPM is the allocation of scarce land and water resources to competing uses. This is not a new problem, but it is becoming increasingly critical as demand increases and supply diminishes. It is a problem with a strong historical component or "memory": existing land and water users generally have very strong claims to continued use, either through legislation or political lobbying power, and they are naturally reluctant to cede their individual rights in the common interest. The history of land and water resources allocation in most western nations may perhaps be divided into four main phases, as follows. The first was a "squatter" or "scramble" phase, when firstcomers used resources largely at their own discretion, with very little central control. Evidently this phase took place very much earlier in Europe than in the USA or Australia, and the types of land and water use, and associated management practices, differed substantially in consequence. The second phase occurred when the activities of different users began to impinge upon each other, leading to the introduction of planning

---

[1] To these five I would now (in 1990) add EPM in tourism, and in particular the potential of green tourism as a conservation tool.

controls, water quality legislation, and so on: but still with a strong presumption of individual resource rights.

In the third phase, particular resources became so severely degraded, as a result of poor or misguided management practices, that land and water uses were forced to change, irrespective of individual rights or social controls. Salinisation of irrigated agricultural land is a case in point. The first phase also involved major modification to resources, such as clearance of timbered land for agriculture, but at that period the changes were perceived as improvements which increased the value of the resource. Changes occurring in the third phase are perceived as degradation which reduces the value of the resource. In some areas, irreversible resource degradation, the third "phase", occurred before resource competition and partitioning, the second.

Finally, in the fourth phase, the loss of resources during the third has led to public perception that land and water allocation and management should not be left to the individual or to an unregulated market mechanism if this jeopardises national assets[2]. This has led to calls for a more integrated planning approach, based on "total catchment management" (TCM) and similar strategies[3].

Hence, it appears that the social climate is now amenable to procedures for land and water resource allocation (LWRA) in which resource capability and suitability are given greater weight, relative to historical patterns of occupation, tenure, and use, than has occurred previously. This does not solve the basic problem of how best to allocate land and water resources to competing uses, but it provides a milieu in which techniques for improving LWRA are likely to receive a constructive hearing. Such techniques, however, must still operate within the constraints of past and present uses.

Depending on the spatial and temporal scales considered, some land and water uses can occur contemporaneously or sequentially: others cannot. Multiple and sequential land-use strategies have a major role to play in the sustainable use and conservation of resources, but decisions on the allocation of land and water resources must still be made at any given point in space and time. What information is available to guide such decisions?

---

[2] Note that regulated market mechanisms, however, may provide efficient means for allocating scarce land and water resources with minimal wastage or excess consumption.

[3] Some governments have now passed legislation adopting a TCM approach.

Procedures for allocating land and water resources on the basis of capability and suitability rather than historical rights or present-day politics may be divided into two main categories. One category involves some form of benefit-cost assessment, either with explicit conversion to a single parameter such as a financial unit, or with some implicit trade-off function between different types of value. The other involves entirely non-parametric methods, typically intended to produce or approach some predetermined mix of land and water uses within a given area. The developed western nations tend to rely principally on procedures in the first category. Less developed nations, and in particular those with strongly centralised political economies and limited individual rights, have in some cases attempted to use procedures in the second category.

Non-Parametric Approaches

If some form of benefit-cost analysis is used, the critical problems of LWRA simply become the critical problems of EBCA, which are considered later. Setting these aside for the moment, what are the prospects for non-parametric approaches? The basic idea here is that all the land in a given region should be divided into small homogeneous parcels, so that each parcel is subjected to only a single use at any given time. Evidently, the definition of parcels and uses will depend upon the scale considered: at a large scale, for example, mixed agriculture or mixed-management forestry would be considered as single uses. All the parcels within the region would then be ranked, independently, on the basis of their value and suitability for each possible land use considered, including conservation. This requires techniques for comparison within land uses or economic sectors, but not between them. A measure of suitability must consider both positive aspects such as productive potential under the land use considered, and negative aspects such as sensitivity to disturbances associated with that use (Buckley 1982, 1985).

The next requirement is a ranking of land uses. That is to say, that a particular land use is determined to take priority over others until a given predetermined proportion of the total land has been allocated to that use. Land is then allocated to these land uses in decreasing order of priority; for any given land use, those parcels which have the highest rankings for that use, and which have not already been allocated to a higher-priority use, are selected in decreasing rank order for the use under consideration, until the allotted proportion of land has been assigned to that use.

It is apparent that even if all the necessary information were available to rank parcels according to each potential use, and even if there were no prior-use constraints, such procedures would contain ample grounds for contention in determining the relative priorities of different uses, and the preferred overall mix. Lack of information is a major bone of contention in choosing between mining and conservation, for example: since without exploration the capability of the area for mineral production remains unknown, yet the exploration required to provide that information can seriously reduce the capability of the land for conservation. In addition, the introduction of a new type of land use into an established pattern, as perhaps occasioned by a new farming or mining technique, would create major difficulties.

Despite these problems, this kind of approach does already have a place in western political and social systems, since arguments of this nature are used as a basis or justification for political lobbying and decision-making. It is therefore valuable to try to improve such approaches to a workable technical tool. The critical difficulty, apart from information gaps and prior-use constraints, is that there is no general agreement on preferred land-use mixes or the relative priorities of different land uses: and without these, there will generally not be an unambiguous algorithm for allocating parcels of land to one use or another. Typically, parcels which are of high ranking for one use, such as forestry or arable farming, are also of high ranking for other uses, such as conservation or urban development respectively.

It is here that the prior-use constraints and other practicalities reduce the problem. In practice, the "global" problem, i.e. optimal allocation of land parcels to different uses for an entire region at a single point in time, almost never arises in the developed western nations, because of prior development. Real problems are generally "local" in a conceptual sense, even if not in a geographical one: to choose between a limited number of competing uses for a small number of the land parcels in a given region. In such cases one possible approach would be to compare the existing proportions of land currently allocated to each of the competing uses within that region, with aggregate public perceptions of preferred proportions. Even here it will rarely be necessary to quantify the preferred mix as a whole, but merely to determine whether given land uses are perceived as being over- or under-represented, and to what relative degree.

The problem hence becomes one of defining spatial boundaries for the area to be considered (e.g. local council area, state, nation, or the entire world?); demographic boundaries for the population whose preferences should be taken into account (e.g. only those living in the area concerned, or also those outside it?); and temporal and administrative boundaries for the decision, such as how long it should hold, and to what degree it is reversible. The temporal boundaries are important since public perceptions and values change with time, often substantially. These are questions of political and social choice rather than EPM in the more limited sense, indicating the degree to which EPM is embedded in social and political systems and requires increased administrative integration.

The above considerations suggest that non-parametric approaches in LRWA may well be valuable, at least as an adjunct to EBCA approaches. In particular, they can provide a framework for integrating social preferences such as land-use priorities into LWRA decisions: a framework which forces such preferences to be made explicit and hence subject to rational debate. Such non-parametric approaches are hence well worth further development.

GIS's as Tools in REPM

Irrespective of the LWRA procedure adopted in REPM, it will require spatially organised data: on land and water resources and capability; on existing land and water uses, tenure and rights; and on other anthropogenic modifications such as development infrastructure. It also requires information on directions and rates of change in these patterns. This information needs to be rapidly and readily accessible for use in actual decisions, and it needs to be stored in a form which can be updated promptly as the data change or new information becomes available. If possible, it should also be in a form suitable for modelling the effects of possible LWRA decisions. Such flexible regional environmental databases (FRED's), or geographic information systems (GIS's), are becoming increasingly important technical tools in REPM worldwide; and their continued development is hence a critical direction for research in EPM techniques.

GIS's are currently in use or under development by a number of organisations involved in environmental planning and management worldwide. Within these and associated organisations the debate at present is not so much in regard to whether or how GIS's should be used, but what computer system should be used to support them and to what extent they should be made available to users outside the organisation which owns them. Hence, it is likely that the use of GIS's will become far more widespread in the next few years.

One particularly interesting avenue which does not seem to have been much explored to date is the possibility of including LWRA decision criteria within a FRED or GIS, to produce a regional land- and water-use allocation pattern based on specific and explicit criteria. Evidently this would still be subject to human review, but it would have the advantage that the consequences of different LWRA criteria could be explored rapidly, and their implications compared. Criteria based on land and water capability, prior use, and proximity rules could be compared with those based on an expert systems approach, for example (cf. Walsh 1985; Davis and Nanninga 1985). Such "active" GIS's, to coin a phrase, would seem to be an especially promising direction for research at present.[4]

Integration in Time: Environmental Audit and Operational Feedback

Current EPM techniques suffer from lack of integration in time as well as space. In particular, the value and effectiveness of single-project EIA have been severely limited in many past projects by the perception that it is merely one step in obtaining planning approval or development consent: the "EIS hurdle" approach (Buckley 1986). This perception is changing, as regulatory authorities are gradually insisting on greater involvement throughout the operating life of major projects. The goal is "integrated environmental planning and management" (IEPM), implying full consideration of environmental aspects in every decision from initial project concept to final completion of rehabilitation. As yet, however, IEPM remains more of a catchphrase than a reality.

Perhaps the most critical deficiency at present is the lack or ineffectiveness of feedback links in the EPM process. Typically, EIS's predict a range of impacts with various degrees of probability and physical significance, and prescribe monitoring programmes to determine whether these predictions are in fact fulfilled. Rarely, however, do EIS's prescribe what is to be done if their predictions are not fulfilled. In fact, it is rare even for the results of monitoring programmes to be checked back against the original impact predictions in any systematic way. Such systematic checking is termed an audit of environmental impact predictions (see Chap 6).

---

[4] Since 1988, this approach has indeed attracted further research effort.

Environmental impact predictions will always contain a degree of uncertainty. This does not necessarily mean that projects with uncertain impacts should not proceed; but rather that effective feedback links should be set up so that (1) actual impacts are monitored with an appropriate degree of precision and reliability; (2) monitoring results are regularly compared with impact predictions; (3) if actual impacts are more severe than predicted, immediate management action is taken to reduce them to the predicted level; and (4) automatic penalties are prescribed, before the project starts, to ensure that such management actions actually are taken if necessary.

Public accountability is required throughout this process, which means that all stages in the feedback link must be subject to public scrutiny. In the EIS hurdle system currently used by most western nations, there is only a single opportunity for formal public review of a development, namely the period for public submissions on the Draft EIS or equivalent document. There is no formal mechanism for members of the public to object if their submissions are not adequately addressed in a supplementary or final EIS or in formal assessments of the EIS by regulatory bodies.

Perhaps even more importantly, there is usually no formal mechanism for the public to determine whether environmental protection commitments made by a developer or government in an EIS or associated documents are in fact followed. There is little or no opportunity for public participation in the design of monitoring programmes: and many monitoring programmes are so poorly designed that they simply cannot yield the information required to test impact predictions in a scientifically and statistically competent manner. There is no mechanism for the results of monitoring programmes to be subjected to formal public review. In theory such results are scrutinised by regulatory agencies, but this is not always done and there is no formal mechanism for the public to ensure that it is done competently and without negligence. In addition, environmental regulatory agencies have generally had very little power to bring about changes in operational or management practices, if monitoring programmes show that impacts are more severe than predicted. Public backing might well enhance their capability.

Overall, therefore, audit and operational feedback links exist in theory but are extremely weak in practice: and they seem unlikely to improve until there is (1) a formal mechanism for public scrutiny of the design of, and results from, monitoring programmes, and of operational changes made in response to those results; and (2) legal public accountability of developers, land and water users, and their regulatory authorities.

In many countries and jurisdictions, for example, there is no legal avenue for concerned third parties to compel individuals, corporations or government agencies to comply with environmental legislation, including pollution control regulations or the provisions of an EIS, unless they can claim to be materially disadvantaged by the infringement, and so gain legal standing. Nor is there any legal provision for members of the public to take regulatory agencies to task for negligence in enforcing environmental protection statutes or commitments.[5]

This contrasts with countries such as Papua New Guinea, for example, whose Water Resources Act contains provisions for third-party scrutiny and redress, and prescribes substantial penalties for directors and staff of companies convicted of infringements, and for government agencies and personnel shown to be negligent in enforcement[6].

What steps are being taken to alleviate these failings? Some governments have now made statutory provision for an extended process of public involvement in the preparation of an EIS and for an extended process of government involvement in environmental protection during the operation of a project. Provisions for effective audit, enforcement, and operational feedback, however, are still scant and inadequate. In other states and jurisdictions, and notably in the USA, there is much broader standing for legal challenge by interested third parties.

Audits of Environmental Impact Predictions

The need for more effective audit of environmental impact predictions was recognised in the 1980's in the UK, Australia, New Zealand, Canada and the USA (Tomlinson and Bisset 1983; Bisset 1985; New Zealand Commission for the Environment 1985; Canter and Fairchild 1986; Carley 1986; Orians 1986; Buckley 1987; Cullhane 1987; McCallum 1987; Tomlinson and Atkinson 1987a, b). As yet, however, there appears to be no administrative framework to support routine audits in any of these countries; nor is there any mechanism for public involvement in or scrutiny of such audits. Concern over the lack of effective audit has grown so great in Europe that an independent audit commission was set up

---

[5] This situation has improved slightly since 1988 in some countries, but the concerns listed in these paragraphs still apply in 1990.
[6] Legislation adopted in late 1989 by two of the Australian State Governments has extended liability for breaches of pollution control regulations to corporate directors and management. Similar legislation exists in North America.

Table 1. Potential products from auditing environmental impact predictions

1. A classification of types of development impact according to the tractability, reliability, precision and cost-effectiveness with which they can be predicted.
2. Criteria for determining the apportionment of time and cost effort between the prediction of different types of impact.
3. A set of precision criteria for different types of impact, defining just how precise a prediction is required for impacts of different types, and how much latitude should be permitted in matching performance to prediction.
4. Guidelines for the design of monitoring programmes for impacts of different types, covering: sampling design, layout and frequency, and measurement precision and replication, required to optimise statistical significance, reliability, management utility and cost-effectiveness.
5. Guidelines for the integration of monitoring programmes into management structures so as to maximise the efficiency of feedback from monitoring results to management practices and action.
6. Specifications or guidelines for the modification of monitoring programmes and reporting procedures required when the concept, design, process, technology or operation of a development project is changed.
7. Criteria for assessing the efficacy of safeguards and the appropriateness of standards for different types of impact: where impacts cannot be predicted precisely, design impacts must be reduced to allow a margin of uncertainty between design impact and standard; and where impacts cannot be measured precisely, standards must be conservative to allow for uncertainty in determination.
8. Reasons for inadequate impact prediction and poor design, execution and management use of monitoring programmes in the past, in various industry sectors; critical aspects of relevant institutional structures; and possible improvements.

3 years ago under the auspices of the Government of the Netherlands (Anonymous 1987). Its function, however, is to assess the adequacy of EIS's prepared for development projects in less-developed countries, rather than to examine the accuracy of impact prediction and the effectiveness of monitoring and operational feedback.

Besides its relevance to improving operations at individual projects, systematic audits of environmental impact predictions and associated monitoring results, for a large number of past EIS's, could have several other valuable functions (Table 1). They could provide empirical measures of the levels of confidence that can be assigned to impact predictions for various types of development and impact and for various components of the physical, biological and social environment. These measures of confidence would be of considerable value in assessing the likely accuracy of impact predictions in future EIS's or equivalents. They would also highlight consistent faults in the design of monitoring programmes, which could then receive greater attention in future.

There are a number of technical difficulties in carrying out such a systematic environmental audit, but they can all be overcome. The first step is to identify the set of EIS's under consideration, e.g. all EIS's produced in a particular country in a given time period. The second step is then to select those EIS's covering projects which were expected to produce major quantifiable impacts on specific components of the physical, biological or human environment. Most EIS's will probably fall in this category, but there are some which cover, e.g., building development in an already urbanised area and essentially predict no further significant impacts.

The third step is to select EIS's covering projects which went ahead substantially as planned, and which have been subjected to a routine monitoring programme. In theory this step should not eliminate any of the EIS's, since major modifications to project design should have been reflected in the production of a new or modified EIS, and since all projects whose EIS's predicted significant impacts should have been subjected to monitoring. In practice, however, this does not always occur and there are likely to be projects whose impacts are essentially unmonitored. One spin-off from large-scale systematic audits is to identify such projects at this step.

Having screened the projects and EIS's, the fourth step should then be to isolate actual predictions couched in scientifically testable terms, and to express those predictions in quantitative form, including a measure of error. This is far less straightforward (Duinker and Baskerville 1986; Duinker and Beanlands 1986). Most predictions in most EIS's are relatively vague, and couched in unquantified terms such as "likely", "unlikely", "significant", "negligible" and so on. This difficulty arose in pilot studies by Culhane (1987) and Henderson (1987), forcing them to classify impacts according to their approximate (verbal) level of uncertainty.

Once specific impact predictions have been isolated, the next step is to determine whether the monitoring programme for the projects concerned actually measured the parameters required to test these predictions; and if so, whether the sampling design (e.g. location, frequency and precision of measurements) was statistically adequate to perform such a test. Here again, many monitoring programmes are simply not adequate to test impact predictions in any rigorous manner; and one additional benefit of systematic audits is to show up any consistent flaws in the design of monitoring programmes.

If a large number of well-designed EIS's and monitoring programmes are considered simultaneously, yielding large numbers of rigorously testable predictions, then some form of stratification (e.g. by industry sector or ecosystem component) or data reduction may be necessary at this step. In many cases, project design is modified slightly between preparation of the EIS and project start-up, and again during operations. Impact predictions may need to be adjusted to take account of such modifications; any such adjustments should be made before testing the adjusted predictions against monitoring results.

The final step is then to compare impact predictions and monitoring results, to determine the degree of accuracy with which each prediction was met; and to search for patterns in the accuracy or otherwise of predictions, in relation to, e.g., recentness, geographic location, project type or industry sector, environmental parameters concerned, and so on.

Tomlinson and Atkinson (1987a) proposed a system of terminology for seven different types or points of audit in the standard EIA process: (1) DEIS; (2) decision-point; (3) implementation; (4) performance; (5) predictive-techniques; (6) project-impact; and (7) EIA-procedure audits respectively. Types 1 and 2 cover the assessment of DEIS and EIS by regulatory bodies. Types 3 and 4 cover areas of public accountability mentioned earlier. The type of audit discussed here combines the final three types (5–7), starting with an audit of project impacts audit and using the results to audit predictive techniques and to a lesser extent EIA procedures.

A number of small-scale or pilot-level project-impact audits have been undertaken in recent years, and most of these were reviewed by Tomlinson and Atkinson (1987b). The earliest were concerned only with single projects. These were followed by a pilot study in the UK (Tomlinson and Bisset 1983; Bisset 1985) which examined 791 impact predictions from 4 projects, but found that only 77 of these could be audited. Of these, 57 were rated as "probably accurate". More recently Henderson (1987) examined 122 predictions from two projects in Canada. Of these, 42 could not be audited because of lack of monitoring data, and 10 either because they were too vague or because of modifications to the project. Of the 70 predictions audited, 54 were substantially correct, 13 partly correct or uncertain, and 3 were definitely wrong.

A much broader audit has now been carried out in the USA by Culhane (1987), who examined 239 impact predictions from 29 EIS's, intended to form a "representative cross-section" of EIS's prepared in the USA between 1974 and 1978. The projects were concerned principally with agriculture, forestry, infrastructure, waste management and uranium processing: none were mining projects, for example. Culhane found that most of the impact predictions in these EIS's were very imprecise, with less than 25% being quantified. Few predictions were clearly wrong, but less than 30% were "unqualifiedly close to forecasts".

These studies demonstrated the directions required, and some of the practical difficulties involved, but were all of a pilot nature. Audits which are both more extensive and intensive are urgently required[7].

Economic Integration

Ecological/Economic Exchange Rates

Environmental benefit-cost analysis is a rapidly growing field, and one which promises to play an increasingly important role in EPM at all scales. The general principles of EBCA have been expounded by a number of authors, including Sinden and Worrell (1979), Hufschmidt et al. (1983), Kneese and Sweeney (1985), Leonard (1985), Nijkamp et al. (1985), Dixon and Hufschmidt (1986), and Krutilla and Fisher (1986), and need not be reiterated here. Common to all approaches, however, is the difficulty of measuring ecological values in economic units, or of converting ecological values into economic ones. This may be seen as a problem of determining an appropriate "exchange rate" between ecological and economic values.

Whilst economic values can be measured by the outcome of individual market transactions, the values of ecosystem components generally derive from a diverse range of attributes and functions. As the number and complexity of the links between natural systems and human well-being have come to be better appreciated during recent decades, the values assigned to ecosystem components have steadily increased; and at the same time, techniques for measuring these values have become more complete and inclusive. Reviewing the progress of EBCA over the past decade, say, it is clear that the net effect has been a gradual increase in the effective "exchange rate" used to compare ecological and economic values in EBCA.

Whereas early attempts at EBCA might have compared annual revenue from timber or mineral production in a wilderness area, say, with annual revenue from wilderness recreation, a modern analysis would (or

---

[7] One attempt, the first national audit of environmental impact predictions for Australia, is described in Chapter 6.

should, at least!) include additional surrogate or shadow values for recreation (e.g. travel costs, land price differentials on nearby areas, equivalent value of income forgone in recreation, and so on); measures of existence, option and bequest values, stratified by distance, for the country's entire population, including separate measures for any rare or endangered species as well as the overall wilderness value; measures for additional benefits provided by protection against hazards such as flooding, soil erosion, etc, estimated as direct and indirect damage costs avoided (see, e.g., Clark 1985); and measures of net benefit provided by resources such as water which are derived from the area but are delivered to consumers by a non-market system.

Whilst EBCA techniques have been in use for many years in some areas of planning, notably in water resources planning in the USA, many planning agencies have avoided it on the grounds that it is not yet sufficiently well developed to be a useful planning tool. This was the view of the environmental agency of the Australian Commonwealth Government in 1985; for example (Kent 1985).[8] It is also notable that a review of past EBCA analyses for US water resources projects (Lynn 1984) concluded that most of them had not been carried out correctly. According to Lynn, only one quarter of the dams built by the US Corps of Engineers were justifiable on purely economic grounds, and only one eighth were justifiable if environmental costs and benefits were also considered.

One reason why EBCA has not been generally adopted in environmental planning is perhaps because it has simply seemed to emphasise a conflict of values, between individuals who espouse short-term economic gain and rapid economic growth, and those who believe in the precedence of non-economic values and sustainable or steady-state economies. It is certainly true that there is a major class of values which derive from inner convictions of a religious or related nature; are therefore held as absolute beliefs; and so cannot be expressed in economic or other parametric terms. Through the political process in western democracies, such values are just as significant in environmental planning decisions as are those which are convertible to economic units. There has been a tendency in the past, however, to confuse two distinct classes of values under vague general headings such as "non-utilitarian values" (Wathern et al. 1986). One of these classes is the intrinsically unquantifiable religious values mentioned above: values which to those who hold them are immutable,

---

[8] However, this view has changed in 1990.

non-negotiable and essentially "priceless". Individuals who hold values of this type hold them in the belief that they are set "externally" by a God who is entirely superior to all human knowledge and endeavour. Such values are therefore not subject to human enquiry, quantification or modification. I suspect, however, that not many values fall into this category.

The other class consists of all values which are not based on religious beliefs. This includes values which are based on moral convictions, but which may still be modified if one moral conviction conflicts with another. Many people, for example, believe that mankind has moral responsibilities toward other species or toward future human generations; but also toward alleviating poverty and suffering in present generations. Where these conflict, they can be traded or compromised. This class also includes values which are based on the contribution of natural systems to human well-being, however poorly a particular contribution may be understood. Such contributions include recreation and aesthetic appreciation; maintenance of human health (e.g. clean air and water); contribution to future crop and livestock gene pools; potential future use in the production of pharmaceuticals, vaccines, pest control substances, and so on; and many more. Since all values in this class are "tradeable", they could all in theory be expressed in equivalent or interconvertible units. The difficulty here is technical rather than fundamental: available means for quantifying those values are as yet inadequate. Hence, past estimates of the "exchange rate" between ecological and economic values have been perceived as inappropriate: and it is this, rather than any fundamental conceptual flaw, which has prevented widespread use of EBCA.

The critical problem is hence how to quantify ecological values in a way which takes into account all their different components of value. The critical difficulty is not bias in methods for surveying the values held by individuals at any given place and time, though such bias can indeed be a substantial methodological problem (Loomis and Walsh 1986). Rather, it is lack of information on which individuals can assign meaningful values to ecosystem functions of which they know little or nothing. It has been argued that the average value quoted by a set of individuals for a particular item, such as the continued existence of an area of wilderness, actually is the value of that item: simply because values are a human construct, and there is no other way to determine them. Whilst it may be conceptually attractive, however, this approach does not reflect the common meaning of the term "value".

In many western countries, for example, a proportion of the population receives "free" medical care, paid for by the remainder of the population. If those individuals assign very low values to medical care, does that mean that medical care actually has a very low value? Most of us, I think, would say no: it just means that those individuals do not know what medical care is worth; they are simply ignorant. Again, if they are suddenly compelled to pay for medical care at private-sector prices, because the rest of the population can no longer afford to subsidise them, does that mean that the value of medical care has changed? No, it just means that they did not have to pay for it before, and now they do. The same applies to natural systems whose functions we barely understand, and for which, in the past, we have not had to pay.

Support for this view is gained from the observation that as human understanding of ecosystem processes, and their linkages with human well-being, has increased, so too has the value placed on natural systems by human beings. I should add here that so-called inclusive measures of ecological value, derived from willingness-to-pay (WTP) surveys, suffer from the same problems as attempts to measure ecosystem values directly: they are simply concealed within the process by which the individuals surveyed assign values to the items under discussion. The same applies to refinements of the basic WTP technique, such as willingness to accept compensation, willingness for tax funds to be spent, costless choice, and so on (Churchman 1984; Kellert 1984; Boyle et al. 1985; Loomis and Walsh 1986; Farber and Costanza 1986; Buckley 1987).

Human knowledge of ecosystem functions is still very limited. Despite this, much of what is known has not yet been applied in the estimation of environmental values. This, then, is the first critical task in improving EBCA: a systematic attempt to apply information from all ecological and related disciplines, to the more accurate estimation of ecological/economic exchange rates.

Particular Problems: Land Degradation and Species Extinction

Evidently this is a very large and imprecise problem, which needs to be broken down into specific smaller problems. One particularly urgent requirement is to quantify the option costs (1) of land degradation and (2) of species extinction. Most forms of primary production, including agriculture, pastoralism, forestry and mining, involve some degree of soil or substrate modification, vegetation clearance, and reduction or local extinction of animal populations. This limits or prevents the future use of that land for water catchments, tourism, wilderness recreation and conservation. These potential future uses would yield both economic and non-economic benefits, including direct revenue generation and a range of indirect benefits through the preservation of species and the maintenance of other other ecosystem components and functions.

In addition, demand for these uses is increasing and the supply of undisturbed land is diminishing, so the option costs of immediate land uses causing degradation are increasing. Because they have not been expressed in quantitative terms, such option costs all too often ignored in present-day EBCA and LWRA, biasing the outcome of such procedures. This is particularly relevant where proposed immediate uses for primary production have marginal or even negative real economic return (i.e. are being subsidised), as for example with vegetation clearance in marginal agricultural lands, timber logging in areas where industry royalties do not cover infrastructure costs, and so on. The quantification of option costs of land degradation is hence an urgent and critical problem in EPM.

Of equal concern are the option costs of species extinction. Most conservation values in common use are in some way related to the ultimate aim of preserving species (Buckley 1984, 1985; Diamond and May 1986; Ehrenfeld 1986). To quantify the benefits of preventing species extinction might seem an intractable problem, but has in fact already been approached with some success. The option cost of extinction of plant species, to the American pharmaceutical industry alone, for example, was estimated in 1983 at $US 200 million per species, or approximately US$ 350 million per species in today's dollars (at 8% inflation). This estimate was reached by dividing the average annual sales of plant-based pharmaceuticals by the ratio between the number of plant species used to produce those pharmaceuticals, and the total number of species tested for such use (Farnsworth and Soejarto 1985). Plant species have many other economic uses, however: food crops, textiles, pest control substances, and so on. Analogous calculations need to be performed for these and other uses. Such calculations will probably not be easy or precise, but they are within the scope of present knowledge.

In addition, plants provide food and habitat for animals, and animals provide a range of economically valuable products – also including food, textiles and pharmaceuticals. As well as estimating the option costs of animal species extinctions in their own right, therefore, we should also include a component derived from animal species values in our estimates of option costs for plant species extinction. This requires estimates of the expected number of animal species which would be rendered extinct by the extinction of a single plant species, and by combinations of several plant species. Is this beyond our present ability? Ecological studies of particular species have revealed an incredible complexity of interactions and interdependences. Evidently we do not have information or time enough to examine these dependences for each species in turn and determine the consequences of its extinction. We may, however, be in a position to make a rough estimate of first-order effects by estimating the proportion of animal species which are critically dependent on one or a few plant species.

It is not only the dependence of animals on plants which is relevant in estimating the option costs of species extinction. Animals, and to a lesser extent plants, are also dependent on each other. Many animal species of direct economic importance, for example, prey on other species which have no direct harvest value at present. These prey species, however, then have an economic value through their contribution to the predator species; and this value can be estimated quite precisely, if the dynamics of the predator-prey interaction are known (Ragozin and Brown 1985).

It is clear from the above that attempts to quantify the option costs of species extinction require major contributions from all branches of ecology, from the observations of the field naturalist to the mathematical models of the theoretical ecologist. This, perhaps more than any other specific problem, highlights the overall difficulty in measuring ecological values and ecological/economic exchange rates: our present inability to quantify the enormous diversity of contributions which components of natural systems make to human quality of life, both material and otherwise. As noted earlier, however, much of what is known has not been applied; and the estimation of option costs is one critical area where it could be applied.

Discount Rates in Environmental Benefit-Cost Analysis

Irrespective of the techniques used to value environmental costs and benefits, any EBCA analysis will fail if an inappropriate discount rate is used. Indeed, the choice of discount rate is perhaps the most vexed question in EBCA. The first point to be made here is that the current interest rate in the country concerned is not an appropriate discount rate for EBCA. The interest rate is simply a measure of the opportunity cost of money at that point in space and time. For comparisons between productive uses of indefinitely renewable resources, such as human labour, the real rate of interest, adjusted for inflation, may provide a meaningful discount rate. For goods or services which become progressively more valuable, however, it has been argued that a zero or negative discount rate should be applied.

Evidently, there has been substantial confusion between at least four separate factors: interest rate, currency inflation, barter exchange rates, and the premium on immediacy. As noted above, the current interest rate, i.e. the cost of borrowing money or the return on lending money, is relevant only when considering opportunity costs of using (or not using) money. It is therefore not an appropriate discount rate for EBCA, where money is not the resource considered, but simply a medium of exchange and measurement. Currency inflation produces increases in the assigned monetary values of resources, but this is due to a decrease in the value of money relative to all non-money resources, not an increase in the value of particular resources. The relative values of different non-monetary resources, which economists would call relative prices and I have referred to above as barter exchange rates, also change with time; but these changes, if predictable, should be taken into account before any discounting of future costs and benefits. This includes increases in the relative values of conservation-related resources owing to increasing demand and falling supply.

The only justification for discounting future benefits from environmental resources, and hence the only factor which should be incorporated in the discount rate, is what economists term the pure-time preference rate, and I have called the premium on immediacy: i.e. the value placed on receiving goods or services immediately rather than identical goods or services later. It is this final factor, the premium on immediacy, which should be used as a discount rate in EBCA; whereas in past applications it is all too often the first, the interest rate, which has been used.

Separating these four factors in this way identifies two critical problems. The first is technical: it is extremely difficult to determine the relative values of environmental goods and services at present, let alone in the future: as discussed in the previous section. The demand for environmental resources is expected to increase and the supply to decrease, but the same may be true for many economic resources.

The second is one of viewpoint. From a national, regional, community or policy viewpoint on resource allocation, the appropriate discount rate is determined by the premium on immediacy, the last of the four factors mentioned above. From the viewpoint of the individual or corporate investor, however, all four factors are relevant, and the largest – at present, the interest rate and inflation – will outweigh the others. EBCA analyses presented from a developer's viewpoint, however, should not be used as a basis for a decision on project approval by a government or community: their task is to determine whether the proposal yields a net benefit for the nation, region or community as a whole, and they should set the discount rate accordingly.

Administrative Integration: EPM in Development Aid

International aid is generally considered in two categories: relief aid and development aid. Relief aid is emergency supplies in the form of food, medicines, etc. Development aid includes the provision of equipment, infrastructure, and so on, intended to assist the recipient country in achieving self-sufficiency: or more accurately, to assist it in achieving a self-sufficient, "developed", multi-sector cash-based economy, rather than a localised subsistence one.

After a long history of ignoring environmental concerns, aid donor nations and multi-lateral lending agencies (MLA's) have recognised over the past few years that development aid without adequate environmental assessment, planning and management is likely to produce severe detrimental environmental impacts, particularly in air and water pollution but also in soil erosion and ecosystem degradation (McNamara 1985; Myers 1986). This then increases future requirements for emergency relief aid. To coin a slogan, environment is food not fad. This is particularly true in less-developed countries (LDC's) reliant on subsistence agriculture. The costs of environmental planning and management in development aid may be seen as an insurance premium: funds spent on EPM at an early stage insure against much greater expenditure on relief aid later on. Even though they may recognise that environmental degradation is occurring, individuals in recipient LDC's often have such a narrow margin of survival that they cannot afford to pay even a small insurance premium in the way of environmental protection costs. Donor nations and MLA's, however, can afford such a premium: and it is in their interests to pay it, since otherwise they incur much greater costs in relief aid a few years later.

As an example of the return from environmental protection, it has been estimated (Karrar and Stiles 1984; Tolba 1985) that whilst the total global cost of anti-desertification measures proposed under the United Nations Environment Programme (UNEP) Plan of Action to Combat Desertification (PACD) would be US$ 4.5 billion per year for 20 years, the loss of agricultural production if these works are not undertaken will be US$ 26 billion per year (both sums in 1980 $US): a ratio of approximately 6:1. This is a global rate of return over a 20-year period. The situation will look very different to an individual farmer or landholder in marginal or desertified lands: one cannot expect information on this global benefit/cost ratio to have any direct effect on land-use practices at the grass-roots level. What it should influence, however, is the strategy of aid donors. Aid funds spent on reducing soil erosion and vegetation degradation would effectively reap a six-fold return (corrected for inflation) over a 20-year period: a good basis for investment.

One major difficulty faced by aid donor nations and MLA's has been the demand by LDC's for aid "without strings". Aid recipient nations have insisted that they should specify their own development priorities and practices, and this demand has generally been accepted by aid donor nations and MLA's. Most LDC's, however, have unfortunately been under the misapprehension that "environment is a luxury which developing countries can't afford" – to quote the chief executive of one large Indian public-sector corporation (Buckley 1986). LDC's have tended to assign low priority to environmental protection, and many aid-funded development projects have therefore proceeded without adequate environmental assessment, planning or management. It has now become abundantly clear that international development aid should indeed come with at least one important string, namely an environmental one (see also Chap. 14).

It has been argued by, e.g. Maddox (1987), that if developed western nations (DWN's) want LDC's to conserve their natural ecosystems rather than exploiting them for short-term financial reward, then it is the DWN's which should pay the option costs of environmental conservation, by providing aid funds to compensate the LDC's for income foregone. It is certainly true that aid funds need to be used in sustainable development and improved EPM rather than environmentally damaging projects aimed solely at short-term return in hard currencies. The argument for compensation to LDC's, however, based on the premise that "environmental protection is a self-indulgence of the rich" (Maddox 1987) is unduly simplistic. Firstly, it is generally not the low-income populations of LDC's which profit from exploitation of natural resources, but the shareholders and staff of corporations based in DWN's, and a small number of politicians and businessmen in the LDC's. Hence, the argument that short-term exploitation of natural resources in LDC's alleviates poverty is generally fallacious. The subsistence sectors of LDC populations will commonly be served better by conservation of natural resources than by their exploitation (e.g. Hall and Percy 1986; Chapman 1987). Since decisions on resource use in LDC's are made principally by those who stand to gain most from immediate resource exploitation, however, such human welfare considerations are likely to be ignored in the future as they have been in the past.

Overall, therefore, the DWN's have few means to promote improved environmental planning and management in LDC's: and the main one, as Maddox (1987) concluded, is via international aid and loan funding. If LDC's have sovereign rights to determine their own development priorities and to exploit their natural resources as they see fit, it is equally true that DWN's are under absolutely no obligation to give or lend them money to do it. Aid and loan funding could be a just and powerful tool for global conservation. Rare indeed, at present, is the aid programme whose object is to halt environmental degradation. In future, however, perhaps we can hope that a high proportion of international aid and loan funds will be assigned to environmental protection. Some promising steps have already been taken in this direction in Bolivia, which has effectively "swapped debt for conservation" (Walsh 1987)[9]. If DWN's or MLA's waive repayment of LDC debts in this way, of course, then effectively the citizens of the DWN's are doing precisely what Maddox recommended: paying for conservation in LDC's.

Improving EPM Procedures

Even where LDC's have appreciated the importance of good EPM, they often lack the means to put it into practice. There are two critical aspects where the DWN's can assist: training professional personnel, and strengthening institutional structures. The former, under the name of technology transfer and training, has been a catchphrase in international aid for a number of years. The expertise of professional environmental scientists and planners, however, counts for little unless the country's legislation and planning processes are structured to make full use of that expertise (see Lim 1985; Ramakrishna 1985; UNESCAP 1986; Asian Development Bank 1986; Rees 1986; Bowonder 1987b). DWN's can hardly claim to set an example in this respect: our governments and bureaucracies are very poorly structured for EPM, with environmental portfolios and agencies separated from those responsible for the management of resources such as minerals, energy, forests, agriculture and fisheries, and also from those responsible for infrastructure and finance

---

[9] There have been further such debt-for-nature swaps subsequently, though not many.

(see Mayer-Tasch 1986). Agencies responsible for EPM are often incorrectly viewed as opposed to development, and have limited funds, manpower and status. This applies equally to many international institutions: as noted by Brundtland (1986), many of these were "created under circumstances very different from those prevailing today, and their structures reflect yesterday's priorities".

Equally, however, if the responsibility for EPM is delegated to advisory sections within other portfolios, without executive authority, then these sections are liable to be overridden and their recommendations neglected. It appears that both approaches are needed: environmental sections within every major ministry, and a separate environmental protection agency, including land-use and pollution control aspects, with its own independent budget allocation, legislative backing, and cabinet support. Very few nations as yet have such a system: China is one example.

Whilst institutional structures in DWN's are extremely conservative and hard to change, those in LDC's and MLA's can be much more flexible, so the potential for rapid improvement is perhaps greater. Both the World Bank and the Asian Development Bank (ADB), for example, are currently attempting to modify institutional structures and policies to improve EPM (ADB 1986; Rees 1986; Sinclair 1987): though it remains to be seen whether any changes are effective in practice or merely cosmetic (Fitzgerald 1986).[10]

Another possible means for improving EPM in LDC's would be for each DWN to place the same environmental constraints on overseas operations by its corporations as apply to domestic operations those corporations, enforcing these constraints by means of exchange control regulations (cf. Matthews and Carpenter 1985). In practice, however, such an approach would probably be very hard to implement, monitor and police. It is therefore likely to be more effective to concentrate on strengthening institutional and legislative structures in LDC's, to ensure that those nations are competent to assess and control development projects proposed by external or multi-national agencies, and to assist in the incorporation of environmental considerations in national policy. The current initiative to form an independent international commission, under the auspices of the Government of the Netherlands, to assess EIS's on behalf of LDC's, is particularly commendable in this regard.

---

[10] This concern is still valid in 1990!

A number of nations which receive either aid or MLA loans have recognised the extent of environmental degradation and have changed national policies in attempts to overcome it. In China, for example, the problems of massive air and water pollution, produced by breakneck industrialisation over the past two decades, were officially recognised in the early 1980's. Initial attempts to overcome this pollution concentrated on technical fixes such as downstream pollution control devices: the "bolt-on" or "retrofit" approach (Brundtland 1986). Only very recently has the need for integrated environmental planning and management been appreciated.

Elsewhere, India, for example, is now attempting to introduce a form of large-scale regional environmental planning (Buckley 1986). An REPM approach has also been used in several projects in Asia, notably the ADB-funded Palawan Integrated Environmental Plan in the Philippines (Finney and Western 1986). The ADB, the principal MLA in Southeast Asia, now has a growing environmental unit, and the ADB Board has recognised the need for environmental assessment and environmental protection as part of its official policy (ADB 1986; Rees 1986). The World Bank, castigated in the past for its lack of concern for environmental issues, is also in the process of increasing its environmental staff at present (Myers 1986; Sinclair 1987).

Since national development policies, and also the policies and operations of aid donor nations and MLA's, are cast in economic terms, it is important to know the economic costs and consequences of environmental planning and protection in development aid. These have been established in a few specific instances, such as those mentioned above, but in general remain almost entirely unknown. This, then, is a another critical research problem in EPM: to quantify the economic costs and benefits of measures for environmental assessment, planning and management in development aid.

Environmental Policy Instruments

One critical problem in strengthening institutional and legislative structures in LDC's is the selection of environmental policy instruments. There are three main types of instrument for putting environmental policies into effect: technological, regulatory and economic. The first of these specify the technology to be used, for example in pollution control: typically by means of phrases such as "best available control technology" (BACT), "as low as reasonably achievable" (ALARA), and so on. Technological instruments are widely used in the UK, for example. The regulatory approach, in contrast, prescribes standards (e.g. emission standards) and leaves it to the individual corporation to select appropriate technology to ensure compliance. Regulatory instruments are used in most of the developed western nations, often (as in Australia, for example) to the virtual exclusion of other approaches. The third approach is to promote environmental protection measures by means of economic incentives and disincentives. Examples in pollution control include pollution charges, bubbles and offsets, and tradeable emission rights. Examples in land and water resources allocation include compensation and mitigation payments, conservation credits, development taxes and transferable development credits, marketable or transferable water rights, rehabilitation bonds and so on. Other economic instruments include selective taxes, tax rebates and subsidies: such as those employed in the agricultural sector, for example. Such economic instruments are generally coupled with regulations and legislation as a back-up mechanism.

Current examples from the USA, Scandinavia, West Germany and Australia are summarised by Brown and Johnson (1984), Opaluch and Kashmanian (1985), Ware (1985), Westman (1985), Yapp and Upstill (1985), Schnaiberg et al. (1986), Thompson (1986), Buckley (1987), Griswold (1987) and Heller (1987). Analyses by the OECD have suggested that the use of economic instruments in European countries is likely to increase (Emmelin 1984; Evers 1986). As yet, economic instruments do not seem to have been adopted to any significant degree in LDC's. If they are valuable adjuncts to regulatory and technological instruments in the DWN's, however, why should they not be equally valuable in LDC's?

One major problem in the design of any type of environmental policy instrument is the cost of information. The design of policy instruments requires a balance between control costs and damage costs: for example, between the economic and environmental costs of pollution control systems, and the economic and environmental costs of damage by uncontrolled pollution. To determine the optimum level of control, and so design a policy instrument aimed at achieving that optimum level, requires good information on the control and damage costs associated with different possible strategies; such as different possible emission standards, pollution control technologies, or pollution charges. Acquiring this information incurs costs, often substantial: not only in research funding, but in delays in policy design and implementation. Yet there are also costs and risks associated with lack of information: risks of unforeseen environmental damage, risks that industry will incur costs in fitting additional equipment if standards are revised at frequent intervals, and so on.

In such circumstances a conservative approach would be the most logical, aimed at keeping pollution and other impacts well below those known to cause environmental degradation, at the time when policy instruments are framed. Unfortunately in practice the opposite approach was followed in the past: control costs were minimised, with the risk of then-unforeseen environmental impacts: which have now occurred. Two conclusions may be drawn: firstly, that future environmental policies need to be much more conservative; and secondly, that we should be prepared to incur much greater information costs, since these are small relative to either control or damage costs associated with ill-informed policy instruments.

For LDC's, it could be argued that information costs are negligible, since they can simply adopt standards and practices used in DWN's. This, however, is far from straightforward, since EPM legislation and regulations are far from uniform even within DWN's, let alone between them. Many LDC's – and many DWN's too – have tended to base emission standards, for example, on those set or recommended by the US Environmental Protection Agency (USEPA). Rarely, however, are the USEPA standards applied directly: all too often they are relaxed, often substantially, in particular countries or for particular projects, including aid projects. As further data on the damage costs of pollution have become available in recent years, many of the USEPA emission standards have been tightened. It is clear, therefore, that the previous standards were too lax: the damage costs were substantially greater than the control costs. If LDC's adopt standards which are even more lax, they will subject themselves to even greater damage costs. Just how great is generally unknown: but evidently this should be one important component of the research problem identified earlier, namely to quantify the costs and benefits of EPM in development aid.

Conclusions: How to Improve Public Environmental Awareness

In the preceding pages I have identified and examined a number of EPM research fronts and problems which seem to me to be particularly urgent and critical at present. Research effort in these areas should be particularly effective in improving EPM techniques and procedures. This alone, however, is not enough: new tools have little value unless put into use. New techniques designed to improve the integration of EPM, in any of the four respects considered here, generally require political action of some sort before they are brought into effect: new legislation, a ministerial or administrative directive, or simply the general adoption of a particular technique by government regulatory bodies. Hence, the adoption of new techniques depends upon electoral pressure, and so ultimately on public environmental awareness and opinion. In the long term, all attempts to improve environmental planning and management are ultimately futile unless the general public appreciates the importance of environmental protection in maintaining human well-being. Yet at present there are many groups in western democratic societies who are vociferously "anti-environment". These groups are as dependent as the rest of the human race on the preservation of ecosystem components and processes, but they do not appreciate their dependence.

The improvement of public environmental awareness is a therefore a critical and indeed overriding concern in successful EPM. In the longer term this may be achieved through the normal school education system. Unless public environmental awareness is improved in the short term, however, long-term improvements will be too late. More effective means to communicate the importance of environmental concerns to those in business, government and the general electorate are urgently needed.

One possible approach might be to make use of "grey power": individuals who have retired or are close to retirement from the regular work force, and so are no longer bound by personal ambitions and the demands and pressures of a day-to-day job; but who have education, understanding, contacts, money and votes and are hence in a position to influence present-day decisions – unlike schoolchildren. The success of companies which run natural history tours for older citizens, for example, indicates an increasing level of environmental awareness in this group. The development of improved techniques for reaching and communicating with older citizens is thus another critical direction in EPM: a critical component in environmental education.

Acknowledgements. A previous version of this essay was published in the *Environmental and Planning Law Journal* in 1989.

References

Anonymous (1987) International independent audit commission for EIA proposed. ESCAP Environ News 5 (2):13

Asian Development Bank (1986) Review of the bank's environmental policies and procedures. ADB, Manila

Beanlands GE, Duinker DN (1984) An ecological framework for environmental impact assessment. J Environ Manage 18:267–277

Bisset R (1985) Post-development audits to investigate the accuracy of environmental impact predictions. Z Umweltpolitik 4/84:463–484

Bowonder B (1987) Integrating perspectives in environmental management. Environ Manage 11:305–316

Bowonder B (1987) Management of environment in developing countries. Environmentalist 7:111–123

Boyle KJ, Bishop RC, Welsh MP (1985) Starting point bias in contingent valuation bidding games. Land Economics 61:188–194

Braat LC, van Lierop WFJ (1986) Economic-ecological modelling: an introduction to methods and applications. Ecol Modell 31:1–4

Brouwer F, Nijkamp P (1987) A satellite design for integrated regional environmental modelling. Ecol Modell 35:137–148

Brown GM, Johnson RW (1984) Pollution control by effluent charges: it works in the Federal Republic of Germany, why not in the US? Nat Res J 24:929–966

Brundtland GH (1986) Report of the World Commission for Environment and Development. Journal 86:25–31

Buckley RC (1982) Environmental sensitivity mapping: what, why and how. Miner Environ 4:151–155

Buckley RC (1984) The significance of biological inventories in determining conservation priorities. In: Myers K, Margules CR, Musto I (eds) Survey Methods for Nature Conservation, 2. CSIRO, Canberra, pp 382–386

Buckley RC (1985) Determining conservation priorities. Environ Geochem Health 7:116–119

Buckley RC (1986) Environmental impact assessment and management planning for development of the eastern coalfields of India. AMDEL Report 1603. AMDEL, Adelaide

Buckley RC (1987) Environmental planning techniques. SADME, Adelaide

Burton JR (1985) Land use management and mining. Min Rev 1985:13–20

Butler WH (1985) Multiple land use – an essential part of environmental planning. Aust Petrol Explor Assoc J (1985):311–315

Camara AS, Mano AP, Martinno MP, Marques JF, Nunes et al. (1986) An economic ecological model for regional land-use planning. Ecol Modell 31:293–302

Canter LW, Fairchild DM (1986) Post-EIS environmental monitoring. Impact Assess Bull 4:265–285

Carley MJ (1986) From assessment to monitoring: making our activities relevant to the policy process. Impact Assess Bull 4:286–304

Chapman MD (1987) Traditional political structure and conservation in Oceania. Ambio 16:201–205

Churchman CW (1984) Willingness to pay and morality: a study of future values. In: Churchman CW (ed) Natural Resource Administration. Westview, Boulder, CO, pp 71–76

Clark EH II (1985) The off-site costs of soil erosion. J Soil Water Conserv 40:19–22

Costanza R, Daly HE (1987) Towards an ecological economics. Ecol Modell 38:1–9

Culhane PJ (1987) The precision and accuracy of US environmental impact statements. Environ Monitor Assess 8:217–238

Danby GC (1985) An approximate method for the analysis of uncertainty in benefit-cost ratios. Water Resourc Res 21:267–271

Davis JR, Nanninga PM (1985) GEOMYCIN: towards a geographic expert system for resource management. J Environ Manage 20:377–390

Davos CA (1986) Group environmental preference aggregation – the principle of environmental justice. J Environ Manage 22:55–67

Diamond JM, May RM (1986) Conservation biology: a discipline with a time limit. Nature 317:111–112

Dixon JA, Hufschmidt MM (eds) (1986) Economic valuation techniques for the environment: a case study workbook. Johns Hopkins, Baltimore

Duinker PN, Baskerville GL (1986) A systematic approach to forecasting in environmental impact assessment. J Environ Manage 23:271–283

Duinker PN, Beanlands GE (1986) The significance of environmental impacts: an exploration of the concept. Environ Manage 10:1–11

Ehrenfeld D (1986) Thirty million cheers for diversity. New Sci 110:38–44

Emmelin L (1984) Environmental protection and economic development are not incompatible. Ambio 13:281

Evers FWR (1986) Environmental assessment and development assistance: the work of the OECD. Impact Assess Bull 4:307–320

Farber S, Costanza R (1986) The economic value of wetlands systems. J Environ Manage 24:41–52

Farnsworth NR, Soejarto DD (1985) Potential consequences of plant extinction in the United States on the current and future availability of prescription drugs. Econ Bot 39:231–240

Finney CE, Western S (1986) An economic analysis of environmental protection and management: an example from the Philippines. Environmentalist 6:45–61

Fitzgerald S (1986) The US debate over the environmental performance of four multilateral development banks. Ambio 15:291–295

Goodland R, Ledec G (1987) Neoclassical economics and principles of sustainable development. Ecol Modell 38:19–46

Griswold J R (1987) Conservation credit: motivating landholders to implement soil conservation practices through property tax credit. J Soil Water Conserv 42:41–45

Hall M, Percy S (1986) How aid spreads poverty. New Sci 110:50–55

Heller PW (1987) On the wrong environmental track – the limits of levels. J Environ Manage 24:127–138

Henderson LM (1987) Difficulties in impact prediction auditing. Environ Impact Assess Worldletter, May-June 1987:9–12

Hollick M (1986) Environmental impact assessment: an international evaluation. Environ Manage 10:157–178

Hufschmidt MM, James DE, Meister AD, Bower BT, Dixon JA (1983) Environment, natural systems and development: an economic valuation guide. Johns Hopkins, Baltimore

James DE (1983) Integrated energy-economic-environment modelling with reference to Australia. Australian Government Publishing Service, Canberra

James DE, Chambers J (1986) Managing environmental impacts of energy development: air quality in the Hunter Region, NSW, Australia. Environ Manage 10:421–429

Karrar G, Stiles D (1984) The global status and trend of desertification. J Arid Environ 7:309–312

Kellert SR (1984) Assessing wildlife and environmental values in cost-benefit analysis. J Environ Manage 18:355–363

Kent R (1985) Compendium of case studies on using cost-benefit analysis in the environmental impact assessment process. Australian Government Publishing Service, Canberra, 29 pp

Kneese AV, Sweeney JL (eds) (1985) Handbook of natural resource and energy economics. 3vv North-Holland, Amsterdam

Krutilla JV, Fisher AC (1986) The economics of natural environments

Leonard HJ (ed) (1985) Divesting nature's capital. Holmes and Meier, New York, 299 pp

Leontief W (1986) Input-output economics. Oxford University Press, New York, 436 pp

Lim G-C (1985). Theory and practice of EIA implementation: a comparative study of three developing countries. Environ Impact Assess Rev 5:133–153

Lonergan SC, Cocklin C (1985) The use of input-output analysis in environmental planning. J Environ Manage 20:129–147

Loomis JB, Walsh RG (1986) Assessing wildlife and environmental values in cost-benefit analysis. J Environ Manage 22:125–133

Lynn LE (1984) The role of benefit-cost analysis in fish and wildlife programs. In: Churchman CW (ed) Natural resource administration. Westview, Boulder, Co, pp 53–63

Maddox J (1987) Environment and foreign aid. Nature 326:539

Matthews WH, Carpenter RA (1985) The growing international implications of the US requirements for environmental impact assessments. In: Kato K, Kumamoto N, Matthews WH (eds) Environmental law and policy in the pacific basin area. Univ Tokyo, Tokyo, pp 159–201

Mayer-Tasch PC (1986) International environmental policy as a challenge to the national state. Ambio 15:240–243

McCallum DR (1987). Follow-up to environmental impact assessments: learning from the Canadian Government experience. Environ Monitor Assess 8:199–216

McNamara RS (1985) The challenges for sub-Saharan Africa. Inaugural Sir John Crawford Memorial Lecture. World Book, Washington, DC, November 1985

Miller A (1985) Psychological biases in environmental judgements. Environ Manage 20:231–143

Miller A, Cuff W (1986) The Delphi approach to the mediation of environmental disputes. Environ Manage 10:321–331

Myers N (1986) Economics and ecology in the international arena: the phenomenon of "linked linkages". Ambio 15:296–300

New Zealand Commission for the Environment (1985) Environmental impact assessment workshop: issues. NZCE, Wellington

Nijkamp P, Leitner H, Wrigley N (1985) Measuring the unmeasurable. Martinus Nijhoff, Dordrecht

Opaluch JJ, Kashmanian RM (1985) Assessing the viability of marketable permit systems: an application in hazardous waste management. Land Econ 61:263–271

Orians GH (1986) The place of science in environmental problem-solving. Environment 28:12–18

Preston BJ (1986) Adequacy of environmental impact statements in New South Wales. Environ Plan Law J 3:194–207

Ragozin DL, Brown G (1985) Harvest policies and nonmarket valuation in a predator-prey system. J Environ Econ Manage 12:155–168

Ramakrishna K (1985) The emergence of environmental law in the developing countries: a case study of India. Ecol Law Quart 12:907–936

Raufer RK, Feldman SL, Jaksch JA (1986) Emissions trading and acid deposition control: the need for ERC leasing. J Air Pollut Contr Assoc 36:574–580

Rees CP (1986) Environmental planning and management by the Asian Development Bank in its economic development activities. In: Asian Development Bank, environmental planning and management:29–46. ADB, Manila, 282 pp

Richey JS, Mar BW, Horner RR (1985) The Delphi technique in environmental assessment. J Environ Manage 21:135–159

Ross WA (1987) Evaluating environmental impact statements. J Environ Manage 25:137–148

Russell M, Gruber M (1987) Risk assessment in environmental policy making. Science 236:286–291

Schaeffer DJ, Kerster HW, Perry JA, Cox DK (1985) The environmental audit. I. Concepts. Environ Manage 9:191–198

Schnaiberg A, Watts N, Zimmerman K (eds) (1986) Distributional conflicts in environmental resource policy. Gower, New York

Shopley JB, Fuggle RF (1984) A comprehensive review of current environmental impact assessment methods and techniques. J Environ Manage 18:45–47

Sinclair L (1987) World Bank President announces new environmental policies. Ambio 16:279

Sinden JA, Worrell AC (1979) Unpriced values: decisions without market prices. Wiley, New York

Solomon BD (1985) Regional econometric models for environmental impact assessment. Progr Human Geogr 9:379–399

Suter GW, Barnthouse LW, O'Neill RV (1987) Treatment of risk in environmental impact assessment. Environ Manage 11:295–304

Thompson NJ (1986) Fiscal incentives for Australian bushland. Environ Manage 10:591–597

Tolba M (1985) Heads in the sand: a new appraisal of arid lands management. Address to Conference on "Arid Lands: Today and Tomorrow", October 1985. Organisation of Arid Lands Studies, Tucson, Arizona

Tomlinson P, Atkinson SF (1987a) Environmental audits: proposed terminology. Environ Monitor Assess 8:187–198

Tomlinson P, Atkinson SF (1987b) Environmental audits: a literature review. Environ Monitor Assess 8:239–257

Tomlinson P, Bisset R (1983) Environmental impact assessment, monitoring and post-development audits. In: P.A.D.C. (eds) Environmental impact assessment, 405–425. Martinus Nijhoff, The Hague

(UNESCAP) United Nations Economic and Social Commission for the Pacific (1986) Integration of environment into development: institutional and legislative aspects. UNESCAP, Bangkok, 265 pp

Van der Ploeg SWF, Braat LC, van Lierop WFJ (1987) Integration of resource economics and ecology. Ecol Modell 38:171

Walsh J (1987) Bolivia swaps debt for conservation. Science 237:596–597

Walsh SJ (1985) Geographic information systems for natural resource management. J
    Soil Water Conserv 40:202–205
Wathern P, Young SN, Brown IW, Roberts DA (1986) Ecological evaluation techniques.
    Landscape Plann 12:403–420
Ware JA (1985) Fiscal measures and the attainment of environmental opjectives:
    Scandinavian initiatives and their applicability in Australia. Australian Government
    Publishing Service, Canberra
Westman WE (1985) Ecology, impact assessment and environmental planning. Wiley,
    New York
Wright D.S, Greene JD (1987) An environmental impact assessment methodology for
    major resource developments. J Environ Manage 24:1–16
Yapp TP, Upstill HG (1985) Fiscal measures and the environment: impacts and potential.
    Australian Government Publishing Service, Canberra

Chapter 2

Environmental Sensitivity Mapping:
A Regional Planning Tool

Abstract

Environmental sensitivity maps (ESM's) show the probable environmental impacts of different types of land use or development in a geographic context. They are a valuable and under-utilised tool in regional environmental planning.

Environmental sensitivity refers to the relationship between applied stresses and environmental responses. An ESM must identify likely stresses and responses, estimate sensitivities and map them in a usable form. It thus combines the techniques of environmental impact assessment (EIA) with those of regional planning and mapping.

ESM is not always preferable to project-based EIA. In general, ESM is particularly efficient and cost-effective for environmental planning at a regional scale, in mosaic terrain, in pristine areas, and for accidental impacts.

Introduction

Good environmental planning needs a regional as well as a sectoral or project focus, in order to decide where different uses of land, water and air can best be located relative to each other. Single-project environmental impact assessment (EIA) does not do this efficiently. What is needed is a way to place the probable environmental impacts of different types of potential development in a geographic context. This is the aim of environmental sensitivity mapping (ESM).

To date, however, ESM is not widely used. There are several likely reasons for this. Concern over cumulative and interactive impacts of multiple projects is relatively recent, and in most countries the legal and administrative framework for regional environmental planning (REP) is still very sketchy. There is generally no requirement for either the public or private sector to produce REP's, so there has been no demand for relevant tools. In addition, ESM's have often attempted to show so many different stress-response relationships that they have become too complicated to be immediately comprehensible. As a result, they have not been easy to use and so have not gained wide acceptance by engineers and planners.

Besides poor presentation, ESM's have also suffered from confusion over terminology and techniques. Whilst concepts such as stability, resilience, thresholds and sensitivity have been used in ecological contexts for decades (Colwell 1974; Usher and Williamson 1974), methods for actually measuring them and using them in practical planning have not been well defined. Often ESM's have simply shown some aggregate measure of physical and biological parameters such as slope or plant cover, which are presumed to have some bearing on environmental sensitivity. Indeed they do; but they are not in themselves measures of sensitivity, and such schemes do not realise the potential of ESM's as planning tools. Here, therefore, I attempt to define environmental sensitivity, identify difficulties in estimating it, and specify criteria for using it.

Defining Environmental Sensitivity

In practical terms, environmental sensitivity (ES) is a measure of how easy it is to inflict damage on a particular area or produce serious consequences from limited actions. How can this be expressed as a useful definition? The dictionary definition of *sensitive* is "readily responding to or recording slight changes in condition". The critical point is that sensitivity is a derived parameter rather than a primary one. It cannot be measured directly because it is the relation between an applied stress and the resultant strain or response. The environmental sensitivity of a given environmental unit may usefully be defined as the relation between the response of that unit to a given stress and the severity of the stress. This is directly analogous to the definitions of common engineering terms such as the sensitivity of a meter or the elasticity of a material. It is this definition as a stress-response relation that makes environmental sensitivity a useful parameter for planning. It is dependent on a definition of environmental unit boundaries, but this is not a significant limitation in practice. It is apparent that ES as defined above is not a single scale scalar quantity, but a set of relations which depends on the actual value of the applied stress and its variations in the past. This relation also includes any secondary responses to the initial disturbance by particular components of the environmental unit concerned.

Types of Stress-Response Relation

Environmental stress-response relations can take many different forms. Common features include:

1. *Reversibility*: environmental responses may be reversible or irreversible: if the stress is reduced or removed, does the environmental unit recover? If so, does the recovery track back along the same path as the original response, or is there a hysteresis effect?
2. *Thresholds*: a small stress applied under particular circumstances can produce a disproportionately large response. If an environmental unit is already under some stress, either natural or anthropogenic, a small extra load can produce a very significant and perhaps irreversible degradation.
3. *Response rate*: the rate at which environmental units respond to a given increase or decrease in stress.
4. *Interdependence*: a given stress may produce several linked strains and a given strain may be produced by several different stresses.
5. *Primary, secondary and higher-order responses*, which may constitute positive or negative feedback links. As an obvious example, the primary effect of a bulldozer may be removal of plant cover, but loss of fauna through habitat destruction is a common secondary response. Again, loss of plant cover may destabilise the soil surface, and this may reduce plant cover even further.

As used in everyday speech, the terms "stability" and "resilience" encompass two distinct meanings. The engineer's – and ecologist's – criterion for stability is that if a system is perturbed or forced slightly from a stable configuration, it will return to that configuration. In everyday speech, however, "stable" can also mean that a system is resistant to disturbance in the first place: a large increase in stress produces very little response. Of course, an ecosystem may become stable in this way when it is completely degraded.

In general, a stressed ecosystem will suffer environmental degradation, i.e. disturbance from its initial configuration. If this degradation decreases when the stress is removed, the system is at least partially stable. In other words, the initial response is at least partially reversible. In some cases (e.g. simple predator-prey systems), this recovery may overshoot the initial configuration and oscillate before coming to rest. Where entire environmental units have been stressed by anthropogenic impacts, however, any recovery is more likely to be gradual and incomplete: heavily damped, in engineering terms. More generally, if a given stress is applied and then relaxed, the system may:

– return to its initial state;
– recover only partially;
– remain in the state produced by the stress;
– continue to change initially but then stop; or
– continue to change at an increasingly rapid rate.

It is also important to consider the effects of repeated stresses. The second stress may produce:

– the same response and recovery as the first;
– an exaggerated response; or
– the same response but a different recovery.

Using Environmental Sensitivity Maps

To predict the environmental consequences of a potential development requires prediction of:

1. The specific stresses it will impose on the environment concerned;
2. Other stresses which may also be present;
3. The immediate environmental responses to those stresses; and
4. The secondary and longer-term responses and hence the potential overall consequences.

Environmental sensitivity is a measure of responses, items 3 and 4 above. Hence, a map of environmental sensitivity, if it can be expressed in a usable form, will be an invaluable aid in planning: particularly since "environmental consequences" can include not only the potential destruction of rare species, etc., but also some very practical hazards such as flooding, erosion and increased salinity.

To summarise, the main purposes of environmental sensitivity maps are to alert field planning personnel to the potential impacts of any proposed development, and to enable rapid and rational choice on environmental grounds between alternative engineering options for such developments. They can also be used to define the most critical sites for monitoring the impacts of development.

Steps in ESM

The main stages in preparing an environmental sensitivity map are as follows:

1. *Define area:* using boundaries determined by terrain rather than land tenure, if possible.
2. *Review existing baseline data:* with particular attention to spatial patterns; aerial photography is usually a major component.
3. *Classify environmental types:* including man-made environments, and allowing for within-type variations associated with, e.g., altitude, exposure, aspect, etc.
4. *Assess distribution and conservation status:* of each environmental type and subtype, both within the area concerned and outside it.
5. *Review development in all sectors:* summarise the main past, present, and likely future land and water uses in the area concerned: agriculture and pastoralism, forestry, mineral industries, fisheries, tourism and related industries, residential and urban development, transport corridors, etc.
6. *Define impact types:* each type of development produces a specific set of impacts; different developments may produce impacts which are similar and overlapping, or completely independent, or interacting and synergistic. Before sensitivity relationships can be defined, information on likely developments must be translated into details of potential impacts. In addition, primary and secondary impacts must be distinguished.
7. *Assess affects of mitigation procedures:* the impact of any given development may in some cases be mitigated, to a greater or lesser degree, by environmental protection measures undertaken by the developer. The effects of such mitigation measures must be assessed as a "correction factor" to the impacts.

8. *Determine types of sensitivity:* different environments react to different impacts in different ways, so there are many different types of aspects of environmental sensitivity (Buckley 1982).

9. *Determine sensitivity relationships:* assess sensitivity of each type of environment to each type of potential impact (Buckley 1982). This is the main part of the project and the one requiring greatest expertise and experience from comparable areas elsewhere, as it is on this assessment of sensitivity relationships that the entire ESM exercise ultimately depends.

10. *Determine mapping system:* graphic representation of environmental sensitivities in a manner useful for management is one of the most critical aspects of ESM (Buckley 1982). Sensitivities to the various potential impacts can be combined into aggregate numerical indices according to a range of criteria, or can be represented symbolically in non-quantitative terms.

11. *Determine mapping scales:* for management purposes environmental sensitivities need to be mapped at several different scales, to give both a regional overview and detailed information in specific smaller areas which may be, e.g., particularly diverse and heterogeneous, or particularly fragile, or subject to particularly heavy past, present or future development. An effective choice of mapping scales is crucial to the value of ESM as a management tool.

12. *Pilot project (optional):* having defined the environments, impacts, sensitivity relationships and mapping scales for the area as a whole, it is often valuable to apply them to a small pilot section of the area, to check that the earlier stages have been completed successfully and that the final output is suitable for the required management application.

Estimating Sensitivities

Existing environmental sensitivity involves predicting the consequences of environmental stresses. Except at the coarsest levels, such predictions depends largely on comparison: what were the results of similar actions or events in similar environments in the past? The precision with which stress-response relations can be estimated depends on:

– The extent and relevance of the information available for comparison;

- The level of similarity between the environment and stresses under study and those where the responses are known; and
- The level of confidence with which the known stress-response relations can be specified.

To assess this level of similarity requires data on the characteristics of the environment under study, as well as those used for comparison. The collection of such data is the most conspicuous step in environmental sensitivity mapping, but not the most critical. Without the comparative background, such information provides sensitivity estimates only at the coarsest level of environmental response. If a solid causeway is built across a floodplain, one needs only topographic data to predict the area likely to be inundated during the next wet season. If the last remaining stand of rain-forest in a district is clear-felled, one can confidently predict the disappearance of the rain-forest fauna. It is not so straightforward to predict the precise environmental effects of changes in surface runoff caused by grading a road across an arid-zone sand plain; or the effects on river salinity of using its waters for irrigation; or the effects on crops of prolonged low-level fluoride emissions from an industrial stack; yet each may have significant consequences. Some such situations are amenable to direct experimental investigation. Most practical planning problems, however, are too urgent, too large in scale, or insufficiently replicable for an experimental approach to be feasible. Comparative techniques are therefore essential.

Sensitivity Indices

Once actual sensitivities have been estimated for the various environmental types and development stresses, they must then be combined into some simple aggregate index which can be mapped. This involves three main stages.

The first step is to express the relative sensitivity of each environmental unit to each stress as an index on the scale of, e.g., 1–5, and tabulate these indices for each unit and stress. This involves conversion of physical stress-response data of many different types into numerical values. This inevitably involves a loss of information, but it is a necessary step if the information is to be made available to planners as a single comprehensive map.

The second step is to calculate an overall sensitivity index. This involves further loss of information but is needed for the same reason. There are two main approaches. The overall index for each unit can be set equal either to the sum of the individual indices or to the largest of them. These might be termed "sum" and "maximum" indices respectively. Various intermediates are possible: for example, the stresses could be combined in a few major groups and the indices summed within each group: a "combined" index. Whichever index is used, the final map can be keyed to indicate which stresses contribute most significantly to each mapped index value.

The third step is to divide the overall range of the final index chosen into a small number of sectors for mapping. A "sum" index can take any value between the product of the lowest individual index value and the number of individual indices, and the highest such value and that number. Rarely will it be possible to plot such a range of values on a single map with any clarity, particularly if it has to be a black and white line map for dye-line reproduction. Hence, the overall range must be divided into perhaps three to five sectors for mapping.

Mapping

There are generally four main mapping stages in constructing an ESM. The first, preliminary stage involves:

- collating and combining physical maps, aerial photographs and/or satellite images;
- adding boundaries of major environmental types to produce a base map;
- adding keyed overlay(s) of relevant physical and biological parameters: relative elevation, probable soil type, plant cover, physiognomic or structural vegetation type, dominance of particular plant signature types, etc.

The second stage, not always required, is a ground survey. The scale and detail of the ground survey depends on the area, the development, and the time available. The aims are to check the accuracy of the preliminary maps and add further information. Preferred field parameters are those which can be measured or estimated directly without the need to collect samples, carry out experiments, etc., though this will depend on the project and time available. The broad procedure is as follows:

- Examine several representative central areas in at least two segments (if present) of each environmental unit mapped;
- Check parameters mapped in overlays;
- Determine and record appropriate additional parameters from each station;
- Traverse boundaries between representative sections of the mapped environmental units to assess how they differ in the physical and biological parameters considered.

The third step is to prepare final maps of physical and biological parameters by:

- Correcting the preliminary maps using information from the ground survey;
- Adding additional field information to overlays.

Up to this stage, the maps contain subjective decisions on the boundaries between environmental units, but not on environmental sensitivity. They would therefore be available for reinterpretation if further stress-response information became available subsequently.

The fourth and final stage is to construct an environmental sensitivity map which typically consists of:

- The base map of environmental types;
- Shading or colouring to indicate the value of the overall sensitivity index;
- Symbols showing the main component(s) of that sensitivity.

When to Use ESM

ESM is particularly efficient and cost-effective if applied:

1. *At a regional scale*, i.e. to contiguous and relatively large areas. This is because the primary aim of environmental sensitivity mapping is to indicate the relative sensitivities of a range of different environments to a range of different stresses, before those stresses are likely to occur. In small areas, the types of environment and types of potential stress will be few in number, so that localised impact assessment techniques may be more effective than sensitivity mapping.
2. *To mosaic terrain*, i.e. to areas which contain a relatively small number of discrete environmental types in a heterogeneous spatial arrange-

Table 1. Where ESM works well

---

1. Selecting sites for major developments with potential impact on surrounding flora and fauna, e.g.:
   - Power generation plants, mineral processing plants, plastics manufacturing plants, etc., near agricultural or conservation areas
   - Industrial developments, loading facilities, etc., in coastal areas with mangrove or seagrass communities, or commercial fisheries

2. Routing transport corridors or networks through relatively undisturbed environments, e.g.:
   - Oil and gas pipelines
   - Power transmission lines
   - Road and rail links
   - Exploration tracks

3. Zoning large areas for regional land and water use, development and management planning

4. Planning contingency response strategies for containment and cleanup of spills, e.g.:
   - Crude oil and petroleum products
   - Hazardous chemicals
   - Radioactive substances

---

ment. This is because information on the sensitivities of individual environments to various stresses can be used repeatedly for each patch of that type of environment.

3. *To pristine areas*, which are relatively undisturbed by development and have high conservation value. One reason for this is that the need for environmental planning, i.e. the planning of future development and land and water use to minimise overall aggregate environmental impact of a given level of resource utilisation, is particularly vital in pristine areas, where environmental degradation would represent a greater loss than in areas which are already heavily disturbed; and environmental sensitivity mapping is one of the most basic techniques in environmental planning. A second reason is that in general, the types and locations of potential future developments are known less precisely for relatively pristine areas than for areas where substantial development has already occurred. Hence, a technique such as environmental sensitivity mapping, which examines the potential impacts of a range of possible future stresses for every point within the area concerned, is particularly useful.

4. *For accidental impacts*, impacts whose precise time and place are unknown, but which are liable to have severe environmental conse-

Table 2. Where ESM does not work well

1. Single-site development, site already selected or strongly constrained by non-environmental factors

2. Developments which
   (a) have low off-site impact, so the main aspect of environmental planning is land-use allocation rather than pollution control, and
   (b) are in land of relatively uniform conservation value, so that the precise location of the site does not affect the project's impact

3. Developments where the destination of off-site emissions is known and unlikely to vary: e.g. liquid and effluents discharged into a river system

quences and for which contingency plans for environmental protection are therefore necessary. Transport accidents, notably spills of oil, hazardous materials, etc., are the primary example.

Some examples of situations when ESM is or is not an efficient and cost-effective planning tool are summarised in Tables 1 and 2 respectively.

Conclusions

– Environmental sensitivity mapping is underutilised at present because of inadequacies in definition and presentation.

– Environmental sensitivity can usefully be expressed in terms of stress-response relations.

– The most critical part of environmental sensitivity mapping is not mapping, or collection of physical and biological parameters, but determination or estimation of stress-response relationships.

– This is essentially a comparative process and requires prior knowledge of the environment concerned and similar environments and stresses elsewhere or in the past.

– Expression of a number of stress-response relations as a single sensitivity index involves considerable loss of information, but is necessary to present stress-response information in a form of practical use in planning.

– A critical part of planning is the prediction of consequences of alternative courses of action: environmental sensitivity mapping is designed with precisely this need in mind and is therefore a valuable planning tool.

- Different environmental planning applications require different environmental planning techniques: spatially extensive techniques such as environmental sensitivity mapping are more efficient and cost-effective for some applications; site-based environmental impact assessment techniques for others.
- ESM is particularly valuable for environmental planning at a regional scale, in mosaic terrain, in pristine areas, and for accidental impacts.

References

Buckley RC (1982) Environmental sensitivity mapping: what, why and how. Min Environ 4:151–155
Colwell RK (1974) Predictability, constancy and contingency of periodic phenomena. Ecology 55:1148–1153
Usher MG, Williamson MH (1974) Ecological Stability. Blackwell, London

Chapter 3

Environmental Accounting: Techniques and Limitations

Abstract

Environmental accounting is potentially a very valuable tool in planning, public resource management, pollution control and policy analysis. Its main limitations are as follows:

1. Valuation techniques for environmental goods and services are imperfect and shadow prices are only partial valuations. This applies to both deductive and interrogative techniques.
2. Social values for environmental goods and services are uncertain and change very rapidly.
3. Non-economic values are also important in political processes.
4. Aggregation of individual preferences may not yield a meaningful net social preference.
5. Economic values are marginal and incremental, not absolute and total.
6. Reliable industry data are not readily available.
7. Assumptions underlying standard economic theory and analytical models are often not met.

Existing data on the costs and benefits of environmental protection measures to industry and to national economies are reviewed, as are misconceptions relating to: market prices and utility; hypothetical valuation and social values; willingness to pay or to accept compensation; private property rights in environmental goods and services; and discount rates in economic analysis.

Introduction

What is environmental accounting and why is it important? Accounting means tracking stocks and flows of quantifiable commodities, such as tonnes of coal or wheat, hours of work, or units of currency. It's useful at any scale, from individual to global. It is a management tool: the reason for converting different commodities to commensurate units is to help make decisions.

Environmental accounting is accounting that includes environmental goods and services. It is one branch of environmental economics, with two main distinguishing features. First, it generally involves assigning monetary values to environmental goods and services which are valuable but not traded in markets: a process known as shadow pricing. Such estimates are often highly uncertain, quantified in terms with no fixed conversion to money, or only partly or poorly quantified.

Second, in environmental and resource management applications, many of the assumptions and conditions underlying standard economic theory are not met. Markets are not in equilibrium, consumption is not rival, property rights are not clearly defined, parties to transactions are poorly informed, competition is heavily constrained, and so on (Maler 1984; Common 1988). Conclusions reached by simply including shadow prices in standard benefit-cost, cost-effectiveness or input-output ana-lyses, for example, may therefore be invalid. Sensitivity to failures in assumptions should be tested routinely. Such aspects have been analysed extensively in the environmental economics literature, but often seem to have been ignored in recent public pronouncements on environmental management issues.

Despite these limitations, environmental accounting is important because it could greatly improve the value of economics as a decision-making tool, particularly in determining national policy for resource management.

General Limitations and Obstacles

Poor Valuation Techniques

Environmental accounting requires estimates of the social values of environmental goods and services in terms comparable to goods and services which are regularly traded. Such valuation techniques are still imperfect, sometimes misleading, and often controversial. This is of particular concern for ecosystem components and functions which are only partly understood. Limitations of the main approaches used are summarised in the following sections.

Partial Values

Whilst market values can be measured by the outcome of individual transactions, the values of ecosystem components are derived from a diverse range of attributes and functions, and shadow-pricing techniques generally capture only a few of these. As the number and complexity of links between natural systems and human well-being have been more widely appreciated in the last few decades, the human values assigned to ecosystem components have steadily increased; and at the same time, techniques for measuring these values have become more complete and inclusive. In contrast to market prices, however, shadow prices are still only partial valuations.

Uncertainty in Values

Estimated values for environmental goods and services are often only partly or poorly quantified, or quantified in terms which have no fixed conversion to money. Analyses using these values should explicitly take such uncertainty into account. Such uncertainty exists even for conversion rates determined by markets: forex trading provides an example.

Rapidly Changing Values

Social values placed on environmental goods and services are changing so fast that estimates are likely to be obsolete before they are available for use. These social values are set by the relationship between the quality of the environment and the quality of human life; a relationship which changes with individual perceptions as well as physical circumstances. Note that the relationship between material possessions and material well-being is also a relative one, varying both with the mean or base level of material possessions in the society concerned, and with the individual's material history.

Non-Economic Values

Economics is only one component of politics. There are human values that cannot be expressed in economic terms but which still affect how people vote. Note that both politics and economics are based only on human values; individuals may believe in religious rules or species' rights, but these beliefs are human values. Economics in general, and environmental accounting in particular, will always be only one tool in political decision making; and it will only be useful if for most people, economic values outweigh non-economic ones.

Individual and Aggregate Values

Economics defines social values as the sum or aggregate of individual values. Effectively, it deals with averages. Estimates of the human life, for example, refer to the value of an unspecified life to other people in general. Different individuals, however, have very different relative preferences for different purchasable and unpurchasable goods and services. For example, the relative values of time and money differ between individuals: some prefer paid work, others prefer unpaid leisure. There is therefore no guarantee that these individual preferences can be aggregated in any meaningful way to provide a measure of preferences for society as a whole. Individuals whose values differ from the average will disagree with the conclusions of economic analyses. In our society, such people have two options: using individual political power, or convincing others to change their values.

Incremental and Relative Values

Economic values are relative, not intrinsic or absolute; and they are incremental or marginal, not total. We may know what an ounce of gold is worth today: but what would be the option cost if all the gold in the world suddenly vanished? This is directly analogous to estimating option costs for species extinctions.

Inapplicable Assumptions

The reason for estimating economic values for environmental goods and services is to include those values in benefit-cost, cost-effectiveness, input-output or other economic analyses. Such techniques, however, are based on assumptions; and if these do not apply in particular cases, conclusions based on them may be wrong. So every analysis should make its assumptions explicit, and examine the sensitivity of its conclusions to failures in these assumptions.

Uncertainty and Risks

We need to estimate costs and benefits not just for events which we are confident will occur, but also for those with low probability. We also need to know how to allow for uncertainties in estimates of costs and benefits. This field has received considerable attention lately (Russell and Gruber 1987; Suter et al. 1987). There are many different types of uncertainty: some we can identify and some we have not yet dreamed of. Concern over uncertainty is a major factor influencing decisions both by private corporations and public policy makers.

Lack of Reliable Industry Data

Reliable information on industry costs of environmental compliance is hard to obtain for six main reasons. (1) Industries often have not recorded environmental costs. (2) Extracting records and separating environmental cost categories from others involves considerable time and effort. (3) Industry is concerned over confidentiality, particularly the relation of capital and operating costs to product output; though this problem can be overcome by guaranteeing confidentiality during analysis and reporting only industry aggregate or average figures, or a breakdown by unidentifiable company codes rather than company names. (4) Industry may have a strategic bias to quote maximum figures for environmental costs, so for reliability the accounting basis must be clearly defined and the data verifiable. (5) Different corporations use widely differing accounting systems and there is no standard for which particular costs should be included under the heading of environmental protection. Previous attempts to determine costs and benefits of environmental protection measures in the steel and chemical industries, for example (Odgers et al. 1983a,b) encountered all these difficulties.

Valuation Techniques

Deductive Approaches

These techniques attempt to deduce values assigned to environmental goods and services from observed human behaviour and linkages with traded goods and services. Standard techniques are summarised below:

Surrogate markets: The use of marketed goods and services as environmental surrogates, e.g., valuing plant species from their contribution to the pharmaceutical, food and textile industries, or forested catchments from the water they supply.

Property and land-value differentials (hedonic pricing): Prices are measurably higher for sites with preferred environmental characteristics, such as views, clean air, or access to waterfront or reserves; the aggregate difference defines a minimum value for those characteristics.

Wage differentials: People will accept lower pay to work in areas with preferred environmental characteristics, such as clean air or low noise levels; again, the aggregate differences define a minimum environmental value.

Travel and related costs: The value of a visit to a conservation area must be greater than the costs actually incurred by people going there, including travel costs, time, entrance fees, etc; but only if visiting that area was the sole reason for travel.

Damage costs: If some feature of the natural environment is damaged or removed and this leads to damage to human health or property, then the environmental service is worth at least as much as the cost of the damage.

Repair and replacement costs: In similar circumstances, the environmental service is worth at least as much as the cost of repairing or replacing damaged items.

Preventive expenditures: If some feature of the natural environment provides protection against damage to human health or property, and equivalent protection otherwise requires engineering works or behavioural changes, then the value of the environmental service is at least as great as the cost of those works or changes.

Shadow projects: If some ecosystem function or other environmental service could be completely provided or replaced by human construction or activity, a hypothetical shadow project, then the value of that service is at least as great as the cost of the shadow project.

Foregone earnings (human capital): If environmental damage leads to damage to human health or life, preventing the individuals concerned from working, then the cost of that environmental damage is at least equal to the amount those individuals would otherwise have earned.

Foregone income (opportunity costs): Where individuals spend time on recreation involving environmental goods and services, their value is at least equal to the income foregone by those individuals during that time.

The main limitation of these techniques is that each measures only one component of total value, sometimes a very limited component. So we need to use all applicable techniques simultaneously, identify and exclude overlaps and double counts, and sum the remaining partial values to yield an overall estimate.

Whereas early attempts at environmental benefit-cost analysis, for example, might have compared annual revenue from timber or mineral production in a wilderness area with annual revenue from wilderness recreation, a modern analysis should include additional surrogate or shadow values for recreation (for example, travel costs, land-price differentials on nearby areas, equivalent value of income foregone in recreation, and so on); measures for additional benefits provided by protection against hazards such as flooding, soil erosion, etc., estimated as direct and indirect damage costs avoided (Clarke 1985); and measures of net benefit provided by resources such as water which are derived from the area but are delivered to consumers by a non-market system. It should also include measures of existence, option and bequest values, stratified by distance, for the country's entire population, including separate measures for any rare or endangered species as well as wilderness value *per se*.

A second limitation is that third parties observing a transaction and using price to define values do not know the circumstances which led the vendor to sell and the purchaser to buy. A market price only defines a value to those parties at that time under those circumstances: which might be unusual or short-lived. As an obvious example, stolen goods sell cheap.

Interrogative Approaches

These techniques, also known as contingent valuation methods (CVM), rely on simply asking people what particular environmental goods and services are worth to them personally, by means of surveys and questionnaires. These are hypothetical questions and they yield hypothetical answers. They are commonly used to estimate three classes of value which cannot readily be measured by deductive approaches:

Existence values: The value an individual places on simply keeping something in existence, irrespective of its use or enjoyment by the individual concerned; e.g., the continued existence of whales or quetzl-coatls, even if we never expect to see one personally.

Bequest values: The value placed by an individual on the continued existence and possible enjoyment of something during future generations.

Option values: The value of keeping options open as to the possible future use, enjoyment or consumption of something; e.g., species extinction destroys options for using its genetic resources; clearing forest destroys the option of using it for wilderness recreation.

Questioning techniques (Churchman 1984; Kellert 1984; Boyle et al. 1985; Loomis and Walsh 1986; Samples et al. 1986; Buckley 1987; Farber and Costanza 1987) include:

Bidding games: Respondents are simply asked to offer bids for identified environmental goods or services, either total or marginal.

Trade-off games: Respondents are asked to choose between various options, some of which are environmental goods and services, from a fixed hypothetical total budget.

Costless choice: Respondents are asked to choose between various options of which some are environmental goods and services and others are traded goods and services, the money values of which are known but are not quoted to the respondent.

Priority evaluation: Respondents are asked to rank various options in order of preference, some involving environmental goods and services and others only traded goods and services.

Expert opinion: Valuations are sought only from individuals presumed to be particularly well qualified to provide an assessment.

Delphi techniques: An iterative process intended to derive consensus from a group of experts.

Individual responses may be subject to bias of four main kinds:

Strategic: The response is influenced by the respondent's vested interests in possible practical uses of the survey results.

Starting point: If an interviewer mentions a particular figure as a starting point, the respondent is likely to quote a value near this figure.

Information: Quoted values depend on prior information given to the respondent.

Instrument: Values quoted depend on how the question is framed, and in particular, on whether costs would be met by the respondent, a developer, or from general tax revenues.

Analytical Tools

Commonly used analytical techniques include:

Benefit-cost analysis: This assumes that annual costs and benefits can be identified and quantified into the indefinite future; calculates differences between benefits and costs for each year; and discounts future values to arrive at a single measure of value, such as net present value or benefit-cost ratio.

Cost-effectiveness analysis: Given a set of different possible means to reach a desirable goal, this method compares their relative costs on a similar basis to benefit-cost analysis but without quantifying the benefits of that goal.

Input-output analysis: Standard input-output analysis is a matrix technique for analysing interactions between different economic sectors in a given geographical region, where the outputs from some sectors are inputs to others. Two approaches have been used to extend this to include environmental goods and services. The first is to incorporate environmental components directly into the primary matrix, with natural resources providing inputs to industry sectors and industrial pollution providing negative inputs to environmental sectors. The second is to couple a standard input-output analysis to a residuals model, which defines the amounts and types of pollutants produced by each industry sector per unit production. This predicts the pollution generated by a given overall level of industrial activity. These results can then be coupled to a regional model of the sources and dispersion of each pollutant type, to predict regional pollution patterns in relation to overall industrial activity (James 1983, 1985; James and Chambers 1986).

Applications and Examples

Applications and Requirements

Applications of environmental accounting include:

Planning: Determining whether development approvals should be granted, and under what conditions.

Public resource management: Determining appropriate royalties for private use of publicly owned resources.

Pollution control: Determining appropriate discharge standards, effluent charges, rehabilitation bonds, etc.

Policy analysis: Designing and evaluating environmental policy, with reference to both efficiency and equity.

For such applications we need to know both the marginal costs and the marginal benefits of particular projects or programmes or particular levels of environmental protection. Marginal protection costs are the costs of operations carried out to comply with environmental requirements, less the costs of the same operations as they would be done (if at all) without those requirements. These costs, met initially by industry, appear as social costs through increased prices for commodities and utilities. Marginal benefits can be measured by the marginal damage costs of going without a given investment in environmental protection: the difference between the social cost of environmental damage and degradation which occurs with those environmental protection measures in place, and the greater damage and degradation that would occur without them.

Most applications of environmental accounting require shadow prices, for one of two reasons: either because (1) we cannot establish market values, since the goods and services concerned are never traded; or (2) because we do not want them to be traded, but we do want to know what they are worth.

Costs and Benefits of Environmental Protection Measures to Industry

Some examples of the industry costs of environmental compliance are summarised in Table 1. Sometimes environmental protection produces savings for industry: pollution control investments reduced Alcoa's energy consumption by 30%, cut operating costs at one Dow Chemical plant by US$ 2 million per year; and saved 3M US$ 11 million as a result of process changes (McCloskey 1981). Environmental policy changes can also bring substantial savings: netting, bubbles, offsets and bankable emission rights in the USA saved industry US$ 12 billion relative to the cost of achieving the same overall ambient air quality using only direct regulatory instruments such as discharge standards (Hahn 1989).

Table 1. Costs of environmental policies to industry

Country Industry Period	Costs	Reference and comments
Australia Steel 1960–80	Capital: EC = 5.9% total, = 0.2–1.2% raw steel price Of this, 72% is air, 27% water, 1% noise Operating costs = 3 × capital (cap) costs In 1980, op. environmental costs (EC) = $ 1.73/tonne for air, 98¢ for water	Odgers et al. (1983a) 2 plants, 80% total Aust. capacity No measure of benefits
Australia Chemical 1970's	Capital: average EC = 7% total; varies 0–56% Operating: 0.6–0.7% total, little variation Total EC = 0.8–1.1% total costs, decreasing through time	Odgers et al. (1983b) 14 companies: all >50% overseas owned except one; 7 100% overseas owned. Poor response – incomplete information
USA All industries	1979: National compliance cost = US$ 36.9 billion (B) = 1.5% GNP Of this: air = $22.3 B, 46% cap, 93% private Water: $12.7 B, 58% cap, 53% private 1980 Estimate for 1980's: 1979 US$ 520 B: 58% air, 33% water, 3.4% hazardous waste, 3.3% reclamation, 2.3% other	US Council for Environmental Quality cited by Baldwin (1985). 600 companies produce pollution control equipment; sales >$1.8 B in 1977, growth 2 × average
USA	1987 Measure for 1972–86: $78 B/yr by 1986 = 2% GNP	Farber and Rutledge (1986, 1987), Hahn (1989)
USA Petroleum	Oil-spill prevention and cleanup costs US$ 5.50 per gallon; benefits US$ 7.27 per gallon	Cohen (1986)
USA Mining Late 1970's	Reclamation costs per hectare variously quoted as up to 1979 US$ 7300, typically US$ 3000; i.e. up to 1990 US$ 20000, typically 1990 US$ 7500. Costs range from 1–20% value of coal mined	Buckley (1987)
Australia	Costs of stack precipitators and other environmental protection measures at one power station = 7% of total capital costs and 2.4% of total operating costs	ESAA (1990)

Costs and Benefits of Environmental Protection Measures to National Economies

Environmental protection measures in the USA caused <2% change in employment in 31 industry sectors in the 1970's, and <5% change in output, with increases in some sectors and decreases in others (Baldwin 1985). For every US$1 billion spent on environmental protection, between 67000 and 85000 new jobs were created; the only job losses were in the Great Lakes area, where old and inefficient car manufacturers and heavy industries closed down, largely because of overseas competition (US Council for Environmental Quality (USCEQ), cited by Baldwin 1985). In the 1970's, environmental controls reduced national unemployment by 0.3–0.6%, and in 1972, GNP rose by 1% as a result of environmental expenditure (USCEQ, cited by Baldwin 1985). For OECD countries, the net short-term effect of environmental policies has been to increase overall employment; and the maximum contribution of environmental protection policies and regulations to inflation has been 0.1–0.4% (Emmelin 1984). Overall, therefore, environmental protection measures have not been costly to national economies.

The US Clean Air Act is estimated to have saved 25000 lives and prevented 6 million acute respiratory disorders between 1973 and 1980 (USCEQ, cited by Baldwin 1985). The level of environmental protection provided by existing measures still leads to substantial economic costs through environmental damage: some overseas estimates are summarised in Table 2.

Shadow Prices

Some examples of shadowprices for environmental goods and services are summarised in Table 3.

Option Costs of Species Extinction

The last example in Table 3 is particularly interesting, as it uses a surrogate market approach to place a value on something which is often viewed as impossible to value, namely the extinction of a species. This estimate (Farnsworth and Soejarto 1985) was reached by dividing the average annual sales of plant-based pharmaceuticals by the ratio between the number of plant species used to produce those pharmaceuticals, and

Table 2. Environmental damage costs

Country, date component	Annual costs	Derived from	Reference
UK, 1954 Air pollution	1954 £5 per person		Senate Standing Committee on Air Pollution (1970)
UK, 1970 Air pollution	1985 £6 billion for UK using 1970 controls 1985 £200 per person		Wint (1986) quoting a 1972 UK government study
USA, 1979 Air pollution	1979 US$ 75 per person, i.e. 1979 US$ 16 billion for USA	Commercial costs only; poor visibility, cleaning, corrosion, vehicle crashes, *not* health or amenity	Miller (1980) quoted by Owen (1986)
UK, 1952 Air pollution	4000 Deaths	From smog	Fabos (1985)
USA, 1981	If industry met clean air standards, it would save US$ 36 billion per year	Health costs only	McCloskey (1981)
USA, 1970's Water pollution	Water treatment costs in 1970's totalled US$ 150 billion	(1.5 × total costs of highway construction!)	Fabos (1985)
USA, 1980's Soil erosion	On-farm costs = US$ 40 million Off-farm costs = US$ 3.1 billion	Lost production, cleaning, siltation, etc.	Crosson (1984)
Australia, 1975 Soil erosion	Land management and erosion control (repair costs) = 1975 A$ 675 million, once-off total (~ 1990 A$ 2.8 billion, 1990 US$ 2.2 billion)		Woods (1984)
USA, 1986 Soil erosion	New Mexico only On-farm costs = US$ 10 million Off-farm costs = US$ 466 million	Cleaning, recreation, car damage, paint damage, health	Huszar and Piper (1986)

Table 3. Examples of shadow prices for environmental goods and services

Type of value	Shadow pricing technique	Value of	Environmental value	Reference
Existence only	Survey (WTP)	Nadgee Nature Reserve	1986 A$ 21–33 per adult, i.e. over 1990 A$1 billion for Australia (1990 US$ 0.8 billion)	Bennett (1982)
Option and existence	Survey (WTP)	Section of Colorado River	1978 US$ 133 per household for locals; 1978 US$ 64 per household elsewhere	Walsh et al. (1978, 1982, 1984, 1985)
Existence	Survey (WTP)	Whooping cranes	1983 US$ 573 million per year (1990 US$ 1.2 billion)	Loomis and Walsh (1986)
Recreation (partial)	Travel cost	Warrumbungle National Park	1978 $A 100 per day (cf. running costs of $A 4–5 per day); ca. 85000 visitors per year, total value = 1990 A$ 26 million per year (1990 US$ 21 million)	Ulph and Reynolds (1983)
Recreation (partial)	Park fees	Amboseli Reserve, East Africa	1983 US$ 30/ha, cf. 1983 US$ 0.80/ha from agriculture	Salim (1984)
Option (partial)	Surrogate market (drug sales)	Plant species extinction, to US pharmaceutical industry	1983 US$ 200 million per species, ~1990 US$ 380 million	Farnsworth and Soejarto (1985)

the total number of species tested for such use. This is only a very partial value, however. Plant species have many other economic uses: food crops, pest control substances, genes for pest resistance, textiles, structural materials, industrial chemicals, fuel oils, and so on. Analogous calculations need to be performed for these and other uses. Such calculations will probably not be easy or precise, but they are within the scope of present knowledge.

In addition, plants provide food and habitat for animals, and animals provide a range of economically valuable products also including food, textiles and pharmaceuticals. As well as estimating the option costs of animal species extinctions in their own right, therefore, we should also include a component derived from animal species values in our estimates of option costs for plant species extinction. This requires estimates of the expected number of animal species which would be rendered extinct by the extinction of a single plant species, and by combinations of several plant species. Is this beyond our present ability? Ecological studies of particular species have revealed an incredible complexity of interactions and interdependences. Evidently we do not have information or time enough to examine these dependences for each species in turn and determine the consequences of its extinction. We may, however, be in a position to make a rough estimate of first-order effects by estimating the proportion of animal species which is critically dependent on one or a few plant species.

It is not only the dependence of animals on plants which is relevant in estimating the option costs of species extinction. Animals – and to a lesser extent plants – are also dependent on each other. Many animal species of direct economic importance, for example, prey on other species which have no direct harvest value at present. These prey species, however, then have an economic value through their contribution to the predator species; and this value can be estimated quite precisely, if the dynamics of the predator-prey interaction are known (Ragozin and Brown 1985).

It is clear from the above that attempts to quantify the option costs of species extinction require major contributions from all branches of ecology, from the observations of the field naturalist to the mathematical models of the theoretical ecologist. This, perhaps more than any other specific problem, highlights the overall difficulty in measuring ecological values and ecological/economic exchange rates, i.e. our present inability to quantify the enormous diversity of contributions which components of natural systems make to human quality of life, both material and otherwise. Everything is connected to everything else: but how? It is not an easy task to find out: but as noted earlier, much of what is known has not been applied.

Myths and Misconceptions

Market Prices and Utility

There has been a tendency for mainstream economists to take the attitude, even if they would not admit to it in professionally mixed company, that environmental values are soft greenie nonsense and that it is things like gold and internal combustion engines that provide real hard-nosed consumer utility. This is wrong. Beyond subsistence food, clothing and shelter, market values depend on subjectively perceived contributions to the quality of life. Market prices reflect human desires, not utility. A Van Gogh is no more useful than a piece of cardboard, but it's a great deal prettier – and more expensive. The main thing that makes environmental goods and services different is not utility or value, but the general lack of private ownership, control and benefits: the lack of rival consumption.

Hypothetical Valuations and Social Values

Contingent valuation methods involve asking hypothetical questions, which yield hypothetical answers. The basic assumption of CVM is that these reflect social values. Perhaps they do, sometimes; but there is no way to check, and sometimes they certainly do not. The main problem with CVM, more fundamental than bias, is that respondents simply lack the information they need to assign meaningful values to ecosystem functions. As an analogy, in many western nations a proportion of the population receives "free" medical care, paid for by the remainder of the population. Such individuals typically assign low values to medical care. This does not mean that medical care actually has a low social value, but only that those individuals do not know what it is worth. If the subsidy ends, this does not mean that the value of medical care has changed, but just that those individuals now have to pay for it. The same applies to natural systems whose functions we barely understand – and for which, in the past, we have not had to pay. As human understanding of ecosystem processes and their linkages with human well-being has increased historically, so too have values quoted for natural systems.

Willingness to Pay or Accept Compensation

There is a pervasive misconception regarding differences between willingness to pay to avoid environmental damage (WTP), and willingness to accept compensation for it (WTAC). For a given environmental change, figures quoted for WTAC are typically much higher than WTP. This is generally seen as evidence of strategic bias, not to say greed; and indeed, compensation actually accepted may often be well below the hypothetical figures quoted originally (James and Boer 1988). However, such reduced compensation is often forced rather than negotiated, and there is a perfectly good and ethical reason to expect that WTAC should be higher than WTP.

In either case, the respondent is effectively asked to partition a total budget of goods and services, some material and others not. If the question is phrased as WTAC, however, the total budget is larger than if it is phrased as WTP: because the environmental goods and services concerned are included in the total, as something that can be traded; rather than excluded, as something which must be bought by trading something else. So if you ask someone to value environmental goods and services through WTAC, you are asking a person who is richer than they would be if you asked them to estimate the corresponding value through WTP. If the environmental goods and services concerned are of major importance to that person, then they effectively have a far larger budget to allocate under WTAC than under WTP; perhaps orders of magnitude larger.

As an analogy, consider someone suffering a personal injury or other loss of health. Asking them to value that loss of health by WTP is asking how much they would pay for medical treatment. If they are not well off, they can't pay much. But asking them to value it by WTAC, means to ask them: "If you were perfectly healthy again and someone offered to pay you to be injured, how much would they have to pay you to agree to it?" For a significant injury, assuming that the person valued their health and could already afford basic necessities, the answer would probably be many orders of magnitude higher. How much would you take to have your legs permanently broken? Personally, I wouldn't be tempted by a billion dollars – not for an instant. However, if my legs actually were broken and I thought doctors could fix them, what I would pay would depend on how much I had.

Private Property Rights

It has been argued by some economists (Moran 1990) that in many cases, rather than trying to determine shadow prices, we could simply create private property rights for the goods and services concerned and let the market set their prices. It is true that markets and private property rights can be very efficient and cost-effective tools for influencing individual behaviour. However, it is not necessarily true in the real world that private ownership of resources will lead to optimal resource management. That might be true if the owners were constrained to support themselves and their descendants indefinitely from that resource alone, and if they valued their descendants' welfare as highly as their own. But the real world is not like that at all. In the present global economy, almost any kind of material possession or investment can be traded for almost any other kind, indirectly if not directly. Owners of capital seek to maximise their return on that capital by switching it between different forms of investment, constrained only by transaction costs and uncertainties on future returns. There is no financial incentive to manage a forest for sustainable yield at a low annual return, even if you do own it privately, if you can realise a much higher short-term return by selling it as timber and

Table 4. Comparison of financial and economic analysis (After James and Beer 1988)

Factor	Financial	Economic
Focus	Net returns to private investors	Net returns to national economy
Purpose	Investment decisions	National policy
Prices	Market prices, spot or contract	Market or shadow prices for resources, labour, currency, etc.
Taxes	Operating cost: aim to minimise	Internal transfers
Subsidies	Operating revenue: aim to maximise	Internal transfers
Interest	Operating cost: limits capital available	Transfers, domestic or offshore
Discount rate	Marginal and opportunity cost of money; set by market interest rate	Money: as for financial analysis Natural resources; social time preference rate
Equity	Rarely considered	Important, but generally a separate analysis

cleared land and investing the proceeds elsewhere. A similar problem arises with the separation of ownership from production in the agricultural and pastoral industries. If people working the land don't own the farm, they can't make the best decisions to ensure sustainable future production; particularly if absentee landlords treat farms as a speculative investment on a par with commodities, shares or currency futures. Private property rights are fne for the owner, but are not necessarily an alternative to shadow pricing where national resource management policy is concerned.

It is therefore important to distinguish financial analysis from economic analysis (Table 4). It is also important to remember that economics is only a model of part of our social system and that ownership rights are only one of many factors influencing resource management practices. It was recently noted, for example (Moran 1990), that government-owned elephant herds in Kenya had been severely reduced by poaching over recent years, whereas privately owned herds in Botswana and Zimbabwe had increased over the same period. This is true, but the main reason has nothing to do with ownership. It is simply that Kenya has a much higher and faster growing population density than Botswana or Zimbabwe.

Discount Rates

One of the most crucial aspects in many applications of environmental accounting is the discount rate. Irrespective of the techniques used to value environmental costs and benefits, for example, any environmental benefit-cost analysis (EBCA) will fail if an inappropriate discount rate is used. The first point to be made here is that the current interest rate in the country concerned is not an appropriate discount rate for EBCA. The interest rate is simply a measure of the opportunity cost of money at that point in space and time.

At least four separate factors must be considered: interest rate, inflation, relative prices (barter exchange rates), and the social rate of time preference (premium on immediacy). As noted above, the current interest rate, that is, the cost of borrowing money or the return on lending money, is relevant only when considering opportunity costs of using (or not using) money. It is therefore not an appropriate discount rate for EBCA, where money is not the resource considered, but simply a medium of exchange and measurement. Currency inflation produces increases in the assigned monetary values of resources, but this is due to a decrease in the value of money relative to all non-monetary resources, not an increase in the value of particular resources. The relative values of different non-monetary resources, which economists would call relative prices and which might be described in lay terms as barter exchange rates, also change with time; but these changes, if predictable, should be taken into account before any discounting of future costs and benefits. This includes increases in the relative values of conservation-related resources owing to increasing demand and falling supply.

The only justification for discounting future benefits from environmental resources, and hence the only factor which should be incorporated in the discount rate, is what economists term the pure time preference rate, and which I have called the premium on immediacy; the value placed on receiving goods or services immediately rather than identical goods or services later. It is this final factor which should be used as a discount rate in EBCA; whereas in past applications it is all too often the first, the interest rate, which has been used.

Separating these four factors in this way identifies two critical problems. The first is technical: it is extremely difficult to determine the relative values of environmental goods and services at present, let alone in the future, as discussed in the previous section. The demand for environmental resources is expected to increase and the supply to decrease, but the same may be true for many economic resources.

The second is one of viewpoint. From a national, regional, community or policy viewpoint on resource allocation, the appropriate discount rate is determined by the premium on immediacy, the last of the four factors mentioned above. From the viewpoint of the individual or corporate investor, however, all four factors are relevant, and the largest – at present, the interest rate and inflation – will outweigh the others. EBCA analyses presented from a developer's viewpoint, however, should not be used as a basis for a decision on project approval by a government or community. Their task is to determine whether the proposal yields a net benefit for the nation, region or community as a whole, and they should set the discount rate accordingly.

In this context it is interesting to note that public agencies have often used very low discount rates – well below market interest rates at the time – to justify massive investment of public capital in infrastructure developments such as water supply schemes (Lynn 1984); whilst simultaneously using high rates to justify the rapid exploitation of public natural resources.

Conclusions

In conclusion, it is clear that despite a great deal of effort in recent years, environmental accounting still has many limitations. We need to recognise those limitations and work to reduce them; but meanwhile that should not stop us from using existing techniques, albeit cautiously.

In particular, since environmental policies are intended to have a long life span, we should design them using values which will apply in the future, as far as we can estimate them. Available evidence indicates that human values ascribed to environmental goods and services have increased historically and are continuing to do so, reflecting increasing human awareness of the linkages between ecosystem function and human well-being. Human knowledge of ecosystem functions is still very limited. Despite this, much of what is known has not yet been applied in the estimation of environmental values. This, then, is the first critical task in improving environmental accounting: a systematic attempt to apply information from all ecological and related disciplines, to the more accurate estimation of economic values for environmental goods and services.

Acknowledgements. This review was first written for a national workshop on environmental accounting run by the Environment Institute of Australia in Canberra, April 1990.

References

Baldwin JH (1985) Environmental planning and management. Westview, Boulder CO, pp 216–242

Bennett JW (1982) Valuing the existence of a natural ecosystem. Search 13:232–235

Boyle KJ, Bishop RC, Welsh MP (1985) Starting point bias in contingent valuation bidding games. Land Econ 61:188–194

Buckley RC (1987) Environmental Planning Techniques. SADME, Adelaide

Churchman CW (1984) Willingness to pay and morality: a study of future values. In: Churchman CW (ed) Natural resource administration. Westview, Boulder CO, pp 71–76

Clarke EH (1985) The off-site costs of soil erosion. J Soil Water Conserv Jan–Feb 1985:19–22

Cohen MA (1986) The costs and benefits of oil spill prevention and enforcement. J Environ Econ Manag 13:167–188

Common MS (1988) Environmental and resource economics: an introduction. Longman, London

Crosson P (1984) New perspectives on soil conservation policy. J Soil Water Conserv 39:222–225

Electricity Suppliers Association of Australia (ESAA) (1990) Report on environmental costing methodology: thermal plant. Environment Committee, ESAA, Melbourne

Emmelin L (1984) Environmental protection and economic development are not incompatible. Ambio 13:281

Fabos JG (1985) Land-use planning: from global to local challenge. Chapman & Hall, London

Farber K Rutledge G (1986) Pollution abatement and control expenditures. Survey of Current Business, July 1986:94–105

Farber K, Rutledge G (1987) Pollution abatement and control expenditures, 1982–1985. Survey of Current Business, May, 1987:21–26

Farber S, Costanza R (1987) The economic value of wetlands systems. J Environ Manage 24:41–51

Farnsworth EG, Soejarto DD (1985) Potential consequences of plant extinction in the United States on the current and future availability of prescription drugs. Econ Bot 39:231–240

Hahn RW (1989) A primer on environmental policy design. Harwood, London

Huszar PC, Piper SL (1986) Estimating the off-site costs of wind erosion in New Mexico. J Soil Water Conserv Nov–Dec 1986:414–416

James D, Boer B (1988) Application of economic techniques in environmental impact assessment. Australian Environment Council, Canberra

James D, Chambers J (1986) Managing environment impacts of energy development: air quality in the Hunter Region, NSW, Australia. Environ Manag 10:421

James DE (1983) Integrated energy-economics-environment modelling with reference to Australia. AGPS, Canberra

James DE (1985) Air quality prediction in urban and semi-urban regions with generalised input-output analysis: the Hunter Region, Australia. Urban Ecol 9:25–44

Kellert SR (1984) Assessing wildlife and environmental values in cost-benefit analysis. J Environ Manage 18:355–363

Loomis JB, Walsh RG (1986) Assessing wildlife and environmental values in cost-benefit analysis. J Environ Manage 22:125–133

Lynn LE (1984) The role of benefit-cost analysis in fish and wildlife programs. In: Churchman CW (ed) Natural resource administration. Westview Boulder Co, pp 53–63

Maler KG (1984) Cost-benefit analysis: the basic facts. In: Ahmad YJ, Dasgupta P, Maler KG (eds) Environmental decision-making 2. Hodder & Stoughton, London, pp 1–20

McCloskey M (1981) Environmental protection is good business. Sierra 66(2):31–33

Moran A (1990) Sustainable development. Address to Sydney Institute and to Energy and the Environment Conference. Office of Regulation Review, Canberra

Odgers B, Upstill G, Smith K (1983a) The costs of pollution abatement: the Australian integrated steel industry. AEC Report 13. AGPS, Canberra

Odgers B, Upstill G, Smith K (1983b) The costs of pollution abatement: the Australian petrochemical industry. AEC Report 14. AGPS, Canberra

Owen OS (1986) Natural resource conservation: an ecological approach. Collier Macmillan, London

Ragozin DL, Brown JG (1985) Harvest policies and nonmarket valuation in a predator-prey system. J Environ Econ Manage 12:155–168

Russell M, Gruber M (1987) Risk assessment in environmental policy making. Science
    236:286–291
Salim E (1984) Why conservation? Environmentalist 4:97–108
Samples KC, Dixon JA, Gowen MM (1986) Information disclosure and endangered
    species valuation. Land Econ 62:306–312
Senate Standing Committee on Air Pollution (1970) Report to Parliament. Australian
    Government Publishing Service, Canberra
Suter GW, Barnthouse LW, O'Neill RV (1987) Treatment of risk in environmental impact
    assessment. Environ Manage 11:295–304
Ulph AM, Reynolds IK (1981) An economic evaluation of national parks. Aust Nat Univ
    Cent Res Environ Stud Monog Ser 4: Aust Nat Univ, Canberra
Walsh R, Greenly D, Young R, McKean J, Prato A (1978) Option values, preservation
    values and recreational benefits of improved water quality: a case study of the South
    Platte River basin, Colorado. EPA Report 600/5-780991. Environmental Protection
    Agency, Washington D.C
Walsh R, Gillman R, Loomis J (1982) Wilderness resource economics: recreation use and
    preservation values. Colorado State Univ, Fort Collins, Colo
Walsh R, Loomis J, Gillman R (1984) Valuing option, existence and bequest demands for
    wilderness. Land Econ 60:14–29
Walsh R, Sanders L, Loomis J (1985) Wild and scenic river economics: recreation use and
    preservation values. Colorado State Univ, Fort Collins, Colo
Wint A (1986) Air pollution in perspective. In: van Dop H, Fabian P, Gusten H, Hales
    JM, Wint A (eds) Air pollution: handbook of environmental chemistry: 4A:1–22,
    Springer, Berlin
Woods LE (1984) Land degradation in Australia. AGPS, Canberra

Chapter 4

Equity, Public Resources and National Accounts

Abstract

Social equity is as important a policy goal as economic efficiency.
Equity considerations are particularly critical when public resources are used by private business. Public natural resources are owned
equally by all citizens and are managed on their behalf by
governments. Sale or lease of public resources to private interests at
discounted or subsidised rates is poor resource management and is
inequitable. This is of particular concern when profits accrue to
overseas interests at the expense of domestic taxpayers. This
appears to have occurred in the woodchip industry, for example.
One reason is that conflicts between domestic lobby groups weaken
our national negotiating position in international trade. In addition, governments rely on national economic statistics such as GDP
which measure activity but not asset depletion.

Introduction

There are two main aspects to policy: what is it intended to achieve, and
what are the best instruments to achieve it? Environmental accounting is
useful in design and evaluation of both goals and means (Buckley 1988;
1990; Common 1988; Goodland and Ledec 1987; Hueting 1987; Nelson
1987; Pearce 1987; van der Ploeg et al. 1987; Stavins 1989). Here I examine
the first of these aspects, with particular reference to the management of
publicly owned natural resources.

Policy requirements change over time according to their social
context. Policy makers must assess current and likely future trends so that
policy matches social change rather than lagging behind it. There are
currently three main trends relevant to national environmental policy.

The first is increasing environmental degradation worldwide, and increasing public and political concern about it. Our ability to damage our own well-being through poor environmental management has become increasingly apparent to taxpayers and voters. Policy makers can reasonably conclude that social values placed on environmental goods and services will continue to increase, and that environmental protection should therefore feature highly in future policy design.

The second trend is increasing scarcity of natural resources, which is tending to increase prices for raw materials, technology and capital, and to increase the economic dominance of nations or corporations that control them (Coombs 1990). The third is the increasing globalisation and interdependence of trade and financial markets, whereby economic changes in any one sector or country are reflected ever more rapidly in other sectors and regions.

Equity Issues and Public Resources

Economics is a tool intended to serve social ends, which include equity as well as efficiency. In setting environmental and resource management policies, it is not only net gains that matter; it also matters where the money goes, who gains and who loses. Policy instruments should not convert public goods to private profits. If the net gain is positive but some people would be disadvantaged, then equity demands that before the project is approved or the policy adopted, these people should receive acceptable compensation from those who would benefit, either by private or public means. With respect to government policy, two kinds of equity must be considered: horizontal equity, which requires that people with similar incomes are treated equally; and vertical equity, which requires that any costs are not borne differentially by low-income earners or benefits distributed differentially to high income earners.

It is in industries involving use of public resources by private business interests that equity considerations become most critical. Such industries produce direct material benefits for their shareholders, financiers, employees and suppliers. They may also produce indirect benefits for others who deal with the primary beneficiaries: the economic multiplier effect. If they pay royalties to consolidated public revenue for the use of the resource, this represents a benefit to all taxpayers: a differentially higher benefit for those who pay more tax. They impose costs on those who suffer environmental impacts of any kind; generally not the same group of people as those who reap the benefits. They also impose costs on all citizens of the country, who are equal shareholders in all public resources, by depleting the stock of public assets.

The first criterion for deciding whether private businesses should be permitted to use public resources is net aggregate return to the public purse. Commercial profitability from the viewpoint of the operating corporation is not an adequate criterion if the corporation is foreign-owned; nor is the sales value of its products. What matters is the return to the nation, whether as royalties, export levies and taxes, or as income to its citizens. If this net aggregate return is negative, then taxpayers are simply giving money to private interests. Even if it is positive, it is important to assess whether it represents a reasonable return on the public assets concerned. This is all the more important where the resources concerned can be used once only, as in the mineral or petroleum industries; or where use of the resources reduces their value, as in non-sustainable forestry, fisheries, agriculture or tourism. In such cases the asset, or part of it, is essentially being sold: the return to its owners is a once-off price.

The second criterion for private use of public resources is equity. It is not enough that aggregate net return to the nation is adequate. It is also important that that return is equitably distributed. It would not be equitable, for example, if the entire return went to a small number of company directors. Note here that it is perfectly equitable and reasonable for company directors to be well remunerated for their expertise and judgement; and it is perfectly equitable and reasonable for entrepreneurs to receive a high return from their business ventures to compensate them for the risks involved; but it is **not** equitable or reasonable for them to achieve these profits through the use or sale of public resources, which they have obtained at a discounted price. And what constitutes a discounted price? It is anything less than the price that a private owner of those resources, not associated with the purchaser, and not an anxious seller, would demand. Where royalties are levied for private use of public resources, for example, the critical question is whether those royalties are as high as the price which would be demanded by private owners selling the same resources.

In blunt economic terms, most nations have a history of squandering public natural resources (Greiner 1990). This is not a criticism of the hardworking pioneers of our agricultural, mineral and forestry industries; they lived under different imperatives. Squander is a precise term, not a pejorative one: we have spent our assets without getting full value in return. In many cases, governments have subsidised private interests to exploit them at the taxpayers' expense. The text box summarises an example from the forestry industry; but there are examples from other sectors too, with governments spending more on infrastructure for mineral developments than they receive in royalties, or subsidising poor land management practices in the pastoral industry.

This does not mean that government should own business. Quite the reverse: governments are notoriously bad at business. Business should be owned and run by the private sector. What is in public ownership is natural resources: and the public custodians of these resources should manage them for reasonable return. As one politician said recently, "The Government, on behalf of the community, must act as if it were the owner of these resources" (Greiner 1990). As if? The citizens of any democratically governed nation **are** the owners of its resources. In setting public policy, governments could usefully look on the State, in its legal sense, as a corporate body; with the citizens as shareholders, elected politicians as the board of directors, the public service as the salaried staff, and the country's natural resources as the corporation's capital assets. Taxes would be analogous to calls on shares. The aim of such a corporation should be to use its assets to maximise the return to its shareholders through dividends and increases in the value of shares, subject to three criteria. The first of these is sustainability: the company must not collapse, so its management must be risk-averse; and its future total value should always be at least as great as it is at present. The second criterion is equity: each shareholder must receive the same return from the corporation's use of its assets, since they each own one share. The third is efficiency: the company should minimise its running costs per unit profit. These criteria are of course standard in private corporations.

Using this anaology, it is clear that many countries have not always got a good return on the use of their assets. In most countries we can identify questionable management practices by past and present governments, including: unwise borrowing and sales of equity; poor incentive schemes (tax regimes, subsidies, etc.), which have encouraged behaviour by employees and shareholders that is not in the best interests of the corporation; selling assets cheaply, and allowing assets to be run down; and relying on poor management information and accounting systems.

Why has this happened? Why have we, the shareholders, continued to elect directors who employ poor management practices? There are several reasons. (1) Individual shareholders have opted for immediate improvements in their material wellbeing even at the probable expense of future shareholders. (2) There are so many shareholders that it is in their interests to seek individual profit at the expense of the company and other shareholders. (3) At a national level, the political system in most democratic western nations means that politicians are effectively chosen largely by those shareholders of voting age living in marginal electorates, and these people are generally most concerned about their individual jobs, regardless of the company's overall welfare; minority interests may have a disproportionate say in electing the directors.

In addition, most national economies are tightly linked to the global economy and our politicians often have little power to influence it. However, such power as they do have they do not always exercise in the country's best interests. As one example, Australia has a history of weak negotiation in international trade; all too often we are anxious sellers. Why? Because our trading partners buy commodities from several sectors, and play those sectors off against each other through our domestic political system.

An Example: The Australian Woodchip Industry

Let us take as an example the Australian woodchip industry, as analysed by an economist from the London School of Economics (Parker 1988). The analysis did not consider environmental impacts and costs, but simply set out the operating costs and returns for public and private sector parties in the Australian woodchip industry, in the context of the global trade in woodchips and other forest products in the 1970's and 1980's. Its findings were as follows:

1. In 1985; Australia supplied 6.3% of traded roundwood volume but received only 2.8% of total value, because its sales were mostly low-priced woodchips.
2. The global average price for woodchips is 35% higher than the average price received by Australia
3. The trade between Australia and Japan is the largest single link in international trade in woodchips. In 1985; 45% of global woodchip exports were from Australia, and 76% of global imports were to Japan. In that year, 63% of all Japanese imports were from Australia.
4. Australia does not need to maintain low prices to keep its market share. It captured market share in 1971–73 with prices **above** those of its competitors. Japan is unlikely to import more than two-thirds of its total supply from any one country and Australia already has 63% of total market share. Hence, it should increase its prices.

5. Private capital investment by woodchip corporations is relatively low. These corporations use contractors for logging and transport, and invest capital only in the mills themselves. Public capital investment, on the other hand, is large; in roads and ports in particular, as well as the forest resources themselves.

6. The right to chip public forests has a significant market value. On one occasion, APPM bought an established mill from Tasman Pulp and Forest Holdings for $27 million when the value of its capital assets, excluding its woodchip leases, was only $7 million. The value of the forest concession was three times that of the mill.

7. In Tasmania, royalties to the Forestry Commission are related to the value of exports (10% FOB value in 1988), not to the costs of services provided. In the mid-1980's the Commission spent $20–30 million per year but received only $11–13 million per year. This operating deficit was derived almost entirely from the hardwood chip industry, rather than the softwood sector.

8. In addition, public income from road tolls in the early 1980's was $1.5–2.0 million per year, whilst public expenditure was $4–5 million per year on forestry roads, plus extra maintenance costs for public roads used by logging trucks.

9. During the period examined, the price of Australian woodchips to Japan has halved in yen terms. In real terms, allowing for inflation, it has fallen substantially further. During the same period, as outlined above, the Australian woodchip industry has received a public subsidy of millions of dollars a year.

10. There are four immediate options, not necessarily exclusive, to alleviate this problem.
    a) Increase the charges for public services such as those provided by the Forestry Commission, if necessary by an export levy which could be imposed by the Commonwealth.
    b) Impose a resource rent for use of public resources.
    c) Impose an annual environmental levy on the industry.
    d) Promote value-adding processing of forest products in Australia.

It is worth noting that there are paradoxical divergences between the way each of two major Federal parties in Australia treat such issues, and their avowed political leanings. I should emphasise here that I have no affiliation to any political party and no ideological or economic objections to the forestry industry as such, just the way parts of it are currently run. People currently earning their livelihood from the forestry industry, either as loggers, truckers or mill operators, lobby hard for logging to continue because it provides them with jobs, and because that is the "traditional" employment in their communities. This argument is made even in areas where the remaining timber supply is so low that mills will have to close in a decade or less anyway, leaving the community without employment. But the public return from forestry generally does not meet its public costs; and continued logging in areas of high conservation value depletes public resources which could otherwise be used more profitably in other ways in the future. So those who argue for logging to continue in order to save their jobs are demanding the right to be supported by the State; i.e. by other taxpayers. This is a very socialist attitude; yet it is the the more right-wing parties, avowedly capitalist, which support continued logging!

National Accounts and Statistics

One major reason why many countries mismanage their natural resources is that politicians and their economic advisors receive misleading signals about the state of the economy. They rely on aggregate economic statistics such as GDP or GNP which do not properly distinguish credits and debits, stocks and flows, or foreign and domestic ownership. As noted by Coombs (1990): "There is something wrong with an accounting system which records the running down of capital as a contribution to income. ... Not until our national accounts cease classifying exports of exhaustible resources as income and treat them as the sale of capital assets, reducing our national wealth and impairing our economic future, will our business managers, economists and politicians receive accurate signals about the health of our economy."

There are attempts in several nations at present, including the USA, Canada, France, Norway, Holland and Japan, to calculate an alternative statistic, a net national welfare product, which takes these aspects properly into account. The problem has been reviewed in detail in a recent World Bank publication (Ahmad et al. 1989) with specific reference to the System of National Accounts (SNA) as used in OECD nations such as the USA and Australia.

GDP and GNP do not measure national income. At best, they measure gross sales, without allowing for costs, asset sales, debts and depreciation. Strictly, however, they do not even measure sales, but only the level of economic activity. Relying on GDP or GNP to measure the

Table 1. Techniques for incorporating environmental goods and services in national accounts (After Bartelmus in Ahmad et al. 1989)

Non-monetary environmental statistics and physical accounting, additional to economic indicators in SNA
- environmental indicators and statistics
- materials and energy balances
- environmental input-output analyses
- resource accounting

Monetary accounts for environmental goods and services and natural resources, in parallel with main SNA
- flow accounts for environmental quality and natural resources
- balance sheets and reconciliation accounts to tie into SNA

Full monetary environmental accounting, integrated into SNA, using market or shadow prices for
- environmental costs and expenditures
- natural resource capital
- environmental services

Indicators of sustainable production and expenditure (P&E)
- sustainable net P&E
- sustainable gross P&E
- modified measures of gross or net national product

---

success of national economic policy is rather like relying on the tachometer to drive a car. It tells you how fast the engine is running, but not how much fuel is left, whether the wheels are gripping the track, or whether the car is on the right road.

The most serious limitation of GDP/GNP as an economic indicator is that it does not record sale or depreciation of assets, but only the income produced. Many industries have recorded high economic productivity for a number of years and then collapsed as their resource base was exhausted: e.g. Peruvian anchovies, Australian prawns, the international whaling industry. There are several countries in a similar situation. As an obvious example, Nauru has a high GNP from resource exploitation, but without reinvestment in more sustainable industries, the Nauru economy will soon collapse. Middle Eastern oil-producing nations face similar predicaments. So does Australia, though not quite so obviously, since it has more than one primary industry. In 1963, Libya legislated to ensure that at least 70% of revenue from oil sales was reinvested in other forms of domestic development. In Australia the only analogous requirement is for a minimum level of domestic equity in private corporations exporting natural resources.

The current SNA protocols were set in 1968 and are nearing the final stages of a major review, due for adoption in 1991. The main approaches to national accounting for environmental goods and services, including both consumption of natural resources and deterioration of environmental quality, are summarised in Table 1. At present it seems likely that the revised SNA protocol will treat national environmental accounts as a separate subsidiary set, using both physical parameters and monetized values as far as this is possible, linked to the main national economic statistics by a system of balance sheets and reconciliation accounts.

Conclusions

Public natural resources are owned equally by all citizens of the country concerned. Governments are custodians of these resources as public assets. They are responsible for good management of those assets and should not sell them to private interests at discounted prices. In the past, they have done just this on many occasions, for a variety of reasons. Some of these were socially justifiable, such as encouraging private investment in remote areas. Others were not, and many policy aims that were justifiable in the past are now inappropriate.

Three trends may help to overcome these problems. (1) Electoral pressures for greater accountability by government agencies responsible for planning and resource management, and in particular for greater attention to equity considerations. (2) Increasing recognition by governments that they are responsible for managing publicly owned natural resources in a commercially and socially justifiable manner. (3) Revision of protocols for national economic statistics (SNA) so as to distinguish stocks and flows and include environmental goods and services.

Acknowledgements. This review was first written for a national workshop on environmental accounting sponsored by the Environment Institute of Australia in Canberra, April 1990.

References

Ahmad YJ, Serafy SE, Lutz E (eds) (1989) Environmental accounting for sustainable development. World Bank, Washington

Buckley RC (1988) Critical problems in environmental planning and management. Environ Plan Law J 5:206–225

Buckley RC (1990) Shortcomings in current institutional frameworks for environmental planning & management. In: Sawer M, Kelly J, (eds) Development and the environment: making decisions we can live with. Royal Aust Inst Public Admin, Canberra, pp 1–10

Common MS (1988) Environmental and resource economics: an introduction. Longman, London

Coombs HC (1990) The return of scarcity. Cambridge University Press, Melbourne, 171 pp

Goodland R, Ledec G (1987) Neoclassical economics and principles of sustainable development. Ecol Modell 38:19–46

Greiner NF (1990) The new environmentalism: a conservative perspective. Earth Day Speech, 22. 4. 90. Office of the Premier of NSW, Sydney, 22 pp

Hueting R (1987) An economic scenario that gives top priority to saving the environment. Ecol Modell 38:123–140

Nelson RH (1987) The economics profession and the making of public policy. J Econ Lit 25:44–91

Parker P (1988) Environmental and economic conflict: the Australian woodchip debate and policy options. University of London, Australian Studies Centre, Working Paper 31

Pearce D (1987) Foundations of an ecological economics. Ecol Modell 38:9–19

Stavins RN (1989) Harnessing market forces to protect the environment. Environment 31:5–7, 29–35

van der Ploeg SWF, Braat LC and van Lierop WFJ (1987) Integration of resource economics and ecology. Ecol Modell 38:171–end

Chapter 5

Economic Instruments of Environmental Policy

Abstract

Economic instruments of environmental policy can be both efficient and equitable. They provide incentives for particular actions without removing individual freedom of choice. They generally need to be coupled with or supported by regulatory and technological instruments. From a policy viewpoint they can be used to deter environmentally damaging activities, improve social equity, raise revenue or recover public-sector costs. They are used in few countries at present, but seem to have worked reasonably well to date.

Instruments used to control environmental damage include:

1. environmental damage taxes, charges and levies, such as emission charges, environmental protection charges, and development taxes;
2. input taxes;
3. environmental damage rights and credits, such as emission rights (nets, bubbles, offsets), emission reduction credits, and transferable development credits;
4. performance bonds and guarantees, e.g. for rehabilitation or waste management;
5. subsidies and bounties;
6. tax concessions and rebates; and
7. special purpose grants.

Instruments used to control consumption of natural resources include:

1. tradeable quotas, e.g. in forestry, fisheries and water supply;
2. resource rents and royalties; and
3. sliding charges for utilities.

Instruments which affect both damage and consumption include:

1. differential excise, sales taxes and tariffs;
2. refundable deposits; and
3. broad taxes such as payroll and capital gains taxes.

Introduction

There are three main types of instrument for environmental policy: regulatory, technological and economic. In pollution control, for example, regulatory instruments specify physical standards to be attained, such as discharge limits. They leave decisions on technology and costs to the operating corporations concerned. Technological instruments specify technology to be adopted, such as pollution control devices, but not costs or outcome. Economic instruments set charges for environmental use or degradation, such as pollution charges per unit emission, but do not specify the equipment used or environmental quality objectives to be obtained.

By designing appropriate economic incentives for good environmental management, government can allow many development decisions to be made by project proponents, rather than passed to government. Some types of policy instrument can also have the effect of transferring administrative workload from public regulatory agencies to private-sector insurance and finance industries and the courts.

Economic instruments of environmental policy are used extensively in some European countries, and to a lesser extent in the USA. They are by no means a panacea; they have high information and monitoring costs, and they must be backed up by regulatory and/or technical policy instruments.

Initially, economic instruments of environmental policy were advocated strongly by economists. More recent literature (Vollebergh 1987; Common 1988; 1990) suggests that perhaps economic instruments of environmental policy would not work so well after all; but meanwhile, they have been tried in practice and seem to work fine (Bressers 1987).

As with any other policy instrument, criteria for the choice, design and evaluation of economic instruments or environmental policy (Baumol and Oates 1979, Yapp and Upstill 1985; Common 1988, 1990) include:

Table 1. Criteria for evaluating fiscal instruments (After Yapp and Upstill 1985)

Ojective:
- primary
- secondary

Application:
- preventive
- curative
- remedial
- restorative

Operation:
- incentives
- disincentives

Consistency with other policy objections

Individual freedom: effects on
- individuals
- private organisations
- social groups
- public organisations?

Time frame:
- short- or long-term problem?
- appropriate time frame for instrument?
- will it be overtaken by technological change?
- will it influence the planning horizon of decision makers?

Market system:
- is the problem within or outside the market system?
- is it a market or non-market instrument?

Institutional responsibility:
- federal
- state
- local
- private

Focus:
- inputs, outputs or infrastructure?
- buyers, sellers or owners?
- extraction, production, storage, sale or disposal?
- physical resources or human activity?

Administrative efficiency:
- cost of regulation
- opportunities for avoidance
- understandability to those affected
- adaptability

Fiscal impact: on Treasury
- debits?
- credits?

Uncertainty:
- how confidently can effects be forecast?
- economic and structural data
- forecasting tools and models
- speed of social change

Cash flow
Implications: one-off, annual or frequent transactions
- Treasury
- affected groups

Property rights: impacts

Income stability: impacts

Environmental effects:
- intended
- potential unintended

effectiveness, allocative efficiency, equity, cost-effectiveness, reliability, adaptability, ease of administration, maximum incentive for individual effort, minimal interference with private decisions, robustness in the face of uncertainty, and economy in operation, information gathering, monitoring and enforcement. A more detailed checklist is given in Table 1.

As an example of equity considerations, it might seem at first sight that since air and water are in public ownership, improvements in air and water quality would benefit everyone equally. However, the sources of air and water pollution are not uniformly distributed. Ambient air and water quality differ from one place to another, and changes in air and water quality are concentrated in particular areas. Such changes therefore have greatest impact on people who live, work or play in those areas. As a common example, reductions in smokestack emissions or transport noise in urban industrial areas tend to benefit low income earners who live in those industrial areas more than higher income earners who commute from wealthier suburbs. Similarly, reductions in point discharges into a river will generally only benefit those downstream.

Controlling Environmental Damage

Environmental Damages Taxes, Charges and Levies

These rely on charging for damage to publicly owned environmental goods and services. The most common example is charging firms to discharge wastes into air, water and landfill. Development taxes in the USA provide a second example. From a policy viewpoint, they may be used either as a means of raising general public revenue, as a means of recovering public-sector administrative costs, as a deterrent to environmental damage, or as a social mechanism by which those who reduce the value of public assets are taxed an amount equal to the value of the damage. Alternatively, they may be intended as an incentive to improve pollution control, for example, by imposing a tax on pollution such that the marginal cost of paying the tax is greater than the marginal cost of installing better pollution control equipment. This provides an incentive for plants to upgrade equipment by subjecting them to a financial penalty if they do not, rather than threatening them with immediate closedown.

There is an important distinction between variable charges which depend on the degree of environmental damage, and fixed charges which do not. Only the former provide an incentive to reduce environmental damage.

Environmental damage charges can vary greatly in their precise form, particularly as regards thresholds, sliding charge scales, and coupling with statutory penalties. In the Federal Republic of Germany, for example, effluent charges were introduced in 1976 in addition to

technology-based requirements (Brown and Johnson 1984). Their introduction was supported by sectors of industry which had already adopted
improved effluent-control practices, as the charges gave them a financial
edge over their competitors. In Holland, however, both industry and
conservation groups opposed pollution charges initially, but both now
support them in view of their success (Bressers 1987).

Effluent discharge permits in the FRG specify baseline levels,
discharge standards, monitoring procedures, and maximum permissible
discharge concentrations. If the standard is met, charges are discounted
by 50%. If it is exceeded, the full charge is payable, plus a fine. The actual
charge is calculated from the expected discharge concentration as
specified by the corporation concerned, using damage-unit rates fixed by
law, such as 1 unit/m³ organic settleable solids, 5 units/100 g Hg, etc. This
gives a total expected number of damage units and the charge is then set at
a certain fee per unit. The cost of these charges to the corporations
concerned is less than 2% of sales for even the most heavily polluting
industries, excepting only the pulp, yeast and tanning industries (Brown
and Johnson 1984). The standards are set by industry-government task
forces. Municipalities are subject to the charges in the same way as private
corporations. The revenues raised are used to subsidise investment in
waste treatment technology.

Closely related to emission charges are environmental protection
charges. These are designed to be equal to the profit made by breaking or
disregarding an environmental standard, and apply in addition to any
fines or penalties. These are used in Scandinavia (Ware 1985) and the
USA (Westman 1985), but have high monitoring and enforcement costs.

The main disadvantages of environmental damage taxes as policy
instruments are their unpredictable outcome and high information costs,
especially in measuring damage costs where secondary impacts are
involved. Their advantages are that they are adaptable, they can be
improved iteratively, they raise public funds and they can be both efficient
and equitable.

Input Taxes

One approach to reducing monitoring or metering costs is to tax inputs to
environmentally damaging processes, rather than outputs or actual
damage. In some Scandinavian countries, for example, industries are
taxed on their petroleum consumption, with revenues being used to
subsidise various environmental projects (Ware 1985). Fuels containing

over 1% sulphur are also subject to a sliding tax on sulphur content, to encourage the use of low-S fuels (Ware 1985). The main disadvantage of input taxes is that they do not provide an incentive for good environmental management unless the taxes are related to input quantities by a factor which varies with the ratio between input and pollution generated.

Environmental Damage Rights and Credits

Regulatory or technological instruments give firms the right to produce a certain level of environmental damage. These rights are non-rival and do not limit the total level of environmental damage which can be produced by all firms. An alternative approach is to create damage rights which can be owned and which have a fixed and finite total. Depending on the precise form of instrument, these rights may either be bankable by individual firms only, tradeable between firms under various conditions, or marketable for cash. Options and futures in such rights may also be created and traded (Raufer et al. 1986). The main examples are emission or pollution rights, and transferable development credits. Both of these are currently used in the USA. Different types of emission rights have different generic names, depending on the degree of trading permitted:

nets: between discharge points, within one plant;
bubbles: between plants and discharge points, within one site;
internal offsets: between plants, sites and operations, within one firm;
external offsets: between firms within a regional airshed or water catchment.

Nets and bubbles were introduced to enable a company to cut pollution control costs by reducing emissions from sources where it is cheapest to do so, provided the overall net reduction is more than would have been achieved by reducing emissions from each source equally, as required to meet overall emission standards. Higher emission rates from one source are offset by low emissions from another.

In the USA, the 70 air-quality bubbles approved up to February 1981 led to an average cost saving of US$ 2 million each (Westman 1985). Both internal and external offsets are permitted. In an internal offset, a single corporation is permitted to construct a new plant if it reduces emissions in existing plants by more than the emission from the new plant. The number of times this reduction must exceed the new emission is called the offset factor, and is often high: e.g., 10:1. In an external offset, one company reduces its emissions, giving it an emission-right credit which it can then sell to another company in the same region. A similar offset ratio applies. In either case, new plants must use "best practicable technology" (BPT) or "best available control technology" (BACT), depending on state legislation. Evidently this approach works best where administrative boundaries coincide with airshed boundaries; otherwise emissions released in one state would affect air quality in a second, irrespective of the controls applied in the second. To overcome this, all states within a given airshed tend to apply uniform regulations.

One difficulty with tradeable emission rights is how they should be allocated initially. They may be sold to private interests by the State, for example by auction or tender, or they may be distributed gratis to existing industries in proportion to actual past emissions, a process known as grandfathering. The former means that firms which are using emission rights provided by regulatory instruments effectively have those rights cancelled and have to buy new ones. This may be viewed as unjust, since there was a reasonable expectation that these rights would continue. Grandfathering, however, gives an unfair advantage to firms with poor environmental management or outdated pollution control equipment, since it gives them the right to continue as high polluters, to the detriment of their competitors as well as the community. Some combination of short-term free rights and longer-term purchased rights with a transition period for adjustment seems optimal; and this is in fact what has happened in the USA (Chisholm 1985).

Another difficulty with marketable discharge permits is that they could be used to corner the market for a particular product, by preventing competing manufacturers from operating. This does not yet seem to have occurred in practice.

Marketable emission rights can in theory produce the same economically efficient reduction in total pollution that could be achieved with emission charges, but they have very different social implications (Nelson 1987; Common 1988, 1990). Emission charges imply that all repositories for pollution – air, water, soil and biota – are in full public ownership, and the State therefore has the right to charge private interests to use them. Marketable discharge permits, on the other hand, establish private ownership of pollution rights, at least up to a predefined pollution level.

Performance Bonds and Guarantees

Performance bonds are used by regulatory agencies, both as an incentive for operating corporations to comply with environmental requirements, and as a means to ensure that funds for cleanup, decommissioning, rehabilitation or remediation would be available if the corporation defaulted or went bankrupt. Rehabilitation bonds are commonplace in the mineral and energy sectors, and waste management performance bonds in the manufacturing, chemical, and mineral processing industries. In the future we may well see such bonds covered as one sector of corporate environmental insurance, i.e. operating corporations will pay premiums to underwriters, who will provide regulatory agencies with a guarantee of payment if the operating corporation defaults on its obligations. The whole field of environmental insurance seems likely to burgeon in the near future, as environmental audit is now.

Subsidies and Bounties

Rather than penalise poor environmental performance, governments sometimes elect to reward good performance. In practice, however, it appears that whilst subsidies for environmental research and development (R&D) have been effective, subsidies for improved environmental management by operating firms have often been misused (Hollick 1984).

Some subsidies and bounties lead indirectly to adverse environmental impacts. Drought relief subsidies for the pastoral industry tended to reward graziers whose properties were overstocked rather than those who had managed their herds well. Fertiliser subsidies have led to overuse. Clearance subsidies have converted wooded areas of high conservation value into marginal agricultural land with neither economic nor conservation value.

Where public resources are delivered to consumers by public agencies and charges do not cover the full costs, that too is a subsidy. Water reticulation provides a common example.

Tax Concessions and Rebates

Concessions and rebates have similar effects to subsidies. They can apply either to plant and equipment, such as accelerated depreciation provisions for new pollution control technology; or to operating costs and practices; or to encourage R&D.

Special Purpose Grants

One of the most straightforward ways for government to encourage particular environmental management practices is simply to provide special grants for that purpose. These are costly, however, and rarely used except where they can provide substantial savings on administrative costs.

Instruments Controlling Consumption
of Public Natural Resources

Tradeable Quotas

Just as policy instruments can create tradeable rights to reduce the value of public environmental resources by using them as recipients for wastes, they can also create tradeable rights to reduce the value of public environmental resources by consuming them. Tradeable quotas are directly analogous to tradeable damage rights. They are used extensively in fisheries, forestry and water supply.

Resource Rents and Royalties

Resource rents and royalties represent prices extracted by the public owners of public natural resources for their use by private interests. The distinction between them is that rents are related to the quantity or value of the resource before extraction or use, whereas royalties are determined by the quantity or value of the primary commodity after extraction, e.g. crude oil, condensate, sawlogs, etc.

Royalties and resource rents are already in common use in many countries. If we accept the oft-stated economists' argument that to get the best use of public resources we should create private ownership rights in them, then it is clear that such owners would charge high rents for their use by others. The same argument applies to resources in public ownership. The best way to get private industry to add value to public resources is to charge for those resources at as high a price as the market will bear.

Sliding Charges for Utilities

Many publicly owned resources are currently delivered to industrial and domestic consumers as utilities, e.g., water, gas and electricity. At present, the most common charging systems are either fixed unit rates, or fixed total charges which do not vary with the quantity consumed. To encourage resource and energy conservation, it has been suggested (Coombs 1990) that public agencies supplying these utilities could institute sliding scales of charges. A basic supply would be cheap, but heavy demand would attract higher unit prices (Coombs 1990). At present, most differential tariffs for utilities operate in the opposite direction; large industries typically pay lower unit prices than domestic consumers.

Instruments Influencing Both Damage and Consumption

Differential Excise, Sales Taxes and Tariffs

Excise and sales taxes can be used to modify both waste treatment and resource consumption. An obvious example is provided by differential sales tax for recycled materials. The same applies to differential tariffs and tariff protection, though these are relatively blunt instruments that tend to affect entire industry sectors rather than particular activities.

Refundable Deposits

Refundable deposits, as commonly applied to drink containers of various types, are sharply focussed instruments which can effectively reduce both resource consumption and waste generation.

Broad Taxes

Even very broad tax instruments can have environmental impacts, though this is not their primary aim. In Australia, for example, the present tax regime discourages the use of labour by imposing a payroll tax, and good industrial environmental management is often labour-intensive. Given that Australian domestic industries have to be protected by trade barriers because their labour costs are higher than those of their Asian competitors, and given that Australian government policy is purportedly intended to increase employment and keep labour-intensive value-adding manufacturing processes in Australia, a tax that penalises high staffing levels seems remarkably illogical. Equally illogical is government policy which is purportedly intended to decrease inflation by increasing savings, but penalises domestic saving by taxing it. Given that environmental deterioration locally, nationally, and globally is largely determined by industrial activity and investment in environmental management, and that these are strongly influenced by financial systems, it is clear that factors such as inflation rates, or broad tax instruments such as capital gains or consumption taxes, can affect environmental quality. The effects of using such blunt instruments are unpredictable, but they may be large and cannot be ignored.

Discussion and Conclusions

Economic instruments of environmental policy will rarely be effective alone, but they could be very effective as part of an integrated strategy that also uses regulatory and technological instruments. The US strategy for air quality management, for example, contains planning and zoning controls, emission control regulations and penalties, BPT stipulations, and economic instruments such as bubbles and regional offsets (Westman 1985).

Given the many theoretical advantages of economic policy instruments why are they so rarely used in practice? The main reasons (Common 1988, 1990) seem to be uncertainty as to their outcome, and high information costs associated with monitoring and enforcement. In theory, economic incentives should be preferable to regulation because they should be able to achieve a given environmental protection budget at the lowest aggregate cost to society and with the lowest initial information cost for regulatory agencies. In practice, however: (1) we generally do not know what savings are likely to be achieved, although overseas experience suggests they could be substantial; (2) initial information costs are lower for regulatory instruments since we can simply adopt or adapt information from overseas; and (3) operational information costs for regulatory instruments tend to be lower. In addition, the theoretical argument relies on two assumptions: (1) that both regulating agencies and regulated corporations are well informed as to the costs and benefits of different operational practices; and (2) that discharge levels are continuously variable. Neither of these is true. Major reductions in emissions generally require large capital investment by industry. Since economic uncertainty is always a prevailing aspect of commerce, private corporations will generally seek to minimise capital investment even at the cost of higher operating costs, if this maintains flexibility in financial management.

Despite these limitations, the use of economic instruments of environmental policy is increasing. For example, 16 environmental tax bills were put before the most recent (101st) US Congress, for example: 2 relating to clean air; 4 to oil-spill and hazardous-waste control and cleanup; 5 to recycling and materials conservation; 4 to water and energy conservation; and 1 to infrastructure (Hoerner 1990).

In conclusion, my view is that there is considerable scope and potential for the selective use of taxes and tariffs as instruments of environmental policy, but that they will only be effective if they are highly selective and carefully focussed. Deposits on recyclable containers, sliding taxes on the use of polluting processes, emission charges, recycling rebates, and so on may work well. Broad blunt tax instruments, on the other hand, have broad and unpredictable effects.

Acknowledgements. This review was first written for a national workshop on environmental accounting sponsored by the Environment Institute of Australia in Canberra, April 1990.

References

Baumol WJ, Oates WE (1979) Economics, environmental policy and the quality of life. Prentice Hall, New Jersey

Bressers HTA (1987) Effluent changes can work: the case of the Dutch water quality policy. In: Dietz FJ, Heijman WJM (eds) Environmental policy in a market economy. Pudoc, Wageningen, pp 40–60

Brown GM, Johnson RW (1984) Pollution control by effluent changes: it works in the Federal Republic of Germany, why not in the US? Nat Res J 24:929–966

Chisholm AH (1985) The choice of pollution control policies under uncertainty. Aust Nat Univ Centre Resour Environ Stud Monog 15:1–22

Common MS (1988) Environmental and resource economics: an introduction. Longan, London

Common MS (1990) The choice of pollution control instruments: why is so little notice taken of economists' recommendations? Environ Plan A 21:1297–1314

Coombs HC (1990) The return of scarcity. Cambridge University Press, Melbourne. 171 pp

Hoerner JA (1990) Future bright but hazy for pollution taxes. Tax Notes, April 2, 1990:12–15

Hollick M (1984) The design of environmental management policies. Environ Plan Law J 1:58–71

Nelson RH (1987) The economics profession and the making of public policy. J Econ Lit 25:44–91

Raufer RK, Feldman SL, Jaksch JA (1986) Emissions trading and acid deposition control: the need for ERC leasing. J Air Pollut Control Assoc 36:574–580

Vollebergh RJ (1987) Wishful thinking about the effects of market incentives in environmental policy. In: Dietz FJ, Heijman WJM (eds) Environmental policy in a market economy. Pudoc, Wageningen, pp 40–60

Ware JA (1985) Fiscal measures and the attainment of environment objectives: Scandinavian initiatives and their applicability to Australia. AGPS, Canberra, 24 pp

Westman WE (1985) Ecology, impact assessment and environmental planning. Wiley, New York

Yapp TP, Upstill HG (1985) Fiscal measures and the environment: impacts and potential. AGPS, Canberra

Chapter 6

National Audit of Environmental Impact Predictions

Abstract

Our understanding of natural ecosystems can be measured by our ability to predict their responses to external disturbances. Predictions made during environmental impact assessment (EIA) for major development projects are hypotheses about such responses, which can be tested with data collected in environmental monitoring programmes. The systematic comparison of predicted and actual impacts has been termed environmental impact audit. Ecosystem disturbances associated with major resource developments, though of lesser magnitude than those associated with natural cataclysms, are generally of far greater magnitude than those which can be applied experimentally. Environmental audit can hence provide critical tests of theory in a number of natural sciences. It is also needed to improve the scientific content of EIA. Audits of 4 and 29 EIS's respectively have been carried out previously in the UK and USA. This study, in Australia, is the first national scale audit for any country. It is also the first attempt to select, from the many vague statements in EIS's, only those predictions that are scientifically testable, and to determine and analyse their quantitative accuracies. Its principal results are as follows. The average accuracy of quantified, critical, testable predictions in environmental impact statements in Australia to date is $44 \pm 5\%$ SE. Predictions where actual impacts proved more severe than expected were on average significantly ($p < 0.05$) less accurate ($33 \pm 9\%$) than those where they proved as or less severe ($53 \pm 6\%$).

Introduction

One of the central components of development planning is environmental impact assessment (EIA), and one of the central components of EIA is the accurate prediction of potential impacts. It is therefore important to know how accurate such predictions actually are. This can be determined by checking past impact predictions against actual impacts as revealed by environmental monitoring programmes. Such checks have been termed audits.

The principal advantage of large-scale systematic audit of environmental impact predictions is that it provides a feedback link in environmental planning and management. Impacts are rarely known with certainty when development applications are under review or development approvals granted, and project designs are often modified between approval and startup, and again as operations proceed. Operational environmental management should be, and usually is, based on actual rather than predicted impacts: one of the principal aims of operational environmental management is to modify processes as necessary to ensure that actual impacts comply with standards or other commitments, even if they did not initially prove to be as predicted during environmental impact assessment (EIA). Environmental impact audit provides a measure of the accuracy of the initial prediction, and potentially, of the "environmental management effort" needed to bring actual impacts into line with expectations where initial estimates proved inaccurate. This also provides a "learning function" in EIA as a whole: future predictions can take into account the outcomes of past predictions.

Most of the early literature on environmental audit refers simply to compliance checks on single operations, which may be referred to as external single-project environmental impact audit. A number of examples were reviewed by Tomlinson and Atkinson (1987a).

In the mid- to late 1980's, a number of calls were made for systematic checking of environmental monitoring data against impact predictions: multi-project environmental impact audit, in the terminology outlined above (e.g. Canter 1984, 1985; Bisset 1985; Knight 1985; Moncrieff et al. 1985; NZCE 1985; Henderson 1987; Culhane 1987; Tomlinson and Atkinson 1987a, b; McCallum 1987; Bisset and Tomlinson 1988; Buckley 1987, 1988a, b, 1989a, b, c). Several of these authors also presented data on particular sets of developments, as outlined below.

Five multi-project environmental impact audits have been carried out previously. Bisset (1985) examined 791 impact predictions from 4 projects in the UK, finding that only 77 of these predictions could be audited, and that 57 were "probably accurate". Moncrieff et al. (1985) described an "environmental performance audit", of selected pipeline projects in southern Ontario, Canada. In Australia, Knight (1985) reviewed seven projects in Victoria, principally in relation to the operation of institutional systems for EIA and environmental management planning. His review examined nine particular aspects of each project, and the accuracy of impact predictions was one of these. The seven projects were selected from a total of 90 which had been subject to formal EIA prior to April 1985. They included a dam, two freeway upgrades, a power transmission line, a ski lift, a mini steel plant and a marina. Of the seven EIA documents, only two contained "predictions based on theory or modelling", and only one such prediction was testable: traffic volumes on the Hume Highway had increased slightly faster than predicted. Henderson (1987) considered 122 predictions from two projects in Canada. Of these, 42 could not be audited because of lack of monitoring data, and 10 either because they were too vague or because of modifications to the project. Of the 70 predictions audited, 54 were substantially correct, 13 partly correct or uncertain, and 3 were definitely wrong.

The fifth and most extensive environmental impact audit carried out previously was performed by Culhane (1987), who examined 239 impact predictions from 29 EIS's, intended to form a "representative cross-section" of EIS's prepared in the USA between 1974 and 1978. The projects were concerned principally with agriculture, forestry, infrastructure, waste management and uranium processing: none were mining projects, for example. Culhane found that most of the impact predictions in these EIS's were very imprecise, with less than 25% being quantified. Few predictions were clearly wrong, but less than 30% were "unqualifiedly close to forecasts".

This study was the first audit of environmental impact predictions on a national scale.

Methods

The principal conceptual steps in environmental impact audit are summarised in Table 1. There is no single agency which maintains a list of EIS's produced in Australia: separate lists were kindly provided by agencies of the various State and Commonwealth governments.

Table 1. Steps in an external multi-project environmental impact audit

---

1. Identify the set of EIS's under consideration; in this case, all EIS's produced in Australia to date.
2. Select those EIS's covering projects which were expected to produce major quantifiable impacts on specific components of the physical, biological or human environment.
3. Select EIS's covering projects which went ahead substantially as planned, and which have been subjected to a routine monitoring programme.
4. Isolate actual predictions couched in scientifically testable terms, and express those predictions in a quantitative form, including a measure of error. This will not always be straightforward! (Duinker and Beanlands 1986; Culhane 1987).
5. Determine whether the monitoring programmes for the projects concerned measured the parameters required to test these predictions; and if so, whether the sampling design (e.g. location, frequency and precision of measurements) was statistically adequate to perform such a test.
6. Stratify data by type of development and by environmental parameters considered.
7. Adjust impact predictions to take account of any post-EIS operational modifications.
8. Compare impact predictions and monitoring results to determine the degree of accuracy with which each prediction was met.
9. Search for patterns in the accuracy or otherwise of predictions, in relation to, e.g., recentness, geographic location, project type or industry sector, environmental parameters concerned, and so on.

I screened these lists to identify those development projects for which there were both testable impact predictions, in EIA documents; and the data to test them, from environmental monitoring programmes. There is generally no public right of access to corporate environmental monitoring data in Australia, so I approached the relevant operating corporations directly to request access to their data, under the condition that all information would remain strictly confidential until the corporation concerned authorised its publication.

This approach necessarily suffers from a number of limitations; as follows:

- EIA documents often contain few testable predictions: instead, they simply identify issues of concern.
- Such testable predictions as they do contain often refer to relatively minor impacts, with major impacts being referred to only in qualitative terms.
- Environmental parameters which are monitored often don't correspond with those for which predictions were made.

- Monitoring techniques often do not enable predictions to be tested: for example, the predictions may have been made for one point, but monitoring data collected from another; or predictions (particularly in relation to pollutant concentrations) may have been made for one time period, but monitoring data collected or expressed for a different period (e.g. hourly, weekly or annual averages instead of 3-min, daily or monthly).
- Monitoring data are often inadequate for statistically valid testing of predictions: for example, the data may contain too few samples, too many missing data points, inadequate controls, inadequate information on other possible factors which may influence parameters monitored, etc.
- Environmental audits can only test predictions and predictive techniques which were made or used when EIA documents were compiled several years earlier, and there may have been significant advances in predictive techniques subsequently.
- Development projects are almost always modified, sometimes substantially, between conceptual or design stage as used for EIA, and actual operations.
- Most monitoring data are collected and provided by the operating corporations concerned, which may possibly provide only favourable data.

With regard to this particular study, it seems likely that only those companies with relatively good records in environmental planning and management (EPM) are included. One of the most critical screening criteria is the availability of good monitoring data; and corporations which accord low priority to EPM may simply not have good environmental monitoring data and may thus have been excluded without ever being approached. Of those corporations which I did approach, only one made difficulties about providing data, and one government agency refused to provide data on a particular aspect of its operations.

Results

Number of EIS's and predictions

The project screening phase and subsequent comparisons of impact prediction and monitoring data revealed enormous variation, between

Table 2. Predicted and actual environmental impacts

Component/ parameter	Type of development	Predicted impact	Actual impact	Accuracy/ precision
Emissions to air: particulates	Power station	<0.12 g m^{-3} <0.043 kg GJ^{-1} for each of 2 units	1: 95% <0.12 g m^{-3} 99% <0.2 g m^{-3} 2: 95% <0.07 g m^{-3} 99% <0.2 g m^{-3}	Incorrect: 67%, worse Incorrect: 67%, worse
	Power station	<0.458 g m^{-3}	<0.458 g m^{-3}	Correct
Emissions to air: U in dust	Uranium mine	Calciner stack: 2200 g d^{-1}	Calciner stack: <730 g d^{-1}	Incorrect $<33\%$, better
Emissions to air: SO$_2$	Power station	<1.44 g m^{-3} <0.52 kg GJ^{-1} for 2 units	99.99% of data (67% total time) <1.25 g m^{-3} <0.46 kg GJ^{-1}	?Correct: 87%, better
	Brown coal Liquefaction	Stage 1 7.01 g s^{-1}	<1.0 g s^{-1}	Incorrect: 14%, better
		Stage 2 19.55 g s^{-1}	<1.0 g s^{-1}	Incorrect: 5%, better
		50% from waste-water incinerator	80% from waste-water incinerator	Incorrect: 63%, more
Emissions to air: NO$_x$	Power station	<0.84 g m^{-3} <0.3 kg GJ^{-1} for 2 units	99.99% of data (67% total time) <0.65 g m^{-3} <0.225 kg GJ^{-1}	Correct: 76%, better
	Brown coal Liquefaction	Stage 1 2.83 g s^{-1}	<2.7 g s^{-1}	Incorrect: $<95\%$, better
		Stage 2 5.41 g s^{-1}	<4.5 g s^{-1}	Incorrect: $<83\%$, better

Category	Facility	Prediction	Actual	Assessment
Emissions to air: total F⁻	Aluminium smelter	50% from water incinerator	80% from waste-water incinerator	Incorrect: 63%, more
	Aluminium smelter	12 h: 1.23 ppb	24 h: 0.96 ppb	Close
		Long-term: 0.41 ppb	90 day: 0.32 ppb	Correct: 78%, better
	Aluminium smelter	Annual discharge will meet SPCC standards	Total: 48–64% of limit	Correct: 64%, better
			Potlines: <87%	Correct: 87%, better
			Anode plant: <20%	Correct: 20%, better
			Roof vents: <73%	Correct: 75%, better
		Monthly discharges will meet SPCC targets	Potline stacks: 1984–85: 15% > target by up to 2.40x	Incorrect: 42%, worse
			1987–88: All < target, max. 0.80x	Correct: 80%, better
			Potroom vents: 1984: 2% > target by 1.04x	Incorrect: 96%, worse
			1985–88: All < target, max. 0.88x	Correct: 88%, better
Emissions to air: volatile organic carbon (VOC)	Petrochemical plant:			
	Plant 1	45 kg h⁻¹	37.5 kg h⁻¹	Incorrect: 83%, better
	Plant 2	58 kg h⁻¹	43 kg h⁻¹	74%, better
	Plant 3	25 kg h⁻¹	13 kg h⁻¹	52%, better
	Plant 4	18 kg h⁻¹	2.5 kg h⁻¹	14%, better
	Plant 5	114 kg h⁻¹	105 kg h⁻¹	92%, better
	Plant 6	4 kg h⁻¹	22 kg h⁻¹	18%, worse
	Expanded plants	146 kg h⁻¹	96 kg h⁻¹	66%, better
	All plants	264 kg h⁻¹	223 kg h⁻¹	84%, better

(to be continued)

Table 2 (continued)

Component/parameter	Type of development	Predicted impact	Actual impact	Accuracy/precision
Emissions to air: Rn	Uranium mine	During mining: 14.5–26.4 GBq day^{-1}	During mining: 600 GBq day^{-1}	Incorrect: 3%, worse
Emissions to air: plume strike	Power station	Plume looping 1–2 per year	Plume strikes ≥2 in 1 year	?Correct
Emissions to air: cooling tower visible plume	Power station	Visible plume <300 m for 75% >900 m for <12% of total time	Visible plume <300 m for 60% >700 m for 5% of total time	Incorrect: 80%, better <41%, better
Ambient air quality, particulates	Power station	Dust fallout, Max. = 30 + 80 mg m^{-3}	Max. = 10 mg m^{-3}	Correct: 100%
Ambient air quality: particulate fallout	Power station	Annual mean from all sources <1.8 g m^{-2} month^{-1}	Annual mean from all sources ~2.0 g m^{-2} month^{-1}	?Correct: 90%, worse
	Power station	Maximum =0.124 g m^{-2} month^{-1}	Maximum <0.4 g m^{-2} month^{-1}	?Incorrect: <31%, worse
	Power station	Mean within 10 km =0.04 g m^{-2} month^{-1}	Mean within 10 km =0.033 g m^{-2} month^{-1}	Incorrect: 83%, better
Ambient air quality: SO$_2$	Power station	Annual mean [SO$_2$] <60 mg m^{-3} 24-h Mean [SO$_2$] <260 mg m^{-3}	<5 mg m^{-3} <40 mg m^{-3}	Correct: 8%, better Correct: 15%, better
	Power station	Max. annual mean ~1.3 μg m^{-3}	Max. annual mean ~2 μg m^{-3}	Incorrect: 65%, worse

	Source	Prediction	Actual/Value	Result
	Power station	Max. annual mean ~2.0 µg m⁻³	Max. annual mean ~2-3 µg m⁻³	?Correct: ~67-100%
	Power station	Max. annual mean ~0.95 µg m⁻³	Max. annual mean >0.7 µg m⁻³	Correct: 73%?, better
	Power station	Max. annual mean = 5.0 µg m⁻³	Max. annual mean = 12.4 µg m⁻³	Incorrect: 40%, worse
	Power station	Mean annual mean within 20 km = 0.65 µg m⁻³	Mean annual mean within 11.5 km = 0.25 µg m⁻³	Incorrect: 38%, better
	Power station	Mean annual mean within 20 km = 1.3 µg m⁻³	Mean annual means up to 6.33 µg m⁻³	Incorrect: 20%, worse
	Power station	Max. 3-min mean = 930 µg m⁻³	Max. 3-min mean = 1524 µg m⁻³	Incorrect: 61%, worse
	Power station	Max. 3-min mean = 430 µg m⁻³	Max. 3-min mean = 679 µg m⁻³	Incorrect: 63%, worse
	Uranium mine	At ~10 km from source, Mean [SO₂] ~1.1 µg m⁻³; Max. [SO₂] ~1.3 µg m⁻³	Mean [SO₂] ~0.002 µg m⁻³; Max. [SO₂] ~0.4 µg m⁻³	Incorrect: 0.2%, better; Incorrect: 30%, better
Ambient air quality: NOx	Power stations	[NOx] ~0.7x [SO₂]	0.85x	Incorrect: 82%, worse
Ambient air quality: total F⁻	Aluminium smelter	Annual mean contours predicted	Actual [F⁻] at 6 sites range from 0.3 to 0.75x prediction	Incorrect: 30-75%, better
	Aluminium smelter	Maximum monthly means predicted	Actual maxima at 6 sites range from 0.25 to 0.90x prediction	Incorrect: 25-90%, better
Ambient air quality: F⁻ fallout	Aluminium smelter	Annual mean contours predicted	Actual [F⁻] at 6 sites range from ~0.40 to 0.84x prediction	Incorrect: ~40-84%, better

(to be continued)

Table 2 (continued)

Component/ parameter	Type of development	Predicted impact	Actual impact	Accuracy/ precision
Ambient air quality: gaseous F^-	Aluminium smelter	Seasonal patterns predicted	Monthly means available for 6 sites	Variation: ~30%, less
		Annual mean contours predicted	Actual [F^-] at 6 sites range from 0.3–1.00x prediction	Incorrect: 30–100%, better
		Maximum monthly means predicted	Actual maxima at 6 sites range from 0.3–1.02x prediction	Incorrect: 30–98%, mostly better
Radiation from atmospheric dust fallout	Uranium mine	$U^{234} + U^{238}$ 0.1 mBq m^{-3} (0.08 mSv a^{-1})	$U^{234} + U^{238}$ 0.12 mBq m^{-3} (0.09 mSv a^{-1})	Incorrect: 83%, worse
		Other U-series except Rn and daughters: 0.03 mBq m^{-3} (0.03 mSv a^{-1})	Other U-series except Rn and daughters: 0.17 mBq m^{-3} (0.17 mSv a^{-1})	Incorrect: 18%, worse
Radiation: total lung dose	Uranium mine	Rn and daughters: 0.076 mSv a^{-1}	0.015–0.045 mSv a^{-1}	Incorrect: ~40%, better
		Dust: 0.114 mSv a^{-1}	0.035–0.105 mSv a^{-1}	Incorrect: ~70%, better
Radiation: worker exposure		Mine: 20–40 mSv a^{-1}	12 mSv a^{-1}	Incorrect: 30%, better
		Mill: <60 mSv a^{-1}	12 mSv a^{-1}	Incorrect: 20%, better
		Packing: 20 mSv a^{-1}	1.9 mSv a^{-1}	Incorrect: 10%, better

Fresh water consumption	Coal mine	Consumption 1.6 Mm³ a⁻¹	Consumption 0.75 Mm³ a⁻¹ on average	Incorrect: 47%, better
	Offshore petroleum production	0.7 Mm³ a⁻¹	0.36 Mm³ a⁻¹	Incorrect: 50%, better
Wastewater discharge	Coal mine	No discharge except during floods	Discharge during floods only	Correct
Wastewater discharge, dewatering	Coal mine	Dewatering will yield 10 Ml day⁻¹	Yielded 30 Ml day⁻¹	Incorrect: 33%, more
Wastewater discharge: release from retention ponds	Uranium mine	RP1: 940000 m³ in Year 2; 1230000 m³ in Year 10	2156000 m³ in Year 2; 577000 m³ in Year 10	Incorrect: 44%, worse / Incorrect: 47%, better
Wastewater discharge: cooling tower blowdown	Power station	tds = 700 mg l⁻¹	1000 mg l⁻¹	Incorrect: 70%, worse
	Power station	Blowdown 5 Mm³ a⁻¹, ca. 1583 mg l⁻¹ tds, [Total salts]	Blowdown 9 Mm³ a⁻¹, ca. 928 mg l⁻¹ tds, [Total salts]	Incorrect: 67%, worse / 59%, better / 88%, better
Ash ponds discharge	Power station	120 l s⁻¹ ca. 11000 mg l⁻¹ tds [Total salts] Suspended solids – <10 mg l⁻¹ Heavy metals – <1 mg l⁻¹ pH 8–10	222 l s⁻¹ ca. 5000 mg l⁻¹ tds, [Total salts] / <10 mg l⁻¹ / <1 mg l⁻¹ 8–10	54%, worse / 45%, better / 84%, better / Correct / Correct / Correct

(to be continued)

Component/ parameter	Type of development	Predicted impact	Actual impact	Accuracy/ precision
Surface water quality: salts, pH	Bauxite mine	No detectable increase in stream salinity	None detected	Correct
	Aluminium smelter	pH in surface water within 1 km ≥ 6	pH 7.2–8.7	Correct: 82%, better
	Coal mine	No degradation in stream water quality	Change but no degradation in use pH: $+ 1/2$ unit electrical conductivity: 4–6x Cl: 3–8x SO_4: 40–50x	Correct
	Power station	During drought [Ca] max $= 75$ mg l^{-1} Median $= 30$ mg l^{-1} [Si] max $= 44$ mg l^{-1} Median $= 16$ mg l^{-1}	In 1980–83 Max. $= 57$ mg l^{-1} Median $= 39$ mg l^{-1} Max. $= 13$ mg l^{-1} Median $= 4$ mg l^{-1}	Incorrect: 68%, better 77%, better 30%, better 25%, better
	Uranium mine	Concentrations in tailings dam: 50 µg l^{-1} Cu	Means, 1983–86: 22 µg l^{-1} Cu	Incorrect: 44%, better
		300 µg l^{-1} Pb	27 µg l^{-1} Pb	Incorrect: 9%, better
		80 µg l^{-1} Zn	10 µg l^{-1} Zn	Incorrect: 13%, better
		120 mg l^{-1} Mn	260 mg l^{-1} Mn	Incorrect: 46%, worse
		1.48 Bq l^{-1} Ra^{226}	26 Bq l^{-1} Ra^{226}	Incorrect: 5.7%, worse
		20 µg l^{-1} U	37 µg l^{-1} U	Incorrect: 54%, worse
		9300 mg l^{-1} SO$_4$	8140 mg l^{-1} SO$_4$	~Correct: 87.5%, better

Uranium mine	River: mean concentrations:	River: mean concentrations:	
	2 mg l^{-1} SO$_4^{2-}$	0.4 mg l^{-1} SO$_4^{2-}$	Incorrect: 20%, better
	2 µg l^{-1} Cu	0.75–1.1 µg l^{-1} Cu	Incorrect: $\sim48\%$, better
	1.6 µg l^{-1} Pb	1.1–1.6 µg l^{-1} Pb	Incorrect: 85%, better
	<100 µg l^{-1} Mn	11 µg l^{-1} Mn	Incorrect: 11%, better
	5 µg l^{-1} Zn	2.5–3 µg l^{-1} Zn	Incorrect: $\sim55\%$, better
	0.2 µg l^{-1} U	0.3 µg l^{-1} U	Incorrect: 67%, worse
	0.0074 Bq l^{-1} Ra^{226}	0.019 Bq l^{-1} Ra^{226}	Incorrect: 39%, worse

Uranium mine	River: maximum concentrations:	River: maximum concentrations:	
	7 mg l^{-1} SO$_4$	4.3 mg l^{-1} SO$_4$	Incorrect: 60%, better
	5 µg l^{-1} Cu	3 µg l^{-1} Cu	Incorrect: 60%, better
	3 µg l^{-1} Pb	6 µg l^{-1} Pb	Incorrect: 50%, worse
	<100 µg l^{-1} Mn	42 µg l^{-1} Mn	Incorrect: 40%, better
	15 µg l^{-1} Zn	23 µg l^{-1} Zn	Incorrect: 65%, worse
	5 µg l^{-1} U	1.7 µg l^{-1} U	Incorrect: 30%, better
	0.018 Bq l^{-1} Ra^{226}	0.036 Bq l^{-1} Ra^{226}	Incorrect: 50%, worse

Table 2 (continued)

Component/ parameter	Type of development	Predicted impact	Actual impact	Accuracy/ precision
Surface water quality: Ra	Uranium mine	Tails dam: <1.48 Bq l^{-1} Retention ponds: <1.48 Bq l^{-1}	Tails dam: 30–55 Bq l^{-1} Retention ponds: up to 3.6 Bq l^{-1}	Incorrect: 2.7%, worse Incorrect: 41%, worse
Surface water quality: F^{-}	Aluminium smelter	[F^{-}] <10 g m^{-3}	Max. is 22 g m^{-3}	Incorrect: 45%, worse
	Aluminium smelter	[F^{-}] <10 mg l^{-1}	87% >10 mg l^{-1} Mean weekly max = 20.5 mg l^{-1}	Incorrect: 13%, worse
	Aluminium smelter	Increase in river too small to detect: 0.02 mg l^{-1} cf. background 0.1–1.4 mg l^{-1}	No detectable increase, cf. background fluctuations	Correct
	Aluminium smelter	Increase in reservoir <0.002 mg l^{-1} cf. background 0.1–0.4 mg l^{-1}	No detectable increase, cf. background fluctuations	Correct
Groundwater seepage	Brown coal liquefaction	No seepage from sludge disposal	None detected	Correct
	Uranium mine	Into mine pit: 100–1500 m^3 day^{-1} Mean 800 m^3 day^{-1}	Into mine pit: 300–700 m^3 day^{-1} Mean ?500 m^3 day^{-1}	Incorrect: 63%, better
	Uranium mine	From tails dam: 170 m^3 day^{-1} total; 68% in deep zone	From tails dam: 180 m^3 day^{-1} total; ~39% in deep zone	~Correct: 94%, worse Incorrect: 59%, less

		Seepage from tailings dam	Seepage from tailings dam	
Groundwater quality	Uranium mine	$10 \ \mu g \ l^{-1}$ Cu	$5 \ \mu g \ l^{-1}$ Cu	Incorrect: 50%, better
		$60 \ \mu g \ l^{-1}$ Pb	$2 \ \mu g \ l^{-1}$ Pb	Incorrect: 3%, better
		$24 \ \mu g \ l^{-1}$	$350 \ \mu g \ l^{-1}$ Mn	Incorrect: 7%, worse
		$16 \ \mu g \ l^{-1}$ Zn	$20 \ \mu g \ l^{-1}$ Zn	~Correct: 80%, worse
		$4 \ \mu g \ l^{-1}$ U	$5.2 \ \mu g \ l^{-1}$ U	~Correct: 77%, worse
		$0.3 \ Bq \ l^{-1} \ Ra^{226}$	$0.078 \ Bq \ l^{-1} \ Ra^{226}$	Incorrect: 26%, better
Groundwater quality: F^- in leachate	Aluminium smelter	$<0.6 \ mg \ l^{-1}$	Annual means to $3.5 \ mg \ l^{-1}$	Incorrect: <17%, worse
Groundwater quality: F^- retention in soil	Aluminium smelter	$>85\%$ F^- will be held in soil	$>98.3\%$ Held in soil	Correct: 87%, better
Groundwater quality: F^-	Aluminium smelter	$[F^-] <1.53 \ mg \ l^{-1}$ within $5 \ mg \ m^{-2} \ day^{-1}$ fallout isopleth	$<1.53 \ mg \ l^{-1}$ for 47 out of 48 months in 1985–88; to $14.45 \ mg \ l^{-1}$ max.	Incorrect: 11%, worse
Cooling water discharge: bank erosion	Power station	No bank erosion	No bank erosion	Correct
Cooling water discharge: tidal cycle	Power station	10–15% change in tidal cycle	No change	Incorrect: 85%, better
Cooling water flow rate	Power station	$\sim 20 \ m^3 \ s^{-1}$ per unit	$19.86 \ m^3 \ s^{-1}$ per unit	Correct: 99,3%, better

(to be continued)

Table 2 (continued)

Component/ parameter	Type of development	Predicted impact	Actual impact	Accuracy/ precision
Cooling water discharge: temperature rise	Power station	Anabrach entrances: top: 2.3°C bottom: 2.3°C River mouth: 0.5°C (in summer, at 1 GW output)	>2°C >2°C Unknown	2 Models, out by up to 75% and 300% respectively
Cooling water discharge	Power station	Temperature stratification	Occurred as predicted	Correct
Cooling water discharge: mixing zone	Power station	500 m from outlet	250 m from outlet	Incorrect: 50%, better
Cooling water discharge: salinity	Power station	No increase in lake salinity	No detectable increase	Correct
Cooling water discharge: impacts on aquatic biota	Power station	No impact on aquatic plants	No impact	Correct
	Power station	No impact on commercial fisheries	No impact	Correct
Marine discharge: dilution	Ocean outfall	>100x in undefined initial zone	110–160x but zone may not match	?Correct
	Oil loading terminal	40–200:1 in <60 m	800:1 in 20 m	1 Order of magnitude better

Parameter	Source	Standard	Measured	Assessment
Marine discharge: dissolved oil	Oil loading terminal	Oil content <8 mg l⁻¹ mean <15 mg l⁻¹ max.	Oil content 3–4 mg l⁻¹ mean 5 mg l⁻¹ max.	Correct: 50%, better 33%, better
Marine discharge: impacts of biota	Ocean outfall	Little effect	Little effect	Correct
	Power station	No effects	No effects	Correct
	Power station	Various effects on biota	No effects	Incorrect: better
Marine water quality: dissolved O_2	Ocean outfall	>5.7 g m⁻³	Ocean: 6.3–7.0 g m⁻³	?Correct: 90%, better
			Shoreline: 23 of 26 >5.7 g m⁻³	?Correct
Marine water quality: NH_3–N	Ocean outfall	<600 mg m⁻³	Ocean: <320 mg m⁻³	Correct: 53%, better
			Shoreline: <50 mg m⁻³	Correct: 8%, better
Marine water quality: Pb	Ocean outfall	<8 mg m⁻³	Ocean: <0.5 mg m⁻³	Correct: 6%, better
			Shoreline: <5 mg m⁻³	Correct: 63%, better
Marine water quality: Cd	Ocean outfall	<3 mg m⁻³	Ocean: <0.5 mg m⁻³	Correct: 17%, better
			Shoreline: <5 mg m⁻³	Correct: 60%, better
Marine water quality: faecal coliforms	Ocean outfall	<150/100 ml	Ocean: <64/100 ml	Correct: 64%, better
			Shoreline: 24 of 26 <150/100 ml	?Correct:

(to be continued)

Table 2 (continued)

Component/parameter	Type of development	Predicted impact	Actual impact	Accuracy/precision
Marine dredging and spoil dumping	Offshore petroleum production	Spoil area 500 ha: plume travel 4–5 km per tide; plume settling in 6 h; minor damage to corals	300–1200 ha: N–S; 4–5 km; 3.5–6 h; No damage	?Correct Correct Correct Correct Incorrect: better
Marine pipeline	Offshore petroleum production	Seafloor will recolonise in a few years	As predicted	Correct
Marine blasting	Offshore petroleum production	No fish kills in reef outcrops	No kills	Correct
Terrestrial flora: effect of particulates	Power station	No significant impacts	Small increase in foliar boron content	Correct
Terrestrial flora: SO_2 damage	Bauxite refinery	No SO_2 damage to vegetation	Little or none	?Correct
Terrestrial flora: SO_2 damage	Power station	Minimal SO_2 damage	Minimal damage	Correct
Terrestrial flora: NO_x damage	Power station	No NO_x damage to vegetation	No damage	Correct
Terrestrial flora: effects of F^-	Aluminium smelter	Change in vegetation where annual mean $[F^-]$ > 0.5 mg m^{-3}	Increased leaf fall and foliar $[F^-]$ in this zone	Correct
Terrestrial flora: fungal disease spread	Bauxite refinery	Dieback area <1 ha/ha mined	Area is <0.5 ha/ha mined	Correct: 50%, better
Mangroves: effects of F^-	Aluminium smelter	No effects	Elevated $[F^-]$ but no ill effects	Correct

		Order of return predicted	Predictions met	
Terrestrial fauna: recovery	Bauxite mine			Correct
Terrestrial fauna: rare species	Offshore petroleum production	No rare species affected	None affected	Correct
Terrestrial fauna: effects of F^-	Aluminium smelter	Increased bone $[F^-]$ where ambient $[F^-] > 0.3$ mg m^{-3}	Increases at 9 sites in this zone	Correct
Aquatic fauna: disturbance	Pumping station	Platypus will be displaced	Platypus not displaced	Incorrect: better
Rehabilitation	Bauxite mine	No erosion outside pit	No erosion outside pit	Correct
Rehabilitation	Coal mine	Rehabilitation will require topsoil replacement	As predicted	Correct
Noise	Bauxite mine	Blast noise <115 dBA	90% <115 dBA	Incorrect: 90%, worse
Noise	Power station	<50 dBA, pulses <90 dBA	As predicted	Correct
Noise	Aluminium smelter	Will meet standards	Has met standards	Correct
Population	Coal mine	Emerald, in 1981: 5076 in 1986: 5765	8435 9462	Incorrect: 65%, more
Work force	Power station	395	349	Incorrect: 88%, less.
Work force	Aluminium smelter	1500 During construction	Up to 2500	Incorrect: 60%, more
Work force	Aluminium smelter	800 during operations	940	Incorrect: 88%, more
Payroll (1988 $)	Aluminium smelter	$30–32 Million	$30 Million	Correct: >94%
Power consumption	Aluminium smelter	14% of power station output	15%	Incorrect: 93%, more

individual development projects, in the number and detail of testable environmental impact predictions.

Between 800 and 1000 EIS's and equivalent documents, containing many thousand impact predictions, have been produced in Australia to date, as compared to over 10,000 in the USA (Culhane 1987). Adequate monitoring data to test these predictions, however, are available for only 3% of these EIS's, dated between 1974 and 1982. More recent EIS's also contain testable predictions, but monitoring data are not yet available to test them. The projects covered by these EIS's, the impacts predicted, and any relevant post-EIS operational changes to environmental management practices are detailed in Buckley (1989b).

Overall patterns in the availability of data may be summarised as follows:

– In general, testable predictions and monitoring data were available only for large complex development projects.
– In general, the number and detail of testable predictions and monitoring data are far greater for developments which generated public controversy and were subject to several phases of environmental impact assessment.
– In general, environmental monitoring programmes are aimed at monitoring compliance with standards rather than testing impact predictions.

These EIS's contain a total of ~200 major and 175 subsidiary predictions. Data to determine the logical correctness of the prediction, and the relative severity of actual and predicted impacts, are available for 181 of the major predictions, summarised in Table 2. Of these 181, 32 were in relation to atmospheric emissions, 30 to ambient air quality, 2 to freshwater consumption, 14 to wastewater discharge, 34 to surface water quality, 13 to groundwater, 10 to cooling water discharge, 17 to marine discharge and water quality, 7 to marine disturbance, 7 to impacts on flora, 4 to impacts on fauna, 2 to rehabilitation, 3 to noise and 6 to social impacts.

It is important to note that any attempt to summarise these results, by impact category or type of developments, requires a substantial degree of simplification from the detailed project information, so that predicted and actual impacts of very different types, from very different projects, can be expressed in commensurate or at least comparable terms. This simplification is necessary in searching for general patterns in the accuracy and precision of impact predictions. In any evaluation with respect to individual development projects, however, the detailed descriptions in Buckley (1989b) should be used, since these include relevant information on applicable standards, baseline parameters, any changes in environmental management practices, and so on, which are necessary for interpretation of raw monitoring data.

Criteria for Assessment

There are two distinct approaches to assessing the accuracy of an environmental impact prediction: the logical correctness of the prediction, or the relative severity of the impact. In cases where actual impacts proved less severe than anticipated, predictions may still be logically incorrect if they were expressed as "impact parameter will be equal to predicted numerical value", rather than "impact parameter will be less than or equal to predicted numerical value". The distinction between predictions which are logically incorrect, but where actual impacts were less severe than predicted, and predictions which are logically correct, with actual impacts within the predicted range, is hence largely semantic rather than technical. The relative severity of actual impact as compared to predicted impact is hence a more useful and meaningful criterion of accuracy than logical correctness of prediction: in comparing predicted and actual impacts for different types of development and impact, it is most useful to distinguish between impacts which proved as or less severe than predicted, on the one hand, and those which proved more severe than predicted on the other.

Whether or not a prediction proved correct in a strictly logical sense also depends largely on how precise the prediction was in the first place. If an EIS contains a best possible estimate of a particular pollutant emission or ambient level, for example, then it is likely that that level will be exceeded on occasion. If, on the other hand, the EIS simply states or predicts that emissions will comply with a relatively lax standard, then it is highly likely that that prediction will be fulfilled. Hence, the mere fact that a high proportion of predictions in an EIS have proved correct in a logical sense does not in itself demonstrate good environmental planning and management. It may simply show that the predictions were vague or unlikely to be falsified. For minor impacts, this distinction is of little importance. It is enough for government and public to know, with a high degree of confidence, that generally applicable standards will be met or that impacts will be within some broadly defined range. For impacts which are not likely to become significant environmental management issues, it is inefficient to devote resources to precise prediction.

The quantitative accuracy and precision of predictions is important, however, for critical impacts, i.e. those which approach most closely to general standards, or perhaps require the setting of a site-specific discharge limit or other environmental protection commitment. These are the impacts which generally raise the greatest degree of public controversy, which may determine whether development approval is granted, and on which the environmental performance of the development will be judged. In such cases there is a choice between setting a relatively stringent target, with the expectation that it will on occasion be exceeded; or a less stringent one, with a higher confidence that it will always be met. One possible approach, currently becoming more common, is to specify a range of targets with corresponding allowable exceedence frequencies. This reflects the probabilistic nature of many impact predictions, and also makes compliance monitoring more straightforward, and less subject to wrangles over interpretation.

The environmental monitoring data available for this project also varied considerably in degree of precision. Some companies provided me with raw data, which enabled me to calculate the means and standard deviations for the parameters concerned with a high level of precision, but occupied considerable time and effort in the process. Others simply stated whether predictions had been met; this saved me considerable effort, but did not allow me to determine a degree of precision. Often the only environmental monitoring data formally reported to regulatory agencies are the number of times, if any, on which specified levels or limits were exceeded: and accordingly, this may be the only information which is retained and available.

Accuracy and Precision of Predictions

Actual impacts proved as or less severe than predicted for 131 (72%) of the 181 testable predictions, and more severe for 50 (28%). If there is any single factor linking the cases where actual impacts were more severe than predicted, it may perhaps be that the environmental parameters concerned were critical or limiting in technical or perhaps economic terms.

Not all of these predictions are of equal significance. For many developments, there are hierarchical sets of predictions for particular parameters, at different scales in space and time. For an air quality parameter, for example, these may range from an annual mean over a 20-km radius to monthly maxima at individual sites. Similarly, water quality predictions may cover a suite of parameters that all vary in a similar way with gross throughput or with effectiveness of pollution control systems. Aggregate statistics for the quantitative precision of predictions must be based on a set of predictions at equivalent scales. Selecting only the most aggregated or the most critical of the fully quantified predictions in each major impact category for each development reduces the total to 68 predictions (Table 3). Of these, 11 relate to atmospheric emissions, 18 to ambient air quality, 2 to freshwater consumption, 7 to wastewater discharge, 10 to surface water quality, 7 to groundwater, 3 to saltwater cooling, 4 to marine discharge and water quality, and 6 to social impacts. Predictions related to marine disturbance, impacts on flora and fauna, rehabilitation and noise were generally unquantified. For these 68, actual impacts proved as or less severe than predicted for 40 (59%) and more severe for 28 (41%).

The quantitative accuracy or precision of a prediction may be expressed as the ratio of actual to predicted magnitude (or occasionally, frequency) of impact. For calculating aggregate measures of accuracy, I used a $|\ln|$ transform of these ratios to normalise the sample distribution and minimise heteroscedasticity. Using this transform, the overall mean accuracy of all 68 critical predictions is $e^{-0.82}$ or 44%, $\pm 5\%$ (1 SE). The accuracies of individual predictions differ by over three orders of magnitude, with actual impacts ranging from $0.05\times$ to $37\times$ prediction. Note that this refers only to the accuracy of predictions, not to compliance of actual impacts with legislated standards. An actual impact which was not accurately predicted may still fall within acceptable limits, whilst one which was predicted quite accurately may exceed such limits. Mean accuracies of predictions for different categories of impact range from 30% for those referring to groundwater to 80% for social impacts (Table 2), but because of the scatter between individual predictions, these differences are not statistically significant ($p > 0.10$). Nor is there a significant difference between the mean for all predictions relating to air and all those relating to water. Primary predictions, such as those referring to the characteristics of emissions to air or water, are on average more accurate (52%) than secondary predictions, such as those referring to ambient air and water quality (39%) but the difference is not statistically significant. Predictions where actual impacts proved more severe than expected are on average less accurate ($33 \pm 8\%$) than those where they proved less severe ($53 \pm 6\%$); the difference is significant at $p < 0.05$ (all significance tests performed on $|\ln|$-transformed variables). Predictions for primary mineral production were on average less accurate (28%) than those for electricity generation (61%), with the

Table 3. Accuracy of principal impact predictions

No.	Type of impact predicted	Type of development	Actual predicted magnitude of impact
1.	Emission to air, particulates	Power station	1.49
2.	Emission to air, U in dust	Mine	0.33
3.	Emission to air, SO_2	Power station	0.87
4.	Emission to air, SO_2	Brown coal liquefaction	0.05
5.	Emission to air, NO_x	Power station	0.76
6.	Emission to air, NO_x	Brown coal liquefaction	0.83
7.	Emission to air, total F^-	Smelter	0.78
8.	Emission to air, total F^-	Smelter	0.64
9.	Emission to air, total F^-	Smelter	2.38
10.	Emission to air, volatile organics	Petrochemical plant	0.84
11.	Emission to air, Rn	Mine	33
12.	Ambient air quality, particulates	Power station	1.00
13.	Ambient air quality, particulates	Power station	1.11
14.	Ambient air quality, particulates	Power station	3.23
15.	Ambient air quality, particulates	Power station	0.83
16.	Ambient air quality, SO_2	Power station	0.08
17.	Ambient air quality, SO_2	Power station	1.54
18.	Ambient air quality, SO_2	Power station	1.00
19.	Ambient air quality, SO_2	Power station	0.73
20.	Ambient air quality, SO_2	Power station	0.38
21.	Ambient air quality, SO_2	Mine	0.30
22.	Ambient air quality, NO_x	Power station	1.22
23.	Ambient air quality, total F^-	smelter	0.52
25.	Ambient air quality, F^- fallout	Smelter	0.62
25.	Ambient air quality, gaseous F^-	Smelter	0.65
26.	Radiation, from dust fallout off-site	Mine	1.47
27.	Radiation, total lung dose off-site	Mine	0.53
28.	Radiation, worker exposure on-site	Mine	0.30
29.	Fresh water consumption	Mine	0.47
30.	Fresh water consumption	Petroleum production	0.50
31.	Wastewater discharge, volume	Mine	3.03
32.	Wastewater discharge, volume	Power station	1.85
33.	Wastewater discharge, volume	Power station	1.49
34.	Wastewater discharge, volume	Mine	2.27
35.	Wastewater discharge, salts	Power station	0.45
36.	Wastewater discharge, salts	Power station	0.59
37.	Wastewater discharge, salts	Power station	1.43
38.	Surface water quality, salts	Power station	0.30
39.	Surface water quality, salts	Power station	0.68
40.	Surface water quality, salts	Smelter	0.82
41.	Surace water quality, sulphates	Mine	0.20

Table 3 (continued)

No.	Type of impact predicted	Type of development	Actual predicted magnitude of impact
42.	Surface water quality, base metals	Mine	0.58
43.	Surface water quality, U	Mine	1.50
44.	Surface water quality, Ra^{226}	Mine	2.56
45.	Surface water quality, F$^-$	Smelter	2.22
46.	Surface water quality, F$^-$	Smelter	7.69
47.	Surace water quality, Ra^{226}	Mine	37
48.	Groundwater seepage, volume	Mine	1.06
49.	Groundwater seepage, base metals	Mine	0.31
50.	Groundwater seepage, Mn	Mine	14.3
51.	Groundwater seepage, U	Mine	1.30
52.	Groundwater seepage, Ra^{226}	Mine	0.77
53.	Groundwater quality, F$^-$	Smelter	5.88
54.	Groundwater quality, F$^-$	Smelter	9.10
55.	Cooling water, flow rate	Power station	0.99
56.	Cooling water, mixing	Power station	0.50
57.	Cooling water, tidal cycle	Power station	0.85
58.	Marine discharge, oil content	Oil loading terminal	0.50
59.	Marine water quality, O$_2$	Ocean outfall	0.90
60.	Marine water quality, Cd	Ocean outfall	1.67
61.	Marine water quality, coliforms	Ocean outfall	0.64
62.	Noise	Mine	1.11
63.	Population, local town	Mine	0.65
64.	Work force, operations	Power station	1.14
65.	Work force, operations	Smelter	0.88
66.	Work force, construction	Smelter	0.60
67.	Payroll	Smelter	0.94
68.	Power consumption	Smelter	1.08

difference significant at $p < 0.05$. For mineral processing, however, the mean was 50%, not significantly different from primary mineral production.

Conclusions

The environmental impacts of development can rarely be predicted with certainty. Knowing just how accurate environmental impact predictions actually are is important in day-to-day operational environmental management, in improving the accuracy of future predictions, in rational resource planning and allocation, and in demonstrating to the public that government regulatory agencies are competent to control and manage the activities of resource development corporations, both public and private sector. The precise levels of uncertainty, and the confidence limits on predictions of various types, can be estimated empirically by comparing impact predictions in past environmental impact assessments with actual impacts as determined from monitoring programmes.

Testable environmental impact predictions for a significant number of developments, and the monitoring data required to test them, have not been available until recently; and even now, access to monitoring data is often restricted. Because of the time lag between initial impact predictions in environmental impact assessment documents, and the production of environmental monitoring data once the development concerned has become fully operational, information on the accuracy of predictions will always refer to predictions made 5 years or so previously. Predictions made during current environmental impact assessments may well prove more accurate, but there is no way of knowing this at the time they are made.

There is growing public concern as to whether government regulatory agencies, responsible for controlling the environmental impacts of industry, actually have the ability, resources, and political will to fulfill these responsibilities competently and without negligence. Environmental impact audits provide a means for both industry and government to demonstrate their competence in environmental management to the public.

This study, the first attempt at a national environmental audit for any nation, deliberately selected the best available data from projects with the most detailed environmental impact predictions and the most intensive environmental monitoring programmes. The data were provided by the operating corporations concerned. In this sense it provides a critical test: if these environmental impact predictions proved inaccurate or inadequately monitored, the remainder will be even more so.

The study showed that the average accuracy of quantified, critical, testable predictions in environmental impact statements in Australia to date is $44 \pm 5\%$ SE; and that predictions where actual impacts proved more severe than expected were on average significantly ($p < 0.05$) less accurate ($33 \pm 9\%$) than those where they proved less severe ($53 \pm 6\%$).

Our current management of the planet's natural resources relies to a significant extent on the assumption that we can predict the environmental impacts of development reliably. At present, in Australia at least, our predictions are less than 50% accurate on average and over an order of magnitude out on occasion. Improvement is clearly needed. It is to be hoped that continuing environmental impact audit will provide the feedback link on which such improvement depends.

Acknowledgements. EIS's were made available by Australian Commonwealth and State Governments and environmental monitoring data by the operating corporations concerned. Over 200 individuals and corporations assisted in the compilation of data and detailed comparison of actual and predicted impacts. For most projects, several iterations were required to ensure a valid comparison, since in many cases project design had been changed post-EIS and monitoring results were not obtained or expressed in the same terms as those in EIS predictions. I thank all of the above for their assistance and for their permission to use and publish confidential monitoring data. This study was carried out at the Centre for Resource and Environmental Studies, Australian National University; and first published as a *CRES Monograph* in 1989.

References

Anonymons (editorial) (1975) An audit may be dangerous to your health. Water Wastes Engin. 12:17

Bisset R (1985) Post-development audits to investigate the accuracy of environmental impact predictions. Z. Umweltpolitik 4/84:463–484

Bisset R, Tomlinson P (1988) In: Wathern P (ed) Environmental impact assessment: theory and practice. Unwin Hyman, London, pp 115–157

Blakeslee HW, Grabowski TM (1985) A Practical Guide to Plant Environmental Audits. Von Nostrand Reinhold, New York

Buckley RC (1987) Environmental planning techniques. SADME, Adelaide

Buckley RC (1988) Critical problems in environmental planning and management. Environ Plan Law J 5:206–225

Buckley RC (1988b) A national environmental audit. Aust Inst Min Metall Bull Proc 293:25–26

Buckley RC (1989a) Environmental audit: short course handbook. 7vv. Bond University, Gold Coast

Buckley RC (1989b) Precision in environmental impact prediction: first national environmental audit, Australia. CRES/ANU Press, Canberra

Buckley RC (1989c) What's wrong with EIA? Search 20:146–147

Canter LW (1984) Environmental impact studies in the United States. In: Reidel D (ed) WHO Perspectives on Environ Impact Assess Report. W.H.O. Geneva, pp 15–24

Canter LW (1985) Impact prediction auditing. Environ Profess 7:255

Culhane PJ (1987) The precision and accuracy of US environmental impact statements. Environ Monitor Assess 8:217–238

Duinker PN, Beanlands GE (1986) The significance of environmental impacts: an exploration of the concept. Environ Manage 10:1–11

Hall WN (1985) Environmental audits: a corporate response to Bhopal. Environ Forum 4:36

Harrison LL (ed) (1984) The McGraw-Hill environmental auditing handbook: a guide to corporate and environmental risk management. McGraw-Hill, New York

Henderson LM (1987) Difficulties in impact prediction audition. Environ Impact Assess Worldletter, May/June 1987:9–12

Knight M (1985) Review of seven environmental assessments carried out between 1975 and 1982. Victoria, Ministry for Planning and Environment, Melbourne: unpublished report

Levin MH (1983) An EPA response on confidentiality in environmental auditing. Environ Law Rep 13:10346

McCallum DR (1987) Follow-up to environmental impact assessments: learning from the Canadian Government experience. Environ Monitor Assess 8:199–216

Moncrieff I, Shea ML, Torrens LW (1985) An environmental performance audit of selected pipeline projects in southern Ontario. In: Environment Canada, Proc Conf on Audit and Evaluation in Environ Assessment and Management, Banff, Oct 13–16, 1:145–159

New Zealand Commission for the Environment (NZCE) (1985) Environmental Impact Assessment Workshop: Issues. NZCE, Wellington

Tomlinson P, Atkinson SF (1987a) Environmental audits: proposed terminology. Environ Monitor Assess 8:187–198

Tomlinson P, Atkinson SF (1987b) Environmental audits: a literature review. Environ Monitor Assess 8:239

Wright RS, Tew EL, Decker CE, von Lehmden DJ, Barnard WF (1987) Performance audits of EPA protocol gases and inspection and maintenance calibration gases. J Air Pollut Control Assoc 37:384

Chapter 7
Guidelines for Environmental Audit

Abstract

Environmental audit means a check, assessment, test or verification of some aspect of environmental management. Environmental audits may examine: compliance, monitoring programmes, impact predictions, equipment performance, physical hazards, financial risks, products and markets, baselines and benchmarks, management programmes and structures, planning procedures and legislation. This chapter provides guidelines for each type, in the form of structured sets of questions.

Introduction

What Does Environmental Audit Mean?

Broadly, environmental audit means a check on some aspect of environmental management. Specific meanings vary widely, because:

- "environment" means different things to different people
- "environmental" can refer either to the environment itself, or to the social systems we use to deal with it
- "audit" also has many different meanings.

What Defines Audit?

Audit implies some kind of testing and verification. All types of audit involve three people or groups of people, and three steps or stages. The first person or group audits the second and reports the results to the third. The three groups are:

- **auditor**: the person or people doing the audit;
- **auditee**: the people or things on whom the audit is done;
- **third parties**: people who want to know the results of the audit.

All three groups may belong to the same organisation, but the three roles are still distinct.

The three steps or stages of any audit are:

- **assess**: evaluate how things actually are;
- **test**: compare how they are with how they ought to be;
- **attest**: certify or testify to the results if necessary.

How Do Audits Differ?

Different types of environmental audit differ in:

Origin: who asked for the audit to be done?
- internal: an organisation, corporation or project carrying out an audit of its own operations in order to improve them;
- external: one organisation carrying out an audit of another to check how well it has performed;
- voluntary: the audit is done to improve management, with the consent of all concerned;
- mandatory: the audit is required by law or as a condition of, e.g., an operating licence, currency exchange or export clearance, or insurance cover.

Scale: e.g.:
- number of parameters examined,
- number and size of sites, projects, operations, corporations.

Focus: what aspects the audit is examining: e.g.:
- compliance: whether a project complies with regulations and standards;
- monitoring programmes: how well they are designed and how well they work;
- impact predictions: how accurate they were;
- plant and equipment performance: whether it meets specifications;
- physical risks and hazards: inventory for a particular site or project;
- financial risks and liabilities: from environmental constraints;
- products and markets: whether products are environmentally friendly;
- benchmarks: state-of-the-environment reviews;

- management programmes: whether they are efficient and effective;
- management structures: how well they work;
- planning procedures: how well they work;
- legislative frameworks: how well they are designed.

Timeframe: whether the audit deals mostly with:
- evaluation of past actions or predictions;
- description of present status;
- predictions and recommendations for the future.

The purpose or function of a particular environmental audit defines:

- the size and expertise of the audit team required;
- the time and resources they need;
- the involvement of personnel in the section(s) or organisation(s) under audit;
- reporting requirements, responsibilities and confidentiality provisions.

Increasing Use of Environmental Audit

Environmental audit is a relatively new term, but one which is used more and more widely. However, (1) it means very different things to different people, and (2) much of what is now being done under the name of environmental audit has been done for a long time, but under different names.

There are probably two main reasons for the current interest in environmental audit. The first is that environmental planning and management have grown and changed enormously in the past two decades, with the rapid introduction of new laws, new standards, new equipment, new processes and new techniques. Environmental audits enable us to check back and see how well these tools have worked. The second reason is that public concern over environmental issues has grown markedly in the last few years. This has led to increased penalties for poor environmental management, producing an incentive to evaluate and improve existing systems.

Apart from the emphasis on verification, and the increased commercial risks associated with poor environmental management, there are two other aspects which are new. The first is that in many countries, environmental monitoring programmes have now yielded enough data to test past impact predictions on a large scale. The second is that corporate environmental management structures and programmes, in both private and public sectors, have now grown complex and expensive enough to merit detailed audit.

Guidelines for Carrying Out Environmental Audit

The first step in carrying out any environmental audit is to establish exactly why it is being done and what it is for. This determines the type of audit needed, the critical information required, and the number and expertise of people to carry it out.

The outlines given below are general guidelines. Not all of the points covered will be relevant in all cases, nor will they all have equal significance or require equal emphasis. In addition, in any given case there are likely to be additional aspects not specifically considered below.

These guidelines are written as a series of modules, each with a different focus. Some types of audit will use only one module; others will use several. Audits of compliance with environmental legislation, for example, will examine only that aspect; whereas a comprehensive environmental management audit for a development project would include audits of compliance as just one of a number of factors.

Compliance with Legislation and Standards

Auditing environmental compliance means checking whether a particular operation, process, site, company or project is complying with relevant legislation. For example, are discharges from factories or mines within prescribed limits? Is sewage from hotels and resorts being treated properly before discharge? Are logging patterns following approved plans? Are fish catches within quotas?

Audits of environmental compliance may be carried out by:

- regulatory agencies, on projects or operators
  - as a routine task
  - in response to public concern
- operators, on their own projects:
  - as a regulatory requirement
  - as a routine component of environmental management
  - as insurance against possible future claims

- community groups and non-government organisations (NGO's):
  - as a check on operators and/or regulators.

The main steps are:

- determine applicable regulations and standards and where they are specified.
- determine how they are expressed, e.g.:
  - absolute limits ("must never exceed ...")
  - average limits over a defined time period ("mean must not exceed ...")
  - proportional exceedances ("not more than...% of measurements may exceed ...")
- examine the design of the monitoring programme (see guidelines for audit of environmental monitoring programmes)
- obtain necessary monitoring data:
  - from project operator
  - from regulatory agency
  - by direct measurement
- assess reliability of monitoring data
- compare monitoring data with standards
  - using appropriate tests of statistical significance
- determine whether all standards and regulations have been complied with; and if not, how often and how serious any breaches were.

For references, see Levin (1983), Harrison (1984), Hall (1985), Blakeslee and Grabowski (1985), and Tomlinson and Atkinson (1987a, b).

Design of Monitoring Programmes

Auditing environmental monitoring programmes means analysing their statistical design: (1) to establish just how accurately each monitored parameter needs to be known, and why; and (2) to ensure that measurements are taken to provide an estimate with precisely that degree of precision.

Environmental monitoring has many different functions: controlling day-to-day operations, checking compliance, testing impact predictions, assessing risks, and so on. In each case, it is important to know not only the value of the parameter being monitored, but also the uncertainty of the estimate. Otherwise effort is often wasted making unnecessarily detailed estimates of relatively unimportant parameters, whilst the values of parameters which actually are important in environmental management remain uncertain.

Questions to consider:

What are the environmental parameters that the operator or regulatory agency needs to monitor for the project(s) concerned, and why?

- legislative requirement?
- to check compliance?
- to test predictions?
- to improve management?

How accurately and precisely must these parameters be known?

- e.g., statistical confidence limits?

How do they need to be expressed, e.g.:

- mean and standard error?
- proportion falling outside predefined limits?
- spatial patterns?
- seasonal patterns and long-term trends?

What are the environmental parameters that the operator or regulatory agency actually monitor, for the project(s) concerned, either routinely or casually?

- When?
    - regular, random, casual or event-determined monitoring?
    - how long between samples or measurements?
- Where? how are sampling or measurement points determined?
    - grid?
    - single point?
    - strategic sites?
    - how far apart?
- How? what methods, techniques or equipment are used for measurement and/or sampling and analysis, considering:
    - precision
    - repeatability
    - checks
    - reliability
    - appropriateness
    - data output
    - backups
    - blanks and standards

How are monitoring data in each category analysed?

- routinely or as needed?
- how often?
- what statistical measures?
    - distribution parameters?
    - compare with standard?
    - test statistics?
    - pattern analyses?

Does the present programme measure:

- the required parameters?
- to a sufficient degree of accuracy?

Does it monitor:

- any unnecessary or irrelevant parameters?
- any parameters to greater precision than necessary?
- if so, could this extra information be valuable in the future?

Does the monitoring programme need to be modified, and if so how?

Are monitoring data checked systematically against (1) standards and (2) predictions? (see guidelines for auditing compliance and impact predictions, this Chap.)

- are standards or predictions available?
- are monitoring data in the same formats and units as standards or predictions?
- are monitoring data actually checked against standards or predictions?
    - how often, if at all?
    - using significance tests?
    - with what results?

For references, see Schaeffer et al. (1985), Perry et al. (1985), and Sokolik and Schaeffer (1986).

Impact Predictions

Auditing environmental impact predictions means testing how accurate the predictions in environmental impact statements (EIS's) are, by comparing them with actual monitored impacts once the project is under way.

Table 1. Past audits of environmental impact predictions

Author	Scope	Results
Bisset (1985)	4 projects in UK; 791 predictions	77 of 791 were testable; 57 of 77 were "probably accurate"
Knight (1985)	7 EES's in Victoria	1 testable prediction; reasonably accurate
Henderson (1987)	2 projects in Canada; 122 predictions	70 of 122 were testable; 54 of 70 were "substantially correct"
Culhane	29 EIS's in USA;	$<25\%$ were quantified; of these, $<30\%$ were "unqualifiedly close to forecast"
Buckley (1989a)	All EIS's in Australia with testable predictions and monitoring data	72% of actual impacts as or less severe than predicted; average accuracy of quantified, testable, critical predictions is $44 \pm 5\%$ SE; predictions where actual impacts proved more severe than expected were on average significantly ($p < 0.05$) less accurate ($33 \pm 9\%$) than those where they proved as or less severe ($53 \pm 6\%$)

Example: Water quality in rivers. The national environmental audit for Australia (Buckley 1989a) tested 24 predictions relating to the impacts of major development projects on water quality in rivers. Of these 16 were associated with mining, 4 with mineral processing and 4 with electricity generation. In 7 (24%) of these cases, actual impacts proved more severe than predicted, by factors of 1.5 to over 8 times. It also tested 14 predictions relating to wastewater discharges, 7 to cooling water discharges, and 13 relating to groundwater. Actual impacts were more severe than predicted in at least 12 (35%) of these 34 cases, by factors of up to 2.3 times for wastewater discharges and 14 times for impacts on groundwater.

Knowing just how accurate environmental impact predictions actually are is important in day-to-day operational environmental management, in making and assessing future predictions, in managing the use of natural resources, and in demonstrating to the public or funding agencies that regulatory agencies can successfully manage the activities of resource development corporations, in both the public and private sectors.

Examples: Five multi-project audits of environmental impact predictions have been published (Table 1). Only one of these covers an entire country: the national environmental audit for Australia (see Chap. 6).

Questions to consider:

- What environmental impacts were predicted for the project(s) concerned?
- When and where were the predictions stated?
- What actual impacts have been monitored?
- Where are the results recorded?
- How do actual impacts compare with predicted impacts?

These questions need to be addressed for every relevant environmental parameter. A broad checklist of such parameters is given below.

- Physical environment
  - emissions to air
  - ambient air quality
  - liquid effluents
  - surface water quality (and/or temperature)
  - groundwater seepage
  - groundwater quality
  - solid wastes
  - sedimentation and soils
  - radiation
  - noise

- Biological environment
  - physical structure of communities
  - diversity and species composition
  - population sizes
  - individual species (rare or indicator)
  - reproduction and growth
  - contaminants in tissues
  - diseases and pests
  - other

- Human environment
  - land use and tenure
  - archeology and material heritage
  - anthropology and cultural heritage
  - population and demography
  - infrastructure
  - other

In practice, this generally involves some or all of the following steps.

1. Identify the projects under consideration, and determine whether any environmental impact assessment was carried out for these projects, whether as a formal environmental impact statement (EIS) or as part of project planning, approval or funding documents.

2. Determine whether the project(s) was expected to produce major quantifiable impacts on specific components of the physical, biological or human environment. Some projects are not expected to produce any further significant impacts, e.g., building development in an already urbanised area.

3. Determine whether the project(s) went ahead substantially as planned: some projects are modified considerably between planning and execution, and impact predictions may no longer apply.

4. Determine whether routine monitoring has been carried out for these project(s), and whether and where the results are available.

5. List all individual impact predictions which are specific enough to be testable. If possible, express those predictions in quantitative form, including a measure of error. This is often difficult: predictions are often vague, and use unquantified terms such as "likely", "unlikely", "significant", "negligible" and so on.

6. Determine whether the monitoring programme for the project(s) concerned actually measured the parameters required to test these predictions; and if so, whether the sampling design (e.g. location, frequency and precision of measurements) was statistically adequate to perform such a test. Many monitoring programmes are simply not adequate to test impact predictions in any rigorous manner.

7. Adjust impact predictions, if necessary, to take account of any modifications to the design of the project(s) made after environmental impact assessment. Any such adjustments should be made before testing the adjusted predictions against monitoring results.

8. Compare impact predictions and monitoring results, to determine the accuracy of each prediction.

For references, see Canter (1984, 1985), Bisset (1985), Knight (1985), Moncrieff et al. (1985), NZCE (1985), Munro et al. (1986), Buckley (1987, 1988a, 1989a, b, 1990a, b, c, e), Culhane (1987), Culhane et al. (1987), Henderson (1987), McCallum (1987), Tomlinson and Atkinson (1987a, b), Bisset and Tomlinson (1988), Berkes (1988), CEARC (1988), Sadler (1988), Jagusiewicz (1989).

Equipment Performance

Equipment performance audits are tests of pollution control and monitoring equipment to ensure that they meet operational specifications. To be called audits, they must be carried out in a verifiable manner to predetermined standards. The US Environment Protection Agency (USEPA) for example, has issued testing and performance protocols for particular types of equipment.

The main steps involved are:

1. Determine performance specifications for equipment concerned.
2. Measure its actual performance under defined and controlled conditions; e.g., for pollution control equipment:
   - Measure input/upstream concentrations and/or volume or mass flow rates.
   - Measure output/downstream concentrations and/or volume or mass flow rates.
   - Compare the two sets of measurements to determine actual performance.
3. Ensure that these measurements are repeatable and precise enough for reliable comparisons, and that they cover the entire range of design and actual operating conditions and not merely optimum performance level.

For references, see Oates (1982), Fuerst et al. (1984), Jayanty et al. (1985), and Wright et al. (1987).

Physical Risks and Hazards

An audit of environmental risks and hazards means an assessment of risks to the physical, biological and human environment near an operating site. It involves an inventory of potentially toxic or hazardous materials, a review of events or pathways which could lead to accidental discharges, and an assessment of the most-likely and worst-case consequences.

Questions to ask:

What internally generated environmental hazards might the organisation, corporation or project be subject to:

- Equipment breakdown?
  - valve failure
  - failure of automated control systems
  - pressure vessel explosions
  - leaks
  - other
- Operator errors?
- Strikes, with or without prior notice?

What external hazards does the organisation, corporation or project face?

- Social hazards, e.g.
  - interruptions in supply (of equipment, consumables or services)
  - riot, war, etc.
  - sabotage
- Natural hazards, e.g.
  - earthquake
  - fire
  - flood
  - storms
- Engineering hazards, e.g.
  - impact (e.g. at plant or during product transport)
  - explosion
  - dam collapse
  - soil erosion, landslide

What would the consequences be in each case? Aspects to consider:

- failsafe mechanisms
- expected damage
- worst case scenarios

For references, see Langkamp and Hails (1986), Cahill and Kane (1987), Wong et al. (1989).

Financial Risks and Liabilities

This is an assessment of commercial risks and liabilities associated with any aspect of environmental management. Such risks include: penalties for breaching regulations; costs of cleanup, remediation or rehabilitation orders; compensation claims; and transfer of liabilities when buying or lending to companies with poor environmental management in the past.

Questions to consider:

What legal and financial liabilities might the organisation, corporation or project face from poor environmental management in the past, present or future, either from its own operations or projects or from those it has funded, insured, approved, or is otherwise responsible for or financially associated with?

- statutory penalties for breaching regulations;
- clean-up, repair and rehabilitation costs: e.g. from residual site pollution;
- compensation claims, citizens' lawsuits, class actions, etc. arising from possible past or future impacts on human health and safety, property or amenity values, or other aspects of the environment: e.g. from air, water or noise pollution, radiation, species extinction, etc.;
- costs associated with possible temporary or permanent closure;
- Additional costs of upgrading, retrofitting or replacing systems or equipment to meet more stringent standards;
- costs of delays in approvals for future projects;
- lost market share from poor public image or product boycotts;
- lower share prices and/or dividends;
- higher cost of finance;
- reduced credit from suppliers;
- higher insurance premiums;
- other.

For references, see Bleiweiss (1987), Demeester (1988), Brennan (1990), Ibbotson (1990).

Environmental liabilities can under some circumstances (Ibbotson 1990) be transferred to a financier who:

- becomes involved in management of the business or operation;
- appoints a receiver manager;
- takes possession of a site or assets;
- sells the site or assets;
- enters or inspects or carries out works on the site.

Different countries have different provisions in allocating liabilities for environmental mishaps and mismanagement. Depending on the jurisdiction, liability may be:

- applied to all consequences of an action or operation, irrespective of whether the action or operating practices were legal at the time;

- applied to all consequences of an action or operation, irrespective of whether they were deliberate or negligent;
- applied to all past and present owners and operators for the site(s) concerned, irrespective of the degree to which they actually caused or contributed to the environmental consequences under consideration;
- applied to directors and some or all staff of the corporations or agencies concerned, as well as to the corporation as a legal entity in itself.

Products and Markets

Environmental audit of products means assessing whether retail products will appeal to so-called green consumers; and if not, how to make them do so, e.g. by changes in manufacturing techniques, raw materials or their sources, or packaging.

Questions to consider:

Market characteristics

- What products does the corporation currently produce?
- What products does it intend to produce in the future?
- What are current and potential markets for each product?
- What is the current market share for each product?
- How strong is competition in that market?
- How strong is brand loyalty by consumers or purchasers of that product?
- How great is the risk of losing market share, or how great is the opportunity to gain market share?
- How important are environmental considerations in influencing consumer choice for each product, relative to other factors?

Raw materials

- What raw materials are used for each product and in what quantities?
- What are the environmental consequences of supplying these materials?
- How great is public concern over these consequences?
- How could the environmental impacts per unit raw material be reduced, and at what economic cost?
- What substitutes are available for each raw material used, and how do they compare in terms of environmental impact and price?

Manufacturing processes
- What manufacturing processes are used for each product?
- What are the environmental consequences of these processes?
- How could the environmental impacts per unit product be reduced, and at what economic cost?
- What process modifications or alternative processes or process steps are available, and how do they compare in terms of environmental impact and operating costs?
- How would such changes affect product storage, transport requirements and shelf life?

Packaging
- How are the corporation's products currently packaged?
- How are these packaging materials manufactured, and with what environmental impacts in terms of raw materials, process effluents, etc.?
- How are packaging materials disposed of, and with what actual and potential environmental impact?
  - wholesale packaging?
  - retail packaging?
- How could packaging be reduced, and how would such a reduction affect:
  - marketability?
  - product price?
  - environmental impacts of packaging?
  - consumer perception?
  - market share?
  - total receipts?
- What substitute materials could be used for packaging, e.g.:
  - recycled materials?
  - biodegradable materials?
- What opportunities are provided for recycling used packaging materials
  - by the corporation?
  - by local councils?
  - elsewhere?
- Is packaging designed with recycling in mind, e.g. with minimum mixed materials?
- How are products labelled and advertised?
- Does labelling and advertising accurately reflect the environmental friendliness of the product and packaging?

- Does it emphasise features which would appeal to green consumers?
- How could the various options to modify raw materials, manufacturing processes and/or packaging best be combined and integrated?
- For each of these integrated options, what would be:
    - changes to material, manufacturing and packaging costs?
    - effects on unit product price?
    - effects on product sale volume and market share?
    - cross-over effects on sales of other products?
    - overall changes in sales receipts?
    - net costs or benefits to the corporation?

Baselines and Benchmarks

State-of-the-environment audits are reviews of specific environmental parameters, sometimes called environmental indicators, in a defined geographic region. They are commonly carried out either at individual sites, for water catchments or regional airsheds, or for government jurisdictional areas. They serve either to establish an environmental baseline or as a kind of progress report or benchmark.

For small areas, the processes involved are effectively the same as those used in carrying out baseline studies for standard environmental impact assessment (EIA), and need not be repeated here.

For larger areas, particularly those with restricted access, a variety of remote sensing techniques can be useful, particularly if coupled with geographic information systems. The approach, however, remains the same.

Questions to consider:

What is the area of interest, and how are its boundaries defined? e.g.:

- single project site?
- river, lake, lagoon or coastal waterbody?
- catchment?
- airshed?
- national park or conservation reserve?
- state forest?
- coastline?
- local government area?
- larger government area?

What is the environmental or conservation significance of this area? e.g.:

– residential, human health and amenity?
– agricultural, crop productivity and edibility?
– fisheries, fish productivity and edibility?
– tourism, recreational amenity?
– conservation, flora and fauna, biodiversity?

Which of these is most critical?

Which parameters best indicate relevant aspects of environmental quality? e.g.:

– water quality parameters, such as tds, pH, BOD, metals, organics;
– air quality parameters, such as SO_2, NO_x, dust;
– diversity or abundance of plant and animal species.

Which of these are most likely to change as a result of human impacts?

In view of all of the above, which environmental parameters would provide the best indicators of likely future changes in environmental quality?

Precisely how would these parameters need to be monitored to provide a statistically significant and sufficiently accurate measure of any such changes? (see guidelines for audit of environmental monitoring programmes)

Which of these parameters are currently monitored in the area concerned?

Are they monitored in sufficient detail to provide a current baseline or benchmark against which to measure possible future change; and if not, what changes to the monitoring programme are required?

Which of these parameters are not currently monitored but could be monitored in future, and at what cost?

Which of these parameters have been monitored in the past, and is historical information sufficient to determine past changes and current trends?

For references, see DAHE (1986), NSW SPCC (1986), Walker (1988), QDEC (1990).

Management Programmes

Auditing environmental management programmes means checking whether they are adequate, reliable, efficient and cost-effective. It covers aspects such as monitoring programmes, research (e.g. on rehabilitation, pollution control, process modifications etc.), planning, budgeting, and day-to-day operations.

Many of the aspects considered are directly analogous to those considered in auditing environmental management structures (see below) but the emphasis is different. Audits of environmental management programmes focus on *what* is being done; audits of environmental management structures focus on *how* it is done.

Questions to consider:

What environmental management is currently carried out by the organisation or project concerned? e.g.:

– in planning projects and gaining development approvals and finance
   – environmental feasibility assessments;
   – environmental baseline studies of relevant sites;
   – environmental design of projects, plants and processes;
   – formal environmental impact assessment (EIA);
   – public environmental consultation.
– in controlling and monitoring emissions and discharges
   to the atmosphere, from
   – point sources such as stacks
   – diffuse sources such as stockpiles or bare ground
   to surface water bodies, freshwater or marine, from
   – point sources such as outfalls or drains
   – diffuse sources such as sheet runoff
   to groundwater and soil, by seepage from
   – tanks and ponds
   – leaks or breaks in pipes, gutters and drains
   – earth drains and contaminated watercourses
   – solid waste disposal sites
   – sewage systems
   noise levels
   – on site
   – off site
– in minimising operational environmental impacts
– in rehabilitation and remediation
– in research to improve all of the above

What environmental management practices are required in each of the above categories by regulatory agencies, financiers or insurers?

What are the economic costs and benefits of current environmental management practices:

- to the operator?
- to nearby residents and communities?
- to the nation?
- to financiers and insurers?
- internationally?

If these costs and benefits are not known, what information is needed to determine them?

Are current environmental management practices:

- adequate to satisfy external requirements?
- efficient, cost-effective and equitable?
- well-informed and flexible?
- capable of improvement, and at what cost or saving?

For references, see Henz (1984), Perander et al. (1986), Bleiweiss (1987), Cheremisinoff and Eyck (1987), Reed (1987a, b) Thurman (1987) Allison (1988), Demeester (1988), Austin (1989), Graham-Bryce (1989), Underwood (1989), Brennan et al. (1990).

Management Structures

Environmental management structures include personnel, funds and procedures which any corporate body in either the public or private sector uses to carry out environmental management. Auditing such structures means testing whether they function as intended. For example, if an organisation has to comply with environmental legislation, and its directors or executives allocate funds and employ staff to carry out the necessary work, then they need to be sure that the work actually gets done and the regulations are actually obeyed. This is particularly important where directors and executives may be held personally accountable for any breaches of environmental regulations. Note that it is not the same as an audit of actual compliance.

Audits of environmental management structures must examine many different components of the organisation concerned:

- commitments, requirements and policy
- authorities and responsibilities: line, budgetary, advisory
- information flow: into, out of and within the corporation

- records: form, content, storage, access
- feedback: speed, effectiveness, flexibility, blocks
- alerting signals: speed and reliability
- training: procedures and programmes

The main questions to be asked are summarised under the subheadings below.

Commitments: What environmental protection commitments is the organisation, corporation or project obliged or expected to meet?
- pollution control standards, general or special;
- other general legislated standards;
- commitments made or imposed during development or funding approval:
  - in special legislation such as indentures or ratification acts
  - in environmental impact assessment documents
  - in government assessments or approvals of these documents
  - in finance or insurance arrangements
  - in other forms (or informally)

Monitoring: What environmental monitoring is the organisation, corporation or project obliged or expected to undertake, and what does it actually undertake? (see guidelines for audit of environmental monitoring programmes, this Chap.)

Reporting: What reporting procedures is the organisation, corporation or project obliged or expected to follow, and what procedures does it actually follow?

- form
- content
- frequency
- recipient
- approval/verification

Policy: Is there an environmental policy for the organisation, corporation or project?

- is it formal or informal?
- are all staff required to know it?
- are all staff required to follow it?
- are contractors bound to adhere to it? how? e.g.

- conditions of contract
- financial penalty clauses, etc.
- other

Authorities and Responsibilities: Who is in charge of and responsible for environmental management in the organisation, corporation or project? (e.g., tree diagram). In particular:

- Do staff involved in environmental management have direct operational authority, or an advisory role only?
- To whom does the most senior member of the environmental management staff report?
- Do all other environmental management staff report to the senior environmental management or to other personnel (e.g. site managers)?

Anyone in an advisory role, or lacking operational authority or control over their own funding, generally cannot be held responsible for failure to perform a particular designated task unless they are proved negligent.

Financial Management: How are funds for environmental management allocated and controlled?

- Who draws up budgets, on what scale, and how often?
- Who approves or negotiates them?
- Who controls them once they are approved?
- Can funds be reallocated subsequently, and if so, on whose authority and according to what priorities?

External Liaison: What liaison is there between operating, regulatory and funding agencies?

- formal procedures
- informal procedures
- means of communication
- records
- what project documents are made available to regulators, financiers and insurers?

Public Relations: What procedures are used in liaison with the public, either domestically or overseas?

- Who answers public enquiries? (single person or many?)
  - written?

- by phone?
- in person?
- What project documents are made available to the public?
- Is there a deliberate programme of public communication?

Downward Communications: How are project or corporate management decisions communicated to the people who have to carry them out?

- Formally?
- Informally?
- How fast?
- How reliably and accurately?
- With what opportunities for discussion and feedback?

Upward Communications: How is information from these personnel communicated back to project or corporate management?

- Routine data (e.g. monitoring data)
- Non-routine data, e.g.:
  - breaches of regulations
  - faults in equipment
  - unusual environmental conditions
- Information on the operation of environmental management structures

Records: How are data, instructions and decisions recorded?

- Routine environmental monitoring data?
- Non-routine data, e.g.:
  - breaches
  - faults
  - other
- Data or information used for ongoing environmental management, e.g.:
  - average and peak emission levels
  - average and extreme ambient conditions
  - other
- Instructions for changes in environmental management procedures, e.g.:
  - modifications to monitoring programmes
- Requests for changes in environmental management procedures?
- Decisions?

How are these records stored, and for how long?

- Hard copy, electronic or both?
- How many copies?
- Where?
- What indexing?
- Who knows where they are?

How can they be retrieved?

- By whom?
- With what authority?
- What if that/those individual(s) are no longer available?
- How long does retrieval take?

How are they analysed, if at all?

- Graphically?
- Tabulations?
- Statistically?
    - means and standard errors?
    - ranges and extreme values?
    - correlations, regressions, factor or component analysis?
    - comparison with fixed values? what test statistics?

Who has access to them?

- Routinely?
- By special request?
- With whose authority?

Feedback and Failsafe Mechanisms:

- If procedures are not working, how will anyone know?
- What can they do about it?
- How long does it take to improve the procedures?
- What happens if someone vital leaves or is sick?
- What checks are there that everyone is doing their job properly?
- What checks are there that all equipment is functioning properly?

Technical and Design Aspects:

- Who designed the environmental management programme?
- Were they qualified to do so?
    - how?

- how do you know?
- would they be recognised as expert (e.g. in a court)?

For example, how do you know that the following are adequate:

- Monitoring programmes (see guidelines for audit of environmental monitoring, this Chap.)
- Number and expertise of staff:
  - environmental managers and planners
  - environmental lawyers
  - environmental scientists
  - technicians
  - labour
- Recording and reporting procedures

Alerting Signals: What kinds of problems are likely to occur? What events or situations would lead to breaches of environmental regulations, standards or commitments? If they did occur:

- Who would find out, and how soon after the breach?
  - maximum time?
  - average?
  - how do you know?
- Who would they inform?
  - and how soon?
- Who has authority to fix problems?
- Under what circumstances would senior executives or directors be informed?
  - how quickly?
  - before or after any problems are fixed?

Clearly, if the above questions cannot be answered for foreseeable "problem events" and breaches, then the environmental management framework is not adequate!

Training: Does the organisation train staff in environmental management techniques?

- General low-key training for all staff?
  - on induction?
  - at regular intervals?
  - what does it cover?

- As required for particular staff?
  - who decides when and what is required, and for whom?
- For executives?
  - all?
  - all those with direct responsibility for environmental management?
  - all those who control staff with responsibility for environmental management, no matter how indirectly?
- For technical staff?
  - in technical skills only? (e.g. in operating analytical equipment)
  - in general environmental management?
- For labour?
- For contractors?
- For environmental management personnel?
  - in-house or external?
  - regular or occasional?
  - how often?
  - with what emphasis?
    - management?
    - professional?
  - by what means?
    - short courses?
    - conferences?
    - part-time degree programmes?
    - individual training programmes?
    - in-house seminars?
    - on-the-job?

For references, see Buckley (1989c, 1990d), Ibbotson (1990), Osborn and Preston (1990).

Mergers and Acquisitions

When one corporation is taking over another, or buying one of its sites, projects or subsidiaries, it needs to be sure that it is not acquiring environmental liabilities as well as assets. In such mergers and acquisitions, environmental audit means determining: (1) legal and financial liabilities associated with past and present environmental impacts of the takeover target; and (2) which of these liabilities would be transferred during purchase, sale or takeover. Liabilities might include cleanup, rehabilitation and compensation costs associated with past emissions, effluents, or waste disposal, for example.

This type of environmental audit may also be relevant where responsibility for operating, regulating or funding a particular project is transferred from one organisation to another. The steps involved generally correspond to those used for audit of financial risks and liabilities and of environmental management structures.

For references, see Ibbotson (1990), Williamson and Odbert (1990).

Planning Procedures

Audit of environmental planning procedures means testing how well they work. Such audits are generally carried out in response to public concern over the effectiveness of government in regulating industry. They might also be carried out in response to concern in one country over environmental planning procedures in another.

Questions to consider:

What permits, licences, approvals, notices or consents are required for:

- agriculture, horticulture and pastoralism
- forestry, logging, woodchipping, timber and chip exports
- fisheries, aquaculture and mariculture
- mining and petroleum exploration and production
- infrastructure and civil engineering:
    - roads and railways
    - dams, irrigation projects and water supply schemes
    - ports and airports
    - power generation, electricity lines, gas pipelines
- residential, commercial and industrial building and construction
- tourism facilities, marinas, hotels and resorts
- other forms of development

How do these requirements differ for:

- private corporations using private land, water or resources:
    - with domestic majority ownership?
    - with foreign majority ownership?
- public agencies using public land, water or resources?
- private corporations using publicly owned land, water or resources?
- public agencies using privately owned land, water or resources?

- projects funded by bilateral aid?
- projects funded by multi-lateral lending agencies?

What laws of the country concerned govern:

- project planning and development approvals?
- regional and sectoral planning?
- changes in tenure and use of land and natural resources?

What is the institutional framework for this legislation:?

- What organisations administer each of the laws concerned?
- What regulations and administrative procedures have been made under these laws?
- What are the opportunities for public involvement?
- What provisions are there for resolution of disputes?
- Who has standing to bring disputes before the courts?
  - designated government nominees only?
  - anyone with a commercial interest in the dispute?
- Any concerned individual regardless of commercial involvement?
  - citizens of the country concerned only, or foreigners also?
  - How long do such court cases generally take?
- What happens to the projects concerned whilst such cases are in progress?

What laws apply to a corporation's operations overseas and how are they applied? – e.g.:

- trade and tariff protection
- pollution control
- flora and fauna conservation
- other

What planning and assessment procedures are used by:

- financial institutions?
- insurance corporations?

How well do each of these sets of procedures satisfy the following criteria, and how could they be improved to satisfy these criteria better?

- Operate smoothly and routinely without ministerial intervention?
- Provide adequate opportunity for informed public debate on relevant issues?
- Provide adequate and equitable mechanisms for resolution of disputes?

- Produce decisions which are:
    - acceptable to all those directly or indirectly affected?
    - beneficial to the country as a whole?
    - economically efficient and socially equitable?
- Take adequate account of environmental concerns and conservation values?
- Take adequate account of economic and commercial considerations?
- Operate as quickly and cheaply as possible in view of the above?

For References, see Hooson et al. (1985), Knight (1985), Moncrieff et al. (1985), Tomlinson and Atkinson (1987a), CEARC (1988).

Legislation

An audit of environmental legislation in any country is a review of (1) the environmental policy goals it is intended to achieve; (2) how well existing legislation achieves those goals; and (3) how it could best be modified or added to. Most developed nations now have a large body of law either directly or indirectly related to environmental policy, planning and management. In these countries, systematic overall reviews are probably no longer feasible: legislation is generally updated in a piecemeal fashion. For corporations investing in nations with a relatively limited body of environmental law, however, audits of environmental legislation can be very useful.

Questions to consider:

What are the country's policies on:

- Oownership, use and management of natural resources
    - land;
    - water: lakes, rivers, groundwater, estuaries, inshore seas
    - forests, woodland, brush and fuelwood, other wood resources
    - fish, shellfish, cetacea, and other freshwater and marine resources
    - minerals, petroleum, quarriable construction materials, etc.
- maintenance of environmental quality:
    - air
    - water, fresh and marine
    - soil
    - flora and fauna, biodiversity
- control of pollution
- the rights of private property owners

What laws, regulations and administrative procedures does the country have for:

- development planning (see guidelines for audit of planning procedures, this Chap.)
- environmental planning and management, including:
  - environmental impact assessment
  - regional environmental planning
  - environmental accounting, e.g. benefit-cost and input-output analyses
- control of pollution and maintenance of environmental quality

Who has standing to bring actions under this legislation?

- public
- commercial interests
- government only

How much ministerial discretion does the legislation provide, and to which ministers?

- ability to override all normal procedures under any circumstances
- ability to override administrative decisions under particular circumstances
- ability for one minister to influence or change decisions under another's portfolio

What policy instruments does this legislation use for each major policy goal?

- regulatory (e.g. discharge limits, emission standards)
- technological (e.g. requirements for best practicable technology)
- economic (e.g. emission charges, tradeable emission rights)

How does environmental legislation interact with other rights and laws, including:

- those relating to use, lease and sale of private property, such as:
  - transfer of liabilities for past environmental impacts
  - rights to modify, remove and or sell natural resources on the property
  - traditional owners and their customary rights
- those relating to human health and safety
- those relating to the powers of:
  - local government and other authorities

- traditional councils and decision-making bodies
- those relating to torts and contracts?

How does the existing body of policy and legislation provide for the future?

- procedures for coping with uncertainties
- degree of risk aversion in exploitation of natural resources
- environmental rights and intergenerational equity
- ability to adapt to changes in:
  - population size and distribution
  - technology
  - global economy, exchange rates, investment patterns, etc.
  - international politics, conventions, etc.
  - social values

What gaps, deficiencies and inefficiencies can be identified in:

- existing environmental and associated policies
- existing environmental and associated legislation

How would these affect commercial operations and investment?

What new laws or changes to existing laws are needed?

Current Considerations in Environmental Audit

Who Needs Environmental Audits?

Evidently, this depends on the type of audit. Some kinds of environmental audit are carried out on behalf of the public; others by or on behalf of industrial corporations. With regard to the latter, environmental audits are a potentially valuable management tool for any corporation whose operations require any form of planning permission, development approval, or discharge licence; or which uses any publicly owned resource or land; or which produces any product for the retail market, or whose activities could give rise to public environmental concern, irrespective of regulatory requirements. The same applies to any corporation which finances, insures, owns or trades shares in any corporation which falls into one of these categories. Most major development corporations and investment houses, in fact, should at least consider whether they face any commercial risks associated with environmental constraints, however indirectly; and if they do, they should consider the potential advantages of an appropriate form of environmental audit.

Who Does Environmental Audits?

Again, this depends on the type of audit. Large-scale state-of-the-environment reports and multi-project impact prediction audits are generally carried out by government agencies. Compliance audits can be carried out by regulatory authorities, by public interest groups, or by independent consultants working on behalf of the corporation under audit and prepared to testify to their results. Physical risk and hazard audits at operating sites are carried out by a range of environmental consulting firms, typically those to whom you might turn for hazard assessments in the preparation of environmental impact statements. Some of these are associated with insurance corporations. If you want to keep the results confidential you should have the work done through your company lawyers or through a law firm specialising in environmental audit. Financial risk and liability audits are now offered as a service by several financial consulting firms. There is at least one specialist company offering environmental product and market audits. And finally, if what you need is a review or audit of corporate environmental management programmes or structures, then you will need an experienced environmental troubleshooter who is familiar with your particular industry.

Costs of Environmental Audit

Clearly, this depends on the type of audit. At its simplest, you might want to hire an external consultant to review an environmental report produced by your own environmental staff: a summary of your current corporate environmental management programme, perhaps. In a case like that, what you want the consultant to do is to act as the devil's advocate: to pick holes in the report so that you can fix them. So it might only cost a few thousand dollars. At the other end of the scale, the "environmental survey" carried out by the USEPA (Walker 1988) must have cost hundreds of millions of dollars in staff time and expenses. Typically, a detailed single-site environmental audit is likely to cost from $100000 to $1000000 depending on size and scope. The best way to control these costs, as with any such programme, is to divide it into stages, each successively more detailed.

Past Audits of Environmental Impact Predictions

An audit of environmental impact predictions may be defined as a systematic check of actual environmental impacts, as revealed by environmental monitoring data, against predicted impacts as stated in environmental impact assessment documents.

The principal advantage of large-scale systematic environmental impact audit is that it provides a feedback link in environmental planning and management. Impacts are rarely known with certainty when development applications are under review or development approvals granted, and project designs are often modified between approval and startup, and again as operations proceed. Operational environmental management should be, and usually is, based on actual rather than predicted impacts: one of the principal aims of operational environmental management is to modify processes as necessary to ensure that actual impacts comply with standards or other commitments, even if they did not initially prove to be as predicted during environmental impact assessment (EIA). Environmental impact audit provides a measure of the accuracy of the initial prediction, and potentially, of the "environmental management effort" needed to bring actual impacts into line with expectations where initial estimates proved inaccurate. This also provides a "learning function" in EIA as a whole: future predictions can take into account the outcomes of past predictions.

In the mid to late 1980's, a number of calls were made for systematic checking of environmental monitoring data against impact predictions: multi-project environmental impact audit, in the terminology outlined above (e.g. Canter 1984, 1985; Bisset 1985; Knight 1985; Moncrieff et al. 1985; NZCE 1985; Munro et al. 1986; Buckley 1987, 1988a, b, 1989a, b; Culhane 1987; Culhane et al. 1987; Henderson 1987; McCallum 1987; Tomlinson and Atkinson 1987a, b; Berkes 1988; Bisset and Tomlinson 1988; CEARC 1988; Jagusiewicz 1989; Sadler 1988). Several of these authors also presented data on particular sets of developments, as outlined below.

To date, six multi-project environmental impact audits have been published, five at pilot scale and one at national scale (Table 1). Bisset (1985) examined 791 impact predictions from 4 projects in the UK, finding that only 77 of these predictions could be audited, and that 57 were "probably accurate". Moncrieff et al. (1985) described an "environmental performance audit" of selected pipeline projects in southern Ontario, Canada. In Australia, Knight (1985) reviewed seven projects in Victoria, principally in relation to the operation of institutional systems for EIA and environmental management planning. His review examined nine particular aspects of each project, and the accuracy of impact predictions was one of these. The seven projects were selected from a total of 90 which had been subject to formal EIA prior to April 1985. They included a dam, two freeway upgrades, a power transmission line, a ski lift, a mini steel plant and a marina. Of the seven EIA documents, only two contained "predictions based on theory or modelling", and only one such prediction was testable: traffic volumes on the Hume Highway had increased slightly faster than predicted. Henderson (1987) considered 122 predictions from two projects in Canada. Of these, 42 could not be audited because of lack of monitoring data, and 10 either because they were too vague or because of modifications to the project. Of the 70 predictions audited, 54 were substantially correct, 13 partly correct or uncertain, and 3 were definitely wrong.

The fifth and most extensive of these pilot-scale audits was carried out in the USA by Culhane (1987), who examined 239 impact predictions from 29 EIS's, intended to form a "representative cross-section" of EIS's prepared in the USA between 1974 and 1978. The projects were concerned principally with agriculture, forestry, infrastructure, waste management and uranium processing: none were mining projects, for example. Culhane found that most of the impact predictions in these EIS's were very imprecise, with less than 25% being quantified. Few predictions were clearly wrong, but less than 30% were "unqualifiedly close to forecasts".

The only national scale environmental impact audit to date is the recently completed National Environmental Audit for Australia (Buckley 1989a; see also Chap. 6), in which many of Australia's major development corporations took part. It concluded that the average accuracy of quantified, critical, testable predictions in environmental impact statements in Australia to date is $44 \pm 5\%$ SE; and that predictions where actual impacts proved more severe than expected were on average significantly ($p < 0.05$) less accurate ($33 \pm 9\%$) than those where they proved more severe ($53 \pm 6\%$).

Risks and Uncertainties

A significant component of environmental management, for many projects and corporations, is the management of environmental risks. This includes both the risk of particular environmental or social impacts, and the risks of legal liability associated with past, current and/or potential future impacts. An audit of such risks is therefore an important component of environmental management audit, notably in merger and acquisition (M & A) audits. Ideally, it should also be a component of environmental impact audit, but it is very difficult to test impact predictions which are inherently probalistic in nature. Aspects which are relevant in environmental management audit are noted in the relevant guidelines earlier in this chapter.

Corporate Environmental Management Structures

As the influence of environmental legislation on corporate operations continues to grow, the importance of environmental planning to a corporation's overall operations increases; and the responsibility of corporate environmental staff increases in consequence. The effectiveness with which corporate environmental staff can operate depends on their position within the overall corporate structure, i.e. their level of authority and the funds and personnel under their control or otherwise available to assist them. One of the first steps in an environmental management audit is to review the overall corporate management structure as it relates to environmental concerns.

Just as there are major variations in the size, structure and operations of different corporations, there are also major variations in their environmental management structures and in the number, position, authority and responsibility of their environmental personnel. General patterns, compiled by Buckley (1987) from 12 companies in the minerals and energy sectors, are summarised below.

Perhaps the single most significant distinction is whether the role of environmental personnel is a line management one, with operational funds and personnel under their direct control; or purely advisory – the "yapping dog" model, as it has aptly been termed. In at least half of the companies which provided data to Buckley (1987), day-to-day environmental operations are under the control of an operations, projects or site services manager, who is advised but not controlled by the environmental officer. In others, however, the environmental personnel control their own professional staff, labour and operating funds.

Three main types of environmental management structure may be distinguished, depending on the size and structure of the corporation as a whole:

1. Group environmental coordinator:
   - large companies and conglomerates, with diversified operations;

- senior position, typically three in line from Group Managing Director;
- line responsibility generally to group corporate technical services manager or general manager (under various titles);
- covering operations at a number of different sites;
- representing corporation in negotiations with government on environmental matters;
- technical/secretarial staff only, no operating funds or labour;
- advises operations managers of individual projects or subsidiary companies;
- informal responsibility for and control over site environmental or rehabilitation officers, if any;
- titles such as Environmental Coordinator, Group Environmental Planning Officer, etc.;
- professional backgrounds vary widely.

2. Site environmental manager:
   - single-site companies, or subsidiaries of larger companies;
   - generally responsible only at a single site or operation;
   - line responsibility to overall site or operations manager;
   - generally one or two in line from overall site or operations manager;
   - responsible for aspects such as rehabilitation, environmental monitoring, etc.;
   - effective management of on-site labour for environmental work either by direct line control or by close liaison with site services manager or operations manager;
   - generally required to prepare budgets for environmental work even if the funds are not under his direct control;
   - titles such as site environmental officer, rehabilitation superintendent, environmental engineer, etc;
   - professional training generally in environmental sciences.

3. Production manager or engineer with responsibility for environmental concerns:
   - typical in companies where the major component of environmental management involves heavy earthmoving (e.g. overburden removal and replacement), etc.;
   - environmental management seen as part of day-to-day site or project operations management;

- senior position, typically reporting directly to overall site or project general manager or to group general operations or production manager;
- training typically in engineering or relevant primary industry discipline (metallurgy, forestry, etc.) *not* environmental sciences;
- direct control of funds and labour;
- may rely on technical advice from environmental staff elsewhere in corporation, or external consultants on occasion.

In some cases a single person acts as site environmental officer at one site and also as group environmental coordinator, advising operations managers at other sites.

One feature common to many companies is that of dual structures, one formal and the other informal. Under the informal structure, environmental personnel are expected to provide advice at a range of levels and are responsible for technical input to operational planning throughout the country. Under the formal structure, however, their direct authority is much more limited. One common way in which this dual structure is achieved is to have environmental professionals report to an operations manager who has line authority over funds and staff and has to ratify every suggestion made by the environmental staff. One serious disadvantage of this system is that if the operations manager experiences a shortfall in operational funds for any reason, environmental work may be seriously curtailed or postponed.

Quality Management Aspects

Many aspects of environmental management audit could equally well be covered in a quality management programme; or at least, the idea that management action should be based on measured data with known statistical accuracy is common to both approaches. This was the concept propounded by Schaeffer et al. (1985 *et seq*), in one of the early uses of the term environmental audit. Where the physical operations of day-to-day site or project management depend on the value of some environmental parameter, then it is important to know the sensitivity of operational requirements to variation in that parameter. In particular, if the value of the parameter concerned is based on an estimate made during environmental impact assessment, or measured in an environmental monitoring programme, then it is important to have some measure of the uncertainty of that estimate, e.g. confidence limits at some probability level.

For example, the amount of some reagent used in a manufacturing or mineral processing operation, or a municipal waste treatment plant, might be determined by a balance, say, between the need for a complete reaction and the need to minimise residual concentrations of the reagent in a water body receiving liquid effluent discharges. From a process efficiency viewpoint, the best approach might be to use excess reagent. To comply with water quality standards, however, expensive effluent treatment might be needed: e.g. using a treatment reagent to neutralise or break down the residual of the primary reagent. This effluent treatment process might be expensive. In a case like this, the site operations manager would need to know the sensitivity of water quality in the receiving water body to changes in the residual concentration of the primary reagent in the final (after treatment) discharge; the relationship between primary residual concentration, amount of treatment reagent used, and the outcome in terms of the final residual concentration of the primary reagent; the cost of the treatment reagent; and the sensitivity of the primary profit-generating process to variation in the primary reagent concentration.

As another example, a forestry or tourist operation might be required to ensure that the population of some rare arboreal marsupial in the project area is not reduced by more than some predefined proportion. Perhaps this animal needs a particular combination of habitat characteristics, e.g. nesting hollows in large, old, dead trees (stags) perhaps, coupled with particular understorey shrubs on which it feeds. The forest or project manager would first have to identify areas with these habitat characteristics, and estimate the population of the marsupial in those areas. Such areas might be in easily recognised zones, e.g. along creek banks; or they might be scattered throughout the forest. They might generally occur in areas with good millable timber (or high potential for tourist development), or they might generally occur in areas without. There would then be two main options. The first would be complete avoidance of areas with the habitat characteristics for the rare marsupial. The alternative would be selective logging (or careful development) so as to leave some of the stags and understorey shrubs in these areas intact. To plan the actual operations, the manager would need to know the sensitivity of marsupial populations to the numbers of stags and food shrubs (e.g. do they use all the available nest sites, or only a small proportion?); the proportion of stags and shrubs removed by selective logging; and the sensitivity of the marsupial populations to other disturbances associated with logging or development (e.g. noise). In each case, measures of uncertainty are needed both for the form and coefficients of the predictive functions, and for estimates of environmental parameters in the field.

The central concept is that it is essential to examine the relationship between environmental management practices and environmental impacts, and the uncertainties in these relationships.

In such cases, the first step is to identify the principal sources of uncertainty. If the value of some relevant environmental parameter was derived from an expert estimate, or a numerical model, then one could use the same expert or model to provide some measure of its uncertainty. If it is derived from a monitoring programme, then the principal source of uncertainty might be, e.g. infrequency of sampling; imprecision in measurement or analysis; systematic differences between different operators of analytical equipment; or perhaps, imprecisely defined monitoring sites.

The next step is to determine how accurately the parameter concerned needs to be known; either for operational or compliance reasons. One can then take appropriate action to ensure that it is actually known to the required degree of accuracy. This might involve, e.g. starting a specific monitoring programme, if none exists; increasing or decreasing sampling frequency; using an alternative technique or equipment for measurement or analysis; and so on. The aim should be to determine the value of the parameter to just the required degree of accuracy, and no more: as cost effectively as possible. Unless these questions are deliberately addressed, it is all too easy to expend resources making unnecessarily detailed estimates of relatively unimportant parameters, whilst remaining uncertain about the value of parameters which are actually important in environmental management.

Corporate Environmental Audits: Hypothetical Example

Let us turn now to the practicalities of environmental auditing. The first thing to be clear on is why you want an audit done. This depends on the kind of business you are in, using business in its widest sense; and it determines the type of audit, the critical information, and the expertise needed. Do you need an audit to help you make an internal management decision, to insure against future risks, to satisfy an external requirement, or to prove a point to some third party? It is important to be very clear on the purpose of the audit, and to define its tasks very precisely, before you appoint and brief the auditor or audit team: because as indicated above, there are so many different meanings for the term that there are ample opportunities for confusion.

Different audits need different techniques, and evidently I cannot canvass all the possibilities here. So let us suppose, for example, that you are an executive director of a large manufacturing, mineral or industrial processing corporation, or perhaps a public-sector energy-generating corporation. You are planning to expand by taking over an old industrial site and building a new plant. One of your existing plants, however, has received public criticism, purportedly for polluting a public water body. You have a small environmental unit in your head office, which is generally responsible for advising on government planning requirements, and hiring and managing external environmental consultants to carry out environmental impact assessments for new projects. Each of your individual sites and operations has a different environmental management system, because they manufacture different things, they are in different countries or States, some are large and some small, some old and some new; and most importantly, because all aspects of on-site management are left to the chief executives of the individual operations, most of which are subsidiary companies. One of the operations has an environmental officer as such, and most of the others have chemists who are responsible for water quality monitoring as well as process work. How can you use an environmental audit to best advantage, and how should you go about it?

Well, let us start with your immediate problems. You want to get your new expansion approved, and to do that you will have to allay concerns over existing operations. So you need to find out if there is actually a technical problem at that site, or a political one. Is that operation infringing discharge standards and, if so, why, and how can you prevent further infringements? Or is there perhaps a public perception that although the operation is complying with applicable standards, these standards are too lax – perhaps more so than for new plants of similar type – and that your corporation should reduce discharges and improve water quality in the receiving water body? Your staff on-site probably have the actual information you need, but they may have too much personal involvement in the debate to be able to separate fact from opinion. Besides, a report by the company may not carry much weight with regulatory authorities or the public. So there is an obvious case to bring in external expertise to audit operational practices and actual discharges at that site, and place them in a broader context. This has two purposes: firstly, to allay public concern; and secondly, to advise you on whether there really is a technical problem, and if so, what to do about it.

We will proceed to the practical details shortly, but before that, it might be worth considering that you have a number of other operations, none of which has been reviewed lately. There are no complaints at present but there might well be in the future. So it could be useful insurance to have a similar kind of audit done on them too. But as there is no public involvement at present, you can save money by using environmental staff in your head office to carry out these audits, with assistance from relevant personnel on-site. So to make sure they know what they are doing, why not also involve them in the first audit? Alternatively or additionally, retain an external consultant to advise them as need be and review their reports when they have finished. And in the process, it might be worth asking that consultant for comments on environmental management structures and personnel at each site, and for the corporation overall. You have got a problem at one site, and it has cost a lot of money in wasted executive time if nothing else. So it is worth trying to prevent a repetition.

Meanwhile, of course, your company lawyers have been on to you about finalising the purchase of the new site. The last two owners were simply real estate speculators, and it ought to be a straightforward conveyancing job. But ... there is a grassed-over depression in the centre of the site, and the old title maps show this as "pughole". Hmmmmm ... Tell the lawyers to find out exactly what kind of industrial operation the early owners were involved in, and then ask your environmental people just what a "pughole" might have been used for. Sludge disposal, eh? By this time the warning bells should be well and truly ringing. Time for a discreet but intensive environmental audit of the site. Inspection of old business records, licences and so on; collection and analysis of soil and water samples; and a careful legal examination of just whose responsibility any future cleanup or compensation claims might be.

But back to the problem operation at the first site. You cannot let the site manager run the audit because he will automatically be on the defensive. After all, it has been his site for many years and he does not want to be told that he has made mistakes. But on the other hand, if his staff will not help, the audit will take twice as long and cost three times as much as it should. So what should be done? Well, maybe you could put your lawyers nominally in charge, with the site manager, the chief of your head-office environmental unit, and an external environmental audit consultant as the formal team. The first of these, and maybe the second, will delegate other staff to do the legwork, which is fine. But when you are hiring the consultant, make sure you are getting a specific person or persons and not just a company. You are hiring them for experience, expertise and judgement, so make sure you get it. If possible, get someone with troubleshooting experience. Experience in standard environmental impact assessment does not necessarily imply competence in environmental audit.

Well, now you have your core audit team. Maybe that is all you need: one skilled consultant, with immediate access to any of your staff. But if time is short and there are many aspects to cover, or specific technical areas to consider such as air sampling, chemical analysis, noise measurement, or so on, then you will need more people. So tell your core team what the audit is for and roughly what you want covered, let them draft a brief which details timing, staff, costs, and questions to be answered, and use that as a basis for your own decisions on each of these aspects. You will also need to consider confidentiality provisions and reporting requirements.

I will not try and carry the details of this example any further because every audit is different. There is, however, one very important point which is common to all internal audits: they do not work unless all staff appreciate that the audit has strong management backing and that contributing to the audit is an important part of their job.

Conclusions

Environmental audit is a useful concept, albeit poorly defined. Demand for environmental audit, in all senses, is growing rapidly, and this is likely to continue. Governments, aid and lending agencies, and the public are likely to demand audits of impact predictions, compliance, equipment performance, baselines and benchmarks, planning procedures and legislation will be of particular interest. For project operators, concern will probably centre on audits covering risks and hazards, financial liabilities, and management programmes and structures.

Acknowledgements. I thank those who attended my executive short courses on environmental audit, held in October 1989, April 1990, and July 1990 for their comments on previous versions of these guidelines. A modified version, designed for use in international development assistance, was prepared on behalf of the Australian International Development Assistance Bureau in July 1990.

References

Allison, RC (1988) Some perspectives on environmental auditing. Environ Prof 10:185–188

Anonymous (editorial) (1975) An audit may be dangerous to your health. Water Wastes Engin. 12:17

Austin J (1989) A lawyer's view of the environment. Forum Appl Res Publ Policy 4:91

Berkes F (1988) The intrinsic difficulty of predicting impacts: lessons from the James Bay hydro project. Environ Impact Assess Rev 8:201–220

Bisset R (1985) Post-development audits to investigate the accuracy of environmental impact predictions. Z Umweltpolitik 4/84:463–484

Bisset R, Tomlinson P (1988) Monitoring and auditing of impacts. In: Wathern P (ed) Environmental impact assessment: theory and practice. Unwin Hyman, London, pp 117–128

Blakeslee HW, Grabowski TM (1985) A practical guide to plant environmental audits. Van Nostrand Reinhold, New York

Bleiweiss SJ (1987) Legal considerations in environmental audit decisions. Chem Engin Progr 83:15–19

Brennan M, Bisits A, Jamieson R (1990) Legal considerations in environmental audits. In: Calcutt G (ed) Pollution law. Calcutt Watson, Sydney

Buckley RC (1987) Environmental planning techniques. SADME, Adelaide

Buckley RC (1988a) Critical problems in environmental planning and management. Environ Plan Law J 5:206–225

Buckley RC (1988b) Environmental implications of development assistance. Hansard 29.9.88: 549–606

Buckley RC (1989a) Precision in environmental impact prediction: first national environmental audit, Australia. CRES/ANU, Canberra

Buckley RC (1989b) What's wrong with EIA? Search 20:146–147

Buckley RC (1989c) Environmental audit: course handbook. Bond University, Gold Coast. (2nd and 3rd editions, 1990)

Buckley RC (1990a) Shortcomings in current institutional frameworks for environmental planning and management. In: Sawer M, Kelly J (eds) Development and the environment: making decisions we can live with. Royal Aust Inst Public Admin, Canberra, pp 1–10

Buckley RC (1990b) Environmental science and environmental management. Search 21:14–16

Buckley RC (1990c) Adequacy of current legislative and institutional frameworks for environmental audit in Australia. Environ Plan Law J 7:142–146

Buckley RC (1990d) Environmental audit: review and guidelines. Environ Plan Law J 7:127–141

Buckley RC (1990e) How accurate are environmental impact predictions? Ambio (in press)

Cahill LB, Kane RW (1987) Environmental audits. 6th edn. Government Institute Rockville, USA

Canadian Environmental Assessment Research Council (CEARC) (1988) Evaluating environmental impact assessment: an action prospectus. CEARC, Hull, Quebec, 10 pp

Canter LW (1984) Environmental impact studies in the United States. In: Reidel D (ed) W.H.O Perspectives on Environ Impact Assess Report. W.H.O, Geneva, pp 15–24

Canter LW (1985) Impact prediction auditing. Environ Profess 7:255

Cheremisinoff PN, Eyck JT (1987) Environmental auditing; a basic guide. Pollut Eng 19:72–75

Culhane PJ (1987) The precision and accuracy of U.S. environmental impact statements. Environ Monitor Assess 8:217–238

Culhane PJ, Friesema HP, Beecher JA (1987) Forecasts and environmental decisionmaking: the content and predictive accuracy of environmental impact statements. Soc Imp Assess Ser 14. Westview, Boulder, Colorado, USA

Demeester JM (1988) Practical guidance for due diligence environmental auditing. Environ Law Reporter 18:10210–10215

Department of Arts, Heritage & Environment (DAHE) (1986) State of the environment in Australia. (2vv) AGPS, Canberra

Fuerst RG, Hayanty RKM, Logan TJ, Midgett MR (1984) A new audit method for EPA reference method 6. J Air Pollut Control Assoc 34:242

Graham-Bryce I (chair) (1989) ICC position paper on environmental auditing. International Chamber of Commerce, Paris

Hall WN (1985) Environmental audits: a corporate response to Bhopal. Environ Forum 4:36

Harrison LL (ed) (1984) The McGraw-Hill environmental auditing handbook: a guide to corporate and environmental risk management. McGraw-Hill, New York

Henderson LM (1987) Difficulties in impact prediction audition. Environ Impact Assess Worldletter, May/June 1987: 9–12

Henz DJ (1984) Safeguarding confidential business information. Environmental audits and litigation. Pollut Engin 16:30

Hooson JO, Embree RC, Jeffers ML (1985) Environmental appraisal and audits: a case study of their application by the Bonneville Power Administration. In: Environment Canada, Proc Conf on Audit and Evaluation in Environ. Assessment and Management, Banff, Oct 13–16, 2:796–815

Ibbotson P (1990) Environmental audits – what financiers should require. In: Calcutt G (ed) Pollution law. Calcutt Watson, Sydney

Jagusiewicz A (1989) "Cradle to grave" monitoring as an integral part of EIA. In: Paschen H (ed) The role of environmental impact assessment in the decisionmaking process. Erich Schmidt, Berlin 336 pp

Jayanty RKM, von Lehmden DJ, Cooper SW, Decker CE (1985) Evaluation of parts-per-billion organic cylinder gases for use as audits under hazardous waste trial burn tests. J Air Pollut Control Assoc 35:1195

Knight M (1985) Review of seven environmental assessments carried out between 1975 and 1982. Victoria, Ministry for Planning and Environment, Melbourne: unpublished report

Langkamp PJ, Hails JR (1986) Environmental agenda, corporate coal: an Australian case study. Publishing & Marketing Australia, Melbourne

Levin MH (1983) An EPA response on confidentiality in environmental auditing. Environ Law Rep 13:10346

McCallum DR (1987) Follow-up to environmental impact assessments: learning from the Canadian Government experience. Environ Monitor Assess 8:199–216

McNeely JA, Pitt D (eds) (1985) Culture and conservation. IUCN/Croom Helm, London

Moncrieff I, Shea ML, Torrens LW (1985) An environmental performance audit of selected pipeline projects in southern Ontario. In: Environment Canada, Proc Conf on Audit and Evaluation in Environ. Assessment and Management, Banff, Oct 13–16, 1:145–159

Munro DA, Bryant TJ, Matte-Baker A (1986) Learning from experience: a state-of-the-art review and evaluation of environmental impact assessment audits. CEARC, Hull, Quebec, 48 pp

NSW SPCC (1986) Lake Illawarra environmental audit. New South Wales State Pollution Control Commission Report 41. NSW SPCC, Sydney

New Zealand Commission for the Environment (NZCE) (1985) Environmental impact assessment workshop: issues. NZCE, Wellington

Oates JAH (1982) Use of an environmental audit procedure. Clean Air 12:3

Osborn R, Preston P (1990) Liability of directors and managers – NSW and Victoria. In: Calcutt G (ed) Pollution law. Calcutt Watson, Sydney

Perander DR, Corbett RA, Garrett III DC, Kohm RF, Patrick DI (1986) Environmental activity – overview. J Environ Engin 112:638–647

Perry JA, Schaeffer DJ, Kerster HW, Herricks EE (1985) The environmental audit II. Applications to stream network design. J Environ Manage 9:199–208

Queensland Department of Environment and Heritage (QDEH) (1990) State of the environment in Queensland 1990. QDEH, Brisbane, 32 pp

Reed JW (1987) Environmental auditing: Canadian private sector practices. In: Environment Canada et al. Proc 9th Canadian Waste Management Conf, Edmonton, Oct 7–9:215–223

Reed JW (1987) Environmental auditing: practices in Canadian industry. Pulp Pap Can 88:113–116

Sadler B (1988) The evaluation of assessment: post EIS research and process development. In: Wathern P (ed) Environmental impact assessment: theory and practice. Unwin Hyman, London, pp 129–142

Schaeffer DJ, Kerster HW, Perry JA, Cox DK (1985) The environmental audit. I. Concepts. J Environ Manage 9:191–198

Sokolik SL, Schaeffer DJ (1986) Environmental audit III. Improving the management of environmental information for toxic substances. Environ Manage 10:311–317

Thurman J (1987) Establishing and operating a corporate environmental audit program. Proc Int Congr Environ Profess/TVA, Hazardous Materials Management (Pudvan), Chattanooga, Jun 8–12:707–714

Tomlinson P, Atkinson SF (1987a) Environmental audits: proposed terminology. Environ Monitor Assess 8:187–198

Tomlinson P, Atkinson SF (1987b) Environmental audits: a literature review. Environ Monitor Assess 8:239

Underwood JD (1989) Managing hazardous wastes is not enough. Ind Environ 11:29–32

Walker M L (1988) The environmental survey: strategic planning for the environment. Nat Resourc Environ 3:29–33

Williamson D, Odbert J (1990) Impact of the new statutes on commercial transactions. In: Calcutt G (ed) Pollution law. Calcutt Watson & Assoc, Sydney

Wong J Jr, Roig R, Eduljee GH (1989) Environmental audits of hazardous waste disposal and treatment facilities. Waste Manage Res 7:201

Wright RS, Tew EL, Decker CE, von Lehmden DJ, Barnard WF (1987) Performance audits of EPA protocol gases and inspection and maintenance calibration gases. J Air Pollut Control Assoc 37:384

Chapter 8

Environmental Insurance

Abstract

Business operates under environmental constraints. These involve commercial risks as well as operating costs. Green consumers, green voters and green government have raised the stakes. The risks are real and the sums are significant.

Risks derive from both legal and market processes and include: penalties, asset forfeits, cleanup costs, compensation claims, forced closure, and compulsory plant upgrades; and lost market share, lower share prices, higher finance costs, reduced credit and higher insurance premiums.

Liabilities and losses from poor environmental management can now reach several billion dollars: enough to bankrupt all but the largest companies. These risks do not only apply to operating corporations, but also to suppliers, customers, shareholders, arbitrageurs and financiers. Liabilities may also be applied to individual directors and staff. Environmental insurance is therefore an essential component of corporate risk management strategies.

To identify and quantify environmental risks, a company needs comprehensive environmental audits. To control those risks, a company needs good environmental management to minimise environmental damage for which it may be held liable; and insurance, to cover unforeseen environmental damage which may occur nevertheless. There is a rapidly growing environmental insurance industry in most western nations, but it will only underwrite some risks. For others, companies must insure themselves.

Because of legal uncertainties surrounding the application of comprehensive general liability (CGL) policies to environmental damage, specific environmental impairment liability (EIL) policies will generally provide more reliable cover. The wording of EIL policies can be quite restrictive, however, and requires careful scrutiny.

In the next few years, environmental insurance will almost certainly increase rapidly in importance for industry and commerce, insurers and lawyers, and the general community.

Introduction

Almost all corporations face environmental risks; that is, environmental management costs or liabilities which may or may not be incurred. In industrial operations, equipment failures or accidents may cause environmental damage for which the corporation is held responsible. Past operating practices, even if legal at the time, may cause long-term or cumulative environmental degradation which the corporation is required to restore. If so, the corporation will face costs over and above its routine operating costs. These will reduce its profitability and may affect its share price, the value of its assets, and its ability to meet financial obligation. These effects may flow on to the finance sector. So corporations face environmental risks, and as with any other risks, it is sound business practice to identify, quantify, reduce and insure against them.

From an industry viewpoint, environmental insurance is therefore just one component of a corporate risk management and loss prevention strategy (Buckley 1990a). The general aim of such strategies is to minimise total expected costs, subject to special constraints such as high aversion to corporate insolvency, criminal prosecution of directors and so on. There are three components to total expected costs:

- costs of identifying and quantifying risks by means of environmental audits;
- costs of reducing or transferring risks, including mitigation and remediation costs, insurance premiums and legal defence costs;
- expected costs of losses from uninsured risks, i.e. aggregate of (probability of loss X size of loss).

The purpose of incurring costs to reduce or transfer risks is to reduce expected losses by reducing either their size or their probability. The purpose of incurring costs to identify and quantify risks is to determine the relationship between investments in prevention and expected losses.

In general, the optimal strategy will be to incur costs required (1) to avoid any specific predetermined risks of particular concern; and (2) subject to (1), to minimise total expected costs for all three components together. This involves balancing the costs of potential losses against the costs of quantifying and reducing them.

Risks and Liabilities

Types of Risk

Financial risks faced by industry as a consequence of poor environmental management (Buckley 1990b) include costs associated with:

- statutory penalties for breaching regulations;
- forfeiture of assets;
- cleanup, repair and rehabilitation costs;
- compensation claims, citizens' lawsuits and class actions;
- closure by regulatory agencies or court injunctions;
- upgrading, retrofitting or replacing equipment to more stringent standards;
- delays in approvals for future projects;
- lost market share from poor public image or product boycotts;
- falls in share prices;
- higher cost of finance;
- reduced credit from suppliers;
- higher insurance premiums.

Transfer of Liability

In addition, both industry and finance sectors face financial risks from potential transfer of environmental liability (Davey 1990; Fordyce et al. 1990; Ibbotson 1990; Windeyer 1990). Such transfer of liability can occur:

- in corporate mergers and acquisitions;
- through contractual arrangements between operating corporations;
- through equity holdings in operating corporations;

- through loan agreements and other financing arrangements;
- through insurance contracts and their legal interpretation by the courts.

Interpretation of Liability

At present there is a general worldwide tendency for liability provisions to be interpreted more and more broadly and strictly (Buckley 1990b), so that they are applied to:

1. All consequences of an action or operation, irrespective of whether the action or operating practices were legal at the time.
2. All consequences of an action or operation, irrespective of whether they were deliberate or negligent.
3. All past and present owners and operators for the site(s) concerned, irrespective of the degree to which they actually caused or contributed to the environmental consequences under consideration.
4. directors and some or all staff of the corporations or agencies concerned, as well as to the corporation as a legal entity in itself.

Risk Assessment

Identifying Risks

The main tool in identifying environmental risks is environmental audit. The people and processes involved in corporate environmental audits are well documented (Buckley 1990c,d; Prescott and Brossman 1990; USCEQ 1990; Zagaski 1990; see Chap. 7) and need not be reiterated here. For risk management and insurance, the following aspects are most significant.

1. Audits are now generally a precondition of environmental impairment liability cover, the main form of environmental insurance.
2. Audits for financial risk management and environmental insurance must involve at least three different fields of expertise: technical, legal and economic. The technical expertise includes environmental engineers, environmental scientists and environmental managers.
3. The essence of audit is independent verification, so environmental audits will generally involve external professionals as well as company personnel.

4. The process of identifying and quantifying risks is best done iteratively. It is pointless to spend time and money on accurate quantification of small risks; it is foolish not to spend time and money on accurate quantification of large ones.

5. Financial risks and legal risks are not the same. From a management viewpoint, it is not worth spending large sums of money to find out if a particular action is illegal, if you already know that any penalty would be small. Equally, however, an action may be perfectly legal but could still be very costly if it affects the markets for the company's products or shares.

6. It is useful to specify criteria to screen out small risks. In general, risks will be considered significant if they could lead to:

   a) large specified statutory penalties; the threshold will depend on the corporation

   b) statutory penalties which are not specified as fines, but which could potentially be very costly, such as
      - closure of plant or site
      - injunctions to stop particular activities
      - forfeiture of assets
      - compulsory actions
      - statutory compensation

   c) penalties for individuals, including:
      - fines
      - convictions
      - gaol terms

Quantifying Risks

Quantifying environmental risks is not easy; but it is necessary, because it determines how much it is worth investing to avoid them. Estimating the chances of physical events such as spills, leaks, explosions and seepages is difficult enough in itself, but this is only the first step. It is also necessary to quantify the likely financial losses from such events, whether through legal or market processes.

There are three general problems which are particularly commonplace in environmental insurance (Buckley 1990a):

- contingent probabilities
- few past occurrences
- rapidly changing probabilities

The first of these means simply that the chance that a particular final event will occur depends on a set of preliminary events. The chance that a development application will be rejected on environmental grounds depends on the environmental design of the project, the content of the EIS, the environmental policies of government and the degree of public concern. The chance that a discharge standard will be breached depends on the technical and engineering design of the project and plant, the efficiency of environmental management structures, and the skill and will of individual personnel. The chance that a breach will lead to a fine or other costs depends on the chance that the breach will be detected or reported; the level of concern by regulatory agencies, community groups and local residents; the resources available to them to pursue these concerns; and in the last resort, the outcome of the judicial process. To estimate the probabilities of possible final outcomes we need to know both the links in such chains of events, and the probabilities of individual components. Such techniques are commonplace, for example, in calculating industrial hazards.

The second problem is that events in which we are interested, contributory as well as final, have not occurred often enough to estimate their probabilities reliably from historical frequencies. And the third is that at least some of these probabilities are changing so rapidly that estimates derived from historical frequencies will not apply in the future. Changing public opinion, for example, is particularly difficult to quantify. The chance that a given design of a boiler may accidentally explode, or that a person working with asbestos for a given period of time will contract asbestosis, is unlikely to change with time. Our estimates of these probabilities may change with time, but only asymptotically; becoming more and more precise as more and more data become available. We can only measure public opinion reliably, however, by observing its effects: e.g., on applications for new project approvals. If public opinion actually changes in the interval between relevant events, such as successive development applications, we will never be able to measure it accurately enough for insurance purposes. Indeed, for such factors it is more important to predict future trends, even roughly, than to estimate current values precisely.

From an insurer's viewpoint, the main concern is the total anticipated payout as compared to the number and size of premiums. Expected payout is the driving factor and determines the size of premiums. Recent examples from the USA indicate that multi-million dollar environmental cleanup costs are commonplace (Black et al. 1988; Gordon and Westendorf 1989; Pruett 1990). The largest single-site clean-up, at a hazardous waste site, cost over US$ 2 billion (Black 1989). The courts ruled that since the company concerned was aware of the environmental impairment, its insurers were not required to cover this cost. It has been estimated that cleaning up the 25000 sites classified as hazardous by the USEPA will take 50 years (Ashley 1987), and cost over US$ 700 billion (Black 1989): an average cost of US$ 28 million per site. Insurers have reacted to such figures by setting ceilings on total cover. If these ceilings are well below likely liability, however, they greatly reduce the value of insurance cover.

Risk Management

Risk Management Tools

Once an operating corporation has identified and quantified financial risks and liabilities associated with environmental management, it must then decide what to do about it. As with any insurance problem, there is a choice of risk management tools. The corporation can reduce risks by changing operations; it can absorb them itself; or it can convert them to operating costs by transferring the risks to an underwriter in return for a premium. Or it can opt for some combination of these. Which of these is commercially preferable will depend on the expected costs and benefits of each: e.g., how cheaply it can reduce risks; what risks an underwriter will insure and at what premium; and how large a loss it could absorb without becoming insolvent. Whether a corporation's risks are underwritten by the corporation itself or an external insurer, the corporation still has to calculate those risks and assess how much to invest to reduce those risks most cost effectively. Part of this investment may be paid as a premium to an external underwriter, and part to reduce risks by improving operating procedures for environmental management.

Duties of Care

Whether corporations decide to cover their own environmental risks or pass them to external underwriters, they must still consider how broad a policy they want, what its conditions and exclusions are, and what risks they face if they do not comply with them (Buckley 1990a). Most insurance policies of any kind contain at least two major sets of exclusion provisions, related respectively to observance of the law and a duty of responsible care. Your car insurance may not cover you if you drive through a road intersection against a red light; your house and contents insurance may not cover you if you consistently leave the doors wide open. Companies sometimes argue that legislative discharge standards should be taken as guidelines rather than strict limits. I do not think a traffic cop would be impressed by this argument in relation to speed limits. From an insurance viewpoint there are two separate questions here. If you elect to breach a standard on a regular basis, whether it be by exceeding discharge standards or by routinely parking in a no parking zone, then you have to assess the chance of being detected and prosecuted and the likely cost if you are convicted; and as a general principal of insurance law, insurance policies do not pay fines or other statutory penalties (O'Shea 1990).

If you set out to follow the letter of the law, however, all you need to insure against are accidental breaches. The penalty for an accidental breach, as well as its probability, may well be much lower than for an intentional one, but only if you can demonstrate that it was accidental. In the case of a discharge, a corporation would need to show that it had equipment, staff and management systems designed to prevent such breaches under normal circumstances, and that such systems normally operated effectively. The corporation would also need to show that for the particular instance concerned, the breach was not due to negligence.

In environmental insurance litigation, the courts have treated these issues of intention, expectation and diligence as very important. In general (McDonald 1990), they are likely to hold that insurance cover does not apply where the insured corporation:

- deliberately and knowingly caused the environmental damage concerned
- deliberately acted in a way which could reasonably be expected to cause environmental damage, especially if it did so repeatedly or continually
- installed systems or procedures deliberately designed to circumvent or avoid statutory obligations for environmental protection
- did not take reasonable care to determine potential environmental damage from its actions
- did not take reasonable care to comply with environmental obligations

For example (McDonald 1990), companies have been held directly liable, and not covered by insurance, where they have:

- repeatedly breached discharge standards
- repeatedly dumped toxic materials
- allowed environmentally damaging leaks, spills or equipment failures to occur repeatedly with only temporary repairs
- used advance warning systems to reduce discharges when the plant was under inspection

In other words, ignorance of potential problems is no excuse; and once you know of potential problems, then if you do not take reasonable steps to avoid or reduce them, you will be held to blame for any consequences.

Type of Cover

Overview

There are several types of policy which can potentially insure against environmental losses and liabilities:

- CGL: comprehensive or commercial general liability
- OHS: occupational health and safety
- PL: product liability
- EIL: environmental impairment liability

CGL and EIL are the most important of these. OHS cover is principally concerned with human health and safety on-site. It may be involved when environmental damage affects human health. PL cover may be involved when environmental damage is due to the use of a product, such as a pesticide.

CGL Cover

The history of claims and court actions for environmental damages under CGL policies is rather convoluted (McDonald 1990; O'Shea 1990). Different courts in different jurisdictions have reached very divergent conclusions from apparently similar circumstances. Broadly, there seem to have been three main episodes. Early CGL policies did not mention environmental liabilities at all, and so were taken to cover them by default. Subsequent policies contained pollution exclusion clauses intended to avoid environmental liabilities, but the courts often ruled that these exclusions did not hold. Most recently, policies have been rewritten with very strong pollution exclusion provisions, which the insurers trust will prove legally valid and binding. Many environmental damages take a long time to become apparent; groundwater pollution is the classic example. Depending on the precise wording of the policies and the views of the courts, claims may then be made either under current cover or, more often, against long-expired insurance policies which were in force at the time of the original occurrence. Opportunities for protracted litigation are considerable.

There also seem (McDonald 1990; O'Shea 1990) to be complex legal ramifications in determining:

- whether a corporation has an environmental liability
- what form that liability takes; e.g.
  - penalties
  - clean-up costs
  - damages
- whether the liability can be shared or transferred
- whether the liability is covered by insurance
- which insurers share the liability
- what policies are triggered and by what events

EIL Cover

To overcome the difficulties in covering environmental liabilities under CGL policies, many insurance underwriters now offer specialised environmental impairment liability (EIL) cover. These are carefully worded policies where definitions, conditions and exclusions together are almost ten times as long as the insuring agreement itself. Typically, they exclude liability from:

- damage occurring before the policy came into force
- damage that was intended or expected
- actions in breach of statutes or regulatory approvals
- fines and penalties

It is a condition of most EIL policies that the insured must comply with statutory obligations, take all possible precautions to prevent environmental impairment, and make sure that staff and contractors do likewise.

Specific exclusions and conditions, and wording of clauses, differ between policies. Since a single word may determine whether you or your insurer pays, every word clearly deserves very careful scrutiny.

It is not just the wording of the policy itself which is important, but how it interacts with relevant legislation. Both CGL and EIL policies, for instance, differentiate between various types of loss or liability: penalties, expenses, damages, restitution and so on. They also distinguish between costs the insured was forced to pay by civil court actions, those it was forced to pay by actions under statutes, those it had to pay or decided to pay to avoid further damage, and so on.

Commonly, environmental legislation provides for:

- penalties
- compulsory control, prevention and mitigation measures
- recovery of costs, expenses, loss and damages by public authorities
- restraining orders over property, and charges against such property

Penalties are not covered by insurance. But what about the remainder? Suppose an accident occurs and expensive steps are taken to minimise environmental impairment. One policy might cover the costs of this action if it is taken by the insured, but not if it is taken by a regulatory body and recovered from the insured; another might cover the latter, but not the former.

Viability of the Environmental Insurance Industry

Poor environmental management by operating corporations imposes costs on third parties. Pollution of a water body, for example, imposes costs on other users of that water. Those afflicted generally have a civil right to sue for damages. If such damages can be passed on to an insurer, this removes the incentive for good environmental management. Insurance is supposed to cover occasional accidents, not routine sloppiness, and this is one of the principles that courts have used in past environmental insurance litigation. From a social policy viewpoint, it is important that environmental insurance should not be abused.

Equally, however, it is important from a social policy viewpoint that environmental insurance should be available. The function of insurance is to share risk. Accidents do happen, despite precautions. If all the companies in a given industry sector are putting equal effort into good environmental management, environmental insurance provides benefits both for them and the general community (Abraham 1988):

- reduces corporate insolvencies
- safeguards jobs
- provides a pool of funds for cleanup

Insurance underwriters will only offer EIL cover, however, if they can quantify risks and calculate appropriate premiums. Quite apart from the technical difficulties in quantifying environmental risks as discussed earlier, insurers face three particular difficulties (Abraham 1988):

- adverse selection
- moral hazard
- generalised uncertainty

The first two of these occur when those insured can estimate their risks more accurately than the insurer. Adverse selection means that only those who know that they have a high risk of losses take out insurance cover. Since premiums are calculated on the basis of average risk, adverse selection means that the premiums will not cover the payouts, and the pool of funds for that particular cover will be drained. To avoid adverse selection, insurers use screening techniques to decide who they will or will not sell cover to. For EIL cover, they use careful and comprehensive environmental audits.

Moral hazard means that the insured's risk increases after insurance cover is taken out, but the insurer is not informed. Screening does not work in this case; instead, insurers use large deductibles. These are the so-called excess payments which must be met by the insured, with the insurer covering only the remainder. Large deductibles provide an incentive for the insured to reduce risks.

Generalised uncertainty means that insurers cannot estimate risks accurately; e.g., because they cannot predict how courts will assign and calculate liability. This appears to have been a major problem in the USA in recent years. There is less litigation to judge from in most other countries, but just as much uncertainty. The general adoption of EIL policies could reduce this uncertainty considerably (O'Shea 1990).

Conclusions

Environmental insurance was not important in the past, in most countries, because companies did not face real financial risks from poor environmental management. Many plants have continued to operate despite breaching environmental regulations. As the relationship between industry and government comes under increasingly close public scrutiny, however, commercial risks associated with environmental constraints are rapidly becoming very real and substantial.

Corporate environmental liabilities can now reach several billion dollars for a single site or occurrence. Liabilities can be transferred from operating corporations to their bankers and financiers; and may also be extended to individuals, with penalties including large fines and gaol terms.

As a result, environmental management is now a major component of corporate risk management and loss prevention. Treating environmental management as an insurance problem provides a useful perspective in corporate planning and accounting. It is sound business practice to insure against environmental losses and liabilities.

Identifying and quantifying environmental risks is not easy, but the costs and effort are very small relative to potential losses. The main tool for risk assessment is environmental audit.

Some environmental risks can be covered by insurance. Comprehensive general liability policies commonly contain pollution exclusion clauses, and their legal interpretation is uncertain. Specialised environmental impairment liability or EIL cover reduces this uncertainty and is likely to become increasingly common. The precise wording of such policies must be scrutinised carefully to ensure that the cover will actually apply when it is needed. Investment in equipment and management practices to ensure that policy conditions are met may also be required.

Where major underwriters will not accept the risks, individual corporations must define their policies and premiums themselves. This has several important implications. (1) In designing any new development, it is worth considering the costs of complying with likely future environmental requirements as well as existing ones. (2) Corporations, and their directors and staff, must be able to demonstrate at any time that they have environmental management systems designed to ensure compliance with currently applicable legislation, and that these systems have functioned effectively in the past. (3) Any company contemplating a takeover or merger, any bank contemplating a major loan, anybody contemplating a major share purchase, or anyone dealing with financial instruments affected by such transactions should be very careful to ascertain that their targets have no major environmental liabilities.

If a corporation elects not to take out insurance cover against potential environmental liabilities, it will need to ensure that its environmental management practices are up to standard so as to minimise risks. If it does take out EIL cover, it will need to ensure its environmental management practices are up to standard so as to comply with policy conditions. Either way, good environmental management practices are essential to ensure that the corporation is not disadvantaged in any future environmental litigation (McDonald 1990).

Thus, in conclusion, EIL cover is very important, but the best environmental insurance is good environmental management.

References

Abraham KS (1988) Environmental liability and the limits of insurance. Columbia Law Rev 88:942–988

Ashley LJ (1987) Representation of the insurers' interests in an environmental damage claim. Def Counsel J 54:11–28

Black B, Zimmerman GE, Bailey RE, Westendorf R (1988) Toxic and hazardous substances and environmental law: 1987 survey. Tort Insur Law J 23:455–477

Black K (1989) Through the looking glass – perception and reality. Aust Insur Instit J 12:42–52

Buckley RC (1990a) Framework for environmental insurance. Environ Plan Law J 7:229–233

Buckley RC (1990b) Current trends in environmental law and practice. Environ Plan Law J 7:169–170

Buckley RC (1990c) Environmental audits: review and guidelines. Environ Plan Law J 7:127–141

Buckley RC (1990d) Environmental audit: Course handbook (3rd edn) Bond University, Gold Coast 350 pp

Davey C (1990) Financing in the new environment. In: Building bridges (unpag). BRW, Melbourne, 8 pp

Fordyce J, Kofman J, Tay R (1990) Environmental liability: a gun at the lender's head? Int Financ Law Rev May 1990:19–22

Gordon TA, Westendorf R (1989) Liability coverage for toxic tort, hazardous waste disposal and other pollution exposures. Idaho Law Rev 25:567–618

Ibbotson P (1990) Environmental audits – what financiers should require. In: Pollution law. Calcutt, Watson, Sydney, 37 pp

McDonald J (1990) Legal framework for insurance claims. In: Environmental risks and insurance. Calcutt Watson, Sydney, 22 pp

O'Shea P (1990) Environmental impairment liability insurance. In: Pollution law. Calcutt Watson, Sydney, 9 pp

Prescott MK, Brossman DS (1990) The environmental liability handbook for property transfer and financing. Lewis, Boca Raton

Pruett MC (1990) Environmental cleaning costs and insurance: seeking a solution. Georgia Law Rev 24:705–732

US Council on Environmental Quality (USCEQ) (1990) Risk analysis: a guide to principles and methods for analysing health and environmental Risks. USCEQ, Washington

Windeyer C (1990) Environmental hazards to lenders. Company Director 6(8):38

Zagaski CA (1990) Environmental risk and insurance. Lewis, Boca Raton (in press)

Chapter 9

Shortcomings in Institutional Frameworks

Abstract

Existing institutional frameworks for environmental planning and management do work. Their present form reflects their historical development, and they evolve continually. Changes needed now are incremental rather than fundamental.

Current institutional shortcomings include: inconsistencies between countries and states; intervention in EIA by other government sectors; inadequate integration between environmental planning, including EIA, and ongoing environmental management, including monitoring and pollution control; inadequate mechanisms for enforcing environmental regulations; poor mechanisms for incorporating science in EIA; inadequate testing of impact predictions; inadequate audit of environmental management processes; no generally accessible repository of information on previous impact predictions; limited formal public involvement in EIA processes; inadequate frameworks for regional environmental planning; inadequate frameworks for integrating economic and non-economic considerations in development planning; and the lack of a coherent framework for environmental planning and management in overseas aid and trade.

Electoral concern over environmental issues is producing pressure for rapid change, and most of the above shortcomings are currently being addressed. Critical to the success of these initiatives, however, will be the ability of government agencies in different areas and sectors to cooperate rather than compete.

As a kind of case study, this chapter also includes an essay on a recurring institutional problem which may be described as "humungous development syndrome".

Current Frameworks

The aim of environmental planning and management (EPM) is to use existing political and socio-economic frameworks to minimise the environmental degradation associated with human activities. Current frameworks for EPM in most countries may conveniently be classified into three main categories, concerned respectively with land and water resources planning; pollution control, and impact assessment (Buckley 1988a). In most of the developed western nations, frameworks for land and water resources planning were initiated at least a century ago, and are now most strongly developed at local government levels. Frameworks for pollution control have grown since the early part of this century, and are most strongly developed at national government levels. Frameworks for impact assessment have developed only over the past two decades and involve both local and national governments. There are overlaps between these three main categories, but they are by no means fully integrated.

It is important to emphasise at the outset that the institutional frameworks for EPM – legislation, administrative procedures, people and buildings, funding – are all well established in most of the developed western nations, and generally do work. Their present form has been influenced strongly by their historical development; and they are continually changing in response to public and political pressures of various kinds. My aim here is to identify areas where these frameworks could be improved: desirable directions for change. This is not to deny the value and effectiveness of the existing frameworks, which continue to provide the basis for EPM. The changes I shall suggest are incremental rather than fundamental.

I shall concentrate principally on frameworks for environmental impact assessment (EIA), referring to pollution control and planning only as they impinge on EIA.

Environmental impact assessment, involving the preparation of formal EIA documents by development proponents and their consultants, and the assessment of those documents by government and public, has a number of distinct purposes (Buckley 1989a, b). Briefly, EIA is intended to:

– identify environmental issues
– predict environmental impacts
– inform the public
– enable government assessment
– demonstrate proponent competence

– make environmental protection commitments
– assist in plant and process design
– assist in setting lease conditions and discharge standards
– provide a basis for ongoing environmental management

Different governments have given particular emphasis to one or other of these functions at different times.

Current institutional systems for EIA and EMP have been shaped by their historical development, which is therefore relevant in examining both current deficiencies and possible improvements. There has been a gradual increase in the complexity and depth of individual EIS's and equivalent documents. Early EIS's tended to be rather superficial, and contained very few specific or testable predictions. Subsequent EIS's were far more detailed, with predictions set out in extensive supporting documents. Most recently, there has been more emphasis on guidelines and scoping, attempting to identify critical issues at an early stage and concentrate on those.

Until recently, EIA was treated by development proponents and government regulatory bodies alike as a once-off, highly project-specific hurdle in the development approval process. Perception and processes have changed, and are continuing to change, to include:

– consideration of cumulative, synergistic and cross-project interactive impacts;
– treatment of EIA documents as part of ongoing environmental management;
– an increasing level of public information and involvement;
– improvement in predictive techniques, and an increasing number of testable predictions.

Shortcomings

Problems in EPM can occur at three different levels:

1. Technical problems, with no immediate solution.
2. Economic problems, where there is a technical solution but its social cost is so high that it has not been adopted.
3. Institutional problems, where there is a technically and economically feasible solution but which has not been adopted for social or political reasons.

It is the last of these categories which concerns us here. Shortcomings in current institutional frameworks for EPM in the developed western nations may be summarised as follows:

- Processes, procedures and requirements differ between nations, states, and local government areas, and economic competition between these militates against uniformity.
- Where governments do not have specific powers to legislate on environmental issues, but have an electoral responsibility for environmental management, they may be compelled to use a range of unnecessarily complex measures in order to fulfil their environmental responsibilities.
- The EIA process is increasingly subject to intervention by other sections of government, preventing its proper operation, and this encourages proponents to use political rather than public administrative processes to gain development approvals.
- In most countries EIA is seen only as part of development planning, with ongoing environmental management being largely the responsibility of pollution control agencies.
- Mechanisms for regulatory agencies to enforce environmental protection commitments are generally inadequate.
- Science is central to EIA, but EIA is not always conducted in a scientific manner.
- Impact predictions are rarely tested and there is no generally accessible information base of experience gained during EIA for past projects.
- Opportunities for public involvement, especially in actual decision making, are still very limited, as is public standing to seek enforcement of environmental legislation.
- Though EIA is purportedly a public process, there is generally inadequate provision for public audit either of actual environmental impacts or of the operations of government regulatory agencies.
- In general, there is as yet no adequate framework for routine EPM on a regional rather than project-specific basis.
- There is as yet no adequate framework for integrating economic and non-economic considerations in development planning through routine administrative, rather than *ad hoc* political, processes.
- There is no coherent framework for EPM in international aid and trade.

The first five of these have been discussed repeatedly and need no further elaboration here. The next, the role of science in EIA, has been hotly debated of late, and I shall summarise the outcome of that debate briefly.

The final six items refer to the need for increased integration in EPM, identified by a number of authors recently as an important step in improving institutional frameworks (see, e.g. Buckley 1988a, b). My previous review (Buckley 1988a; see Chap. 1) examined particularly critical problems in four main areas:

1. Integration over time: environmental audit, operational feedback and public involvement.
2. Integration in space: regional environmental planning and management (REPM).
3. Economic integration: ecological values and environmental benefit-cost analysis (EBCA).
4. Administrative integration: in particular, EPM in overseas development assistance.

Since that review there has been considerable development in environmental audit techniques and government commitment to audit processes, though opportunities for public audit of either private corporations or government agencies are still limited. I will review this in some detail.

Recent developments in the other three critical areas listed above – REPM, ECBA and EPM in aid – have been less marked, and I shall review them more briefly.

Science in EIA

Since EIA was first introduced, there has been considerable debate over its scientific validity (e.g. Schindler 1976; Ruckelshaus 1983). This debate has surfaced again recently (Buckley 1989a; Fairweather 1989). The main points at issue (Buckley 1990a) are institutional rather than technical or economic, and are reviewed below.

The first issue is the relative pace and timing of scientific investigations and the EIA process. For EIA to have some scientific validity, adequate baseline information is essential; but development corporations are reluctant to invest in environmental studies before they have determined whether the project is financially viable. The cost of establishing a baseline monitoring programme, however, may be viewed as an insurance premium: it ensures against the risk that if the project does prove economically viable, startup will be delayed by the time taken for baseline monitoring. For this premium to be worth paying, the risk insured against must be real: proponents must know that development approvals really will be delayed until their EIA documents are adequate. This means that government agencies must have both the skill and the will to play their part in EIA competently and accountably. If political favours are cheaper and quicker, there is no incentive for an early start to EIA. Overall, therefore, this is an institutional problem rather than a technical or economic one; it is created by the unwillingness to start investing in environmental monitoring at the same time as other feasibility studies. I would like to think that it is lessening with time, at least in some industry sectors. The practice of commencing environmental baseline monitoring at a very early stage in development planning, for example, is now widely followed by many of the larger development corporations in the minerals and energy sector.

A second concern is that EIA often contains out-of-date science (Fairweather 1989). This is not necessarily a problem: EIA involves applied science and there is no reason why this should be at the forefront of the disciplines concerned. The shortage of references to recent scientific literature in EIA documents, however, is a reflection of a more fundamental problem. Commercial constraints in industry and environmental consulting firms make it extremely difficult for individuals to devote the time needed to maintain their scientific expertise. This situation may change if the public and government demand better science in EIA, creating a commercial incentive for environmental consulting firms to give their staff more time to keep abreast of recent scientific progress.

The third main area of dissent is the extent to which academic scientists should be involved in the EIA process. This again is an institutional problem: it is difficult for scientists to ensure that information they provide is used in a way which they would consider responsible. There are two requirements to overcome this problem; both eminently reasonable. The first is that expert opinion should be distinguished clearly from conclusions based on actual data; not only in the expression of opinion itself, but in all documents which quote it subsequently. The second is that where an impact is uncertain, but potentially significant, it should be monitored in sufficient detail to determine whether predictions based on expert opinion were in fact correct; that such monitoring data should be available to the public in order to check the accuracy of such predictions; and that if actual impacts prove significantly more severe than predicted, action should be taken to reduce or mitigate them accordingly.

In summary, therefore, it appears that the scientific validity of EIA would be improved if:

1. Environmental feasibility studies started sooner.
2. Environmental consultants had more time to keep abreast of progress in science.
3. Scientists were more used to expressing expert opinions as well as results.

Public Involvement and Environmental Audit

Opportunities for public scrutiny of environmental planning and management processes are currently few. There is generally only a single opportunity for formal public review of a development, namely the period for public submissions on the Draft EIS or an equivalent document. There is generally no formal mechanism for members of the public to object if their submissions are not adequately addressed in a Supplementary or Final EIS or in formal Assessments of the EIS by regulatory bodies.

Nor is there any formal mechanism for the public to determine whether environmental protection commitments made by a developer or government in an EIS or associated documents are in fact followed. There is little opportunity for public participation in the design of monitoring programmes, and no mechanism for the results of monitoring programmes to be subjected to formal public review. In theory such results are scrutinised by regulatory agencies, but this is not always done and there is no formal mechanism for the public to ensure that it is done competently and without negligence. In addition, environmental regulatory agencies generally have very little power to bring about changes in operational or management practices, if monitoring programmes show that impacts are more severe than predicted.

One important step in overcoming this deficiency is regular audit of environmental impact predictions. The term environmental audit has been used in many different contexts (Buckley 1989b, 1990b, c, d); in this sense it means a check on the accuracy of environmental impact predictions by comparing them systematically with the results of environmental monitoring programmes. This provides a means for the public to evaluate the competence of their governments in controlling the environmental impacts of development, both at the planning stage through competent assessment of EIA documents, and during operating phases through competent supervision of environmental monitoring and enforcement of environmental regulations.

Institutional frameworks for environmental audit need three main components:

1. Provision for audit of environmental impact predictions in relevant legislation and administrative procedures.
2. Provision of personnel and support structures in government to carry out the mechanics of data compilation, analysis, and reporting.
3. Formal public access to corporate environmental monitoring data, either through a requirement for direct publication by the operating corporations concerned; through routine publication by government regulatory bodies; or through use of freedom-of-information (FOI) legislation.

Environmental legislation in most countries has no provision to make government agencies accountable to the public for auditing actual impacts and ensuring that operational changes are made if predictions, or subsequent licence conditions, are not met. The public relies on the government to carry out such an auditing function, but has no means to ensure that it actually does so. In many countries there is no legal avenue for concerned third parties to compel individuals, corporations or government agencies to comply with environmental legislation, including pollution control regulations or the provisions of an EIS, unless they can claim to be materially disadvantaged by the infringement, and so gain legal standing. To overcome this problem, specific provisions for third party standing are often incorporated in new environmental legislation.

In most countries there is no legal provision for members of the public to take regulatory agencies to task for negligence in enforcing environmental protection statutes or commitments; though specific laws in a few nations do contain such provisions.

Routine environmental impact audit will require commitment of substantial resources and staff, as well as legislation. The precise requirements will depend on the institutional system adopted. Several possibilities are available. The simplest of these is that government environmental agencies currently responsible for overseeing environmental management, and monitoring compliance with environmental regulations and standards of various kinds, could require individual operating corporations to provide an annual comparison of actual versus predicted impacts as part of their regular environmental reporting programme. Most corporations already produce annual summaries of environmental monitoring data which compare actual parameter levels with prescribed limits. A comparison with predictions would be a straightforward addition. Alternatively, the primary comparisons of actual versus predicted impacts could be carried out directly by government agencies, using the original EIA documents and corporate environmental monitoring data. This option might require the creation of new environmental audit units within the relevant agencies. Neither of these options would require the provision of additional primary data by operating development corporations.

The third critical aspect of environmental impact audit is that if it is to be of real value, it must be open to public scrutiny. This needs public access to environmental monitoring data – not necessarily all such data, but at least that yielded by formal monitoring programmes prescribed during EIA. There are currently three main avenues for public access to environmental monitoring data. The first is directly from the operating corporations concerned, either by general public release of corporate reports or by special request. This is at the discretion of the operating corporation concerned and is not enforceable; nor is it possible to check the completeness of information released. The second avenue is through government regulatory agencies. In most countries, however, such agencies are not bound to publish or release environmental monitoring data, and have often been reluctant to do so if they fear that public release would jeopardise the continued provision of data by operating corporations. This situation is changing in some nations, but not all.

The third avenue is through FOI legislation, where this exists. Use of FOI legislation by concerned individuals and community groups, however, is limited by a number of factors:

1. FOI legislation often contains provision for government agencies to charge substantial fees for provision of information, and this restricts its use by individuals and groups with limited financial support.
2. There are often long delays in the production of information.
3. FOI legislation often applies only to the information held by government agencies, not private corporations.
4. Where government agencies hold information initially produced by private corporations, FOI legislation commonly contains clauses requiring FOI requests to be referred to the corporations concerned, with provisions which may exempt such data from public release on grounds of commercial confidentiality.

Regional EPM

Regional approaches to EPM are needed to overcome several shortcomings in current institutional frameworks, notably problems associated with cumulative and diffuse impacts (Buckley 1988a; see Chap. 1).

Such approaches have been proposed repeatedly for many years but are unlikely to become routine until there are working mechanisms for:

1. Cooperation rather than competition between the various government agencies concerned with different areas and industry sectors.
2. Equitable cost-sharing between development proponents and planning agencies.

Some countries and states do have legislation which provides for the production of so-called regional environmental plans, but this has not yet overcome the obstacles mentioned above.

A parallel approach with similar overall intentions is the adoption of total catchment management (TCM) legislation of various types. New South Wales, Australia, for example, now has both REPM and TCM legislation. The former has not yet lived up to its promise: the latter is too recent to judge.

Resource Accounting, Ecological Values and Benefit-Cost Analysis

Despite publication of several excellent new books on environmental economics (e.g. Common 1988), there are still several major obstacles to the general adoption of resource accounting (RA) and environmental benefit-cost analysis (EBCA) as routine planning tools. Those include technical as well as institutional difficulties:

1. Techniques for expressing social or other values of ecosystem components and functions in terms of currency units are still very imperfect and in some cases misleading.
2. Social values placed on environmental protection are changing so fast that estimates of those values are likely to be obsolete before they are published.
3. There are categories of values which are not expressible in economic terms but which are expressed through political processes, so EBCA alone will always be inadequate as a planning tool.

Besides economic valuations of environmental quality, politicians would like environmental economists to provide a measure of the economic cost of environmental protection measures in various industry sectors. Professional environmental scientists, myself included, have in fact been trying to obtain such measures for a number of years. It is remarkably difficult to obtain reliable figures, however, for three main reasons. The first is that individual operating corporations treat such information as commercially valuable and endeavour to conceal it from their competitors. The second is that industry associations and individual corporations have vested political and economic interests in quoting maximum figures for such costs, so that figures provided by industry are unlikely to be reliable unless the basis for calculation is clearly defined and the data verifiable. And this leads to the third difficulty, which is that different corporations use widely differing accounting systems and there is no standard for which particular costs should be included under the heading of environmental protection.

This is partly an institutional problem and partly a technical one. What we actually need to know are the *marginal* costs of two sets of environmental protection measures. The first set of marginal costs we need to know is for any operation or activity which is done in a particular way in order to comply with minimum standards prescribed by environmental legislation and regulation, i.e. the cost of that operation as it is done for compliance, *less* the cost of the same operation as it would be done (if at all) in the absence of any environmental legislation. The second set of marginal costs is the difference between those minimal compliance costs, and the cost of operations as they are actually carried out, whether to a higher or lower standard than that required under regulation.

A number of attempts to measure such costs are summarised in Chapter 3. Many figures for rehabilitation costs have been quoted by the mining industry, especially the coal mining industry (Buckley 1987). Unfortunately, the bases for calculation are generally not stated and are probably not comparable. There is a better basis for comparison in the electricity industry, which has several advantages in this regard: a number of essentially similar power stations for comparison (as compared to dissimilar mines); a general lack of competition between individual corporate entities, each of which usually has a monopoly in a well-defined area; and in consequence a good network of communication at both technical and executive levels. The principal environmental protection costs in electricity generation are for stack precipitators, and for flue gas desulphurisation, sulphur recovery processes, and catalytic crackers in those countries where they are used. One such study, for a power station in Australia, has been released recently (ESAA 1990).

The estimates, of course, provide only one side of the equation, i.e. the costs incurred by industry in complying with environmental legislation, which appear as social costs through increased prices for commodities, goods, and energy produced by those industries. For rational planning, we also need to know the marginal *benefits* to society which are produced by that investment in environmental protection; or equivalently, the marginal costs of going without that investment. These are even harder to measure than the industry costs of environmental protection measures. What we need to know is the difference between the social value of environmental damage and degradation which occurs *with* those environmental protection measures in place, and the greater damage and degradation that would occur without them. Many techniques for measuring such costs have been proposed and tested; all need to be treated with considerable scepticism at present, some for practical technical reasons and others for more fundamental conceptual reasons (Buckley 1988a, 1990e; Common 1988; and Chap. 3).

Overall, therefore, government interest in RA and ECBA has grown considerably in the past year or two, but techniques for actually doing it have not improved to the same degree.

EPM in Overseas Development Assistance

This topic has been of particular interest for a number of years. My basic contention is that for purely hard-nosed, self-centred, practical and commercial reasons, the developed nations need to conserve biological measures in the developing nations; and that the only feasible means for doing so at present is via international aid. For that reason I contend that the major proportion of our development aid should be earmarked specifically for projects whose principal aim is environmental protection. Trying to improve EIA for major development proposals, such as hydroelectric schemes, power stations and forestry projects, is commendable (albeit rather too little, too late) but simply not enough. The rationale for this is detailed by Buckley (1988a, c, 1989c), and in Chapter 14.

There have been two significant institutional changes in this field in the last few years. One is greater emphasis on project EIA by international financial institutions, both bilateral aid donor agencies and multi-lateral lending agencies such as the World Bank and Asian Development Bank.

To date, this change has been superficial rather than fundamental, but at least it is in the right direction.

The other interesting change is that global environmental concerns have become major issues in all foreign affairs dealings, whether in terms of general bilateral relations, trade agreements, or even forex rates. This has been reflected by a suddenly increased interest in environmental management by Ministers for Foreign Affairs and Trade; and hence by their supporting agencies and government departments.

Case Study: Humungous Development Syndrome

There is a recurring malfunction in current institutional systems for development planning in many countries, which might be termed "humungous development syndrome" (HDS). We need to recognise this syndrome quickly, because there are many instances at present where it could potentially present serious planning problems. These are its symptoms:

- Someone proposes a multi-million dollar, high-tech, futuristic development.
- In this original concept, this proposal may well (though not necessarily) be a grand vision for a better future.
- Government and industry explore the concept cautiously, each on the assumption that funding would be injected from an unspecified outside source.
- Following initial media coverage, public concern is expressed over possible expenditure of taxpayers' funds.
- Various people suggest that the proposed development would not be commercially viable, usually because of simple and basic considerations, but these people are overruled or ignored.
- The original source of funds proves imaginary, inadequate or at best, nebulous.
- By this time, however, a number of people are making a living simply from *promoting* the proposed development in one way or another, and these people have a vested interest in continuing this activity.
- In addition, a second and much larger group of people have perceived potential commercial opportunities, typically in construction, engineering, infrastructure and ancillary service areas.

- Together these groups form a powerful lobbying force which continues to push for the new development.
- Industry assures government that the proposed new development will be commercially self-supporting and will in fact generate government revenue through the tax system, and government assures the public that no public funds will be required.
- Because of industry lobbying, local or State governments begin to compete for the development to be in *their* area or electorate (if its geographic location is not determined by technical constraints); as this competition becomes more intense, they begin to offer economic incentives.
- Industry and local government interests join in calling for the national government or multi-lateral lending agencies to provide a massive injection of funds for "startup".
- Public opinion becomes polarised, media coverage mounts, and development approvals are fast-tracked, amidst protests of political corruption.
- Construction takes place at the public expense, and takes much longer and costs much more than expected; construction companies make a lot of money; the development is turned over to a government agency and immediately reveals numerous flaws which are corrected at great public expense.
- The development proves to be a commercial white elephant and runs at a heavy loss, subsidised by taxpayers' funds.

Several things are apparent from the above. Firstly, not all large developments necessarily suffer from HDS. It is quite possible for development to be well planned and profitable and to contribute to national and community well-being. Secondly, even if a particular development shows the early symptoms, HDS need not necessarily run its full course. Cures are possible.

Thirdly, the risk of HDS is greatest for large infrastructure developments. Primary resource developments and manufacturing enterprises in any sector can certainly suffer from a range of environmental planning problems. Besides direct adverse impacts on the natural environment, they can often transfer public goods to private profit, sometimes even with public subsidy. They differ fundamentally from large infrastructure projects, however, in that they are based on a defined natural resource which can be exploited to produce goods and commodities which contribute to human material well-being. The problems are generally with environmental impacts and social equity, not gross profitability. In addition, capital investment is commonly by the private sector, which makes its own commercial judgement of financial risks.

Large infrastructure developments are different. Their capital and operating costs are funded, in the long run, by taxpayers, consumers and users. They are often proposed and constructed by private enterprise, but construction is usually funded – often on an open-ended basis – by government, and they are commonly handed over to the public sector to operate. These projects have no fundamental resource base and no guarantee of profitability, and the financial risks are passed to the taxpayer. Planning and approval procedures for such developments therefore need to be particularly careful and conservative: but if HDS strikes, they are quite the reverse. Before we are prepared to credit our elected representatives and their appointed bureaucrats with the skill and will to make sound judgements on the merits of such proposed developments, we should therefore examine the institutional systems under which they operate, and make our own assessment of their effectiveness.

Characteristically, these large infrastructure projects involve: massive capital costs; uncertain market demand and price elasticities; competition either domestically or internationally; free use of public land; taxpayer-subsidised ancillary infrastructure, and so on. They may also involve large, and often unquantified, environmental damage costs. Typically, lobbyists start seeking hefty injections of government money for further studies, and continuing promotion before any rigorous economic analysis, let alone environmental impact assessment, has yet been made available for public scrutiny.

Efficient infrastructure in itself is a laudable aim. The objections arise when taxpayers are compelled to allow, or even subsidise, private corporations to construct massive white elephants which (1) destroy or degrade natural environmental resources of which taxpayers, as citizens, are part-owners and want to keep for future use and enjoyment by the community as a whole and themselves in particular; and (2) run at a loss, forcing taxpayers to forego future goods and services in order to pay more tax to keep the bloody things running and pay the interest on their massive capital costs.

By all means, let private-sector syndicates and advocates prepare their plans and feasibility studies. If they choose to invest their funds in such activities, that is their commercial privilege. Let them ask for government funding or endorsement if they wish; anyone can *ask*. But governments should not give them public money without the opportunity for public scrutiny and debate on the economic basis, and social and environmental consequences, of such projects: because that is HDS, full-blown.

Conclusions

I will conclude with two general considerations.

Firstly, to overcome institutional problems requires public pressure for institutional change. The more the public demands greater account-ability from government agencies, and the more weight the electorate places on good resource management decisions by politicians, the greater the commercial incentive for better environmental management by the proponents of development projects, and for better science in EIA.

Secondly, the most critical current shortcomings cannot be overcome unless government agencies start to cooperate instead of compete. At present, too many Ministers and Departments see themselves as represen-tatives rather than regulators of their particular industry sector. Whilst this persists there is little hope for overcoming institutional barriers. And of course, the same applies to competition between different levels of government. If our politicians cannot overcome these barriers at a practical level, perhaps it will be up to government agencies to do so at an administrative level?

Acknowledgements. A previous version of this essay was first presented at a conference on "Development and the Environment: Making Decisions We Can Live With" held by the Royal Australian Institute of Public Administration in Canberra, Australia, February 1990. A previous version of the essay on "Humungous Development Syndrome" was first published in the *EIA Newsletter* in 1990.

References

Buckley RC (1987) Environmental planning techniques. SADME, Adelaide
Buckley RC (1988a) Critical problems in environmental planning and management. Environ Plan Law J 5:206–225
Buckley RC (1988b) Integration in environmental planning and management. C Resource Environ Bull 11(4):1–2
Buckley RC (1988c) AIDAB's ability in environmental management of aid projects: relative roles of professional and administrative staff. Report to Senate Standing Committee on Environment, Recreation and the Arts, Canberra
Buckley RC (1989a) What's wrong with EIA? Search 20:146–147

Buckley RC (1989b) Precision in environmental impact prediction: first national environmental audit, Australia. CRES/ANU, Canberra

Buckley RC (1989c) Environmental implications of development aid. C Resource Environ Bull 12(1):1–4

Buckley RC (1990a) Environmental science and environmental management. Search 21:14–16

Buckley RC (1990b) Environmental audit: course handbook (3rd edn) Bond University Gold Coast, Australia

Buckley RC (1990c) Environmental audit: review and guidelines. Environ Plan Law J 7:142–146

Buckley RC (1990d) Adequacy of current legislative and institutional frameworks for environmental audit in Australia. Environ Plan Law J 7:127–141

Buckley RC (1990e) Review of Common M 1988; Environmental and resource economics: an introduction. Aust J Ecol 15:247–250

Common M (1988) Environmental and resource economics: an introduction. Longmans, London

Electricity Suppliers Association of Australia (ESAA) (1990) Report on environmental costing methodology: thermal plant. Environment Committee, ESAA, Melbourne

Fairweather PG (1989) Where is the science in EIA? Search 20:141–144

Ruckelshaus WD (1983) Science, risk and public policy. Science 221:1026–1028

Schindler DW (1976) The impact statement boondoggle. Science 192:509

Chapter 10
The Role of Environmental Scientists

Abstract

This chapter consists of three short essays discussing different aspects of the role of environmental scientists in environmental planning and management.

The first discusses the difference between environmental science and environmental management. Science and management have different goals, and so do scientists and managers. Environmental science is a vital component of environmental management, but not the only one. The main problems in environmental planning and management at present are institutional rather than technical.

The second discusses a number of recent proposals for improving EIA. At present, EIA is generally carried out by consultants on behalf of proponents. There have been suggestions that it could be improved if it were carried out directly by the government; by independent consultants nominated by planning agencies; or by judicial inquiries. Alternatively, EIS's could be reviewed by consultants on behalf of government, so that one team of consultants prepared the EIS and another criticised it. It has also been suggested that EIS's should present economic information in the same detail as environmental information.

The third examines the role of ecologists in industry. Ecologists interact with private enterprise both from inside and outside the private sector. In addition, private enterprise includes a wide range of activities not of particular concern to ecologists; and industry includes public-sector corporations such as electricity commissions, as well as private-sector corporations. This contribution is concerned principally with ecologists working in industry.

As an Appendix, the chapter includes a generic environmental policy for industry institutes and associations, easily adapted to specific industries.

Environmental Science and Environmental Management

Science and management are different. The goal of science is knowledge; the goal of management is action. Scientists are not generally trained for management; but scientific information is needed for good management, and many decision makers are scientifically illiterate. Good scientists want to complete and present their work so that it makes an intelligible, accessible, and lasting contribution to the body of human knowledge. Good decision makers want just enough information to make their decisions; once a decision is made, they are interested only in its outcome, and in equally pressing decisions, rather than on the information which went into making the decision. In environmental impact assessment (Fairweather 1989; Buckley 1989a; McIntosh 1989; Odgers 1989), scientists can help managers by: providing data critical to particular applied problems; estimating parameters to a predefined level of precision; designing and carrying out experiments to examine the impacts of particular actions; and providing expert opinion, in the same way as any other professional.

Environmental consultants help decision makers to analyse and define problems and identify and obtain relevant information. They should then be able to compile and present that information in an intelligible form; show how it bears on the decisions to be made; show which information is most critical, where it comes from, and how reliable it is; and identify any missing information and whether it would be likely to affect the decision. Where the critical information is scientific, environmental consultants must either be competent in both science and management or literate in science and competent at managing scientists and liaising between scientists and decision makers. The line between environmental consultants and environmental scientists is blurred. The main distinction is that scientists seek critical problems and rigorous methods, whereas consultants seek answers to other people's problems, on other people's budgets and deadlines.

Problems in environmental science and management may include technical problems, with no immediate solution; economic problems, where there is a technical solution but its social cost is so high that it has not been adopted; and institutional problems, where there is a technically and economically feasible solution but it has not been adopted for social or political reasons.

Development proponents, and politicians with resource portfolios, often complain that EIA delays development approvals so that market windows are missed. This is an institutional problem, caused by starting EIA too late. Baseline monitoring for EIA can indeed take years; but so do economic feasibility studies and project design, particularly where resources must be proved up. If market windows are short, proponents must determine whether a development is economically worthwhile, and how to actually carry it out, well ahead; and keep this information on hand till a window opens. The same should apply to environmental studies. A proponent could even complete EIA and gain development approval in anticipation of future market windows. This costs money, certainly; but so do economic and engineering studies. A completed EIA should also increase a project's value if the original proponent were to sell it: just as a registered motor vehicle is worth more than an unregistered one. The cost of an early start to environmental studies is a small premium to insure against the risk of missing a future market window. For this premium to be worth paying, however, proponents must know that development approvals really will be delayed until EIA documents are adequate; government agencies must have both skill and will for competent assessment. If political favours are cheaper and quicker, there is no incentive for an early start to EIA. In fact, an early start to baseline monitoring is now becoming commonplace in the minerals and energy sectors at least, so this problem may be shrinking.

Science is not the only component of EIA, but it is a crucial one (Odgers 1989; Buckley 1990); and both the government and public are increasingly demanding that it be worthy of the name. The science in EIA documents is sometimes outdated (Fairweather 1989); but only sometimes; and well-tried techniques in applied science may be more reliable than current tenets. If EIS's quote the jargon of discredited theory, however, that exposes a real problem; commercial pressures do not leave consultants with time to keep abreast of recent scientific progress. This may change if the public and government demand better science in EIA, creating a commercial incentive for environmental consulting firms to keep their scientific expertise up-to-date.

Academic scientists often avoid EIA for fear of misrepresentation. Users of science rarely have the same goals, or qualms, as its providers. If consultants present scientific information accurately and intelligibly, academics will be more willing to provide it. It has been incorrectly asserted that scientists can not generalise or guess. They can; but they like to make it clear that guesses are only guesses. In offering expert opinion on likely environmental impacts, scientists expect firstly that opinions should be clearly distinguished from conclusions based on actual data; and secondly that potentially significant impacts should be monitored, to determine whether expert opinions actually proved correct. They also expect that such monitoring data should be publicly available, and that if actual impacts prove significantly more severe than predicted, action should be taken to reduce or mitigate them.

Fairweather (1989) expressed concern over the "cognitive limitations of policy makers". This is not a real problem. Large masses of data may indeed be indigestible and incomprehensible, but that does not reflect on the cognitive limitations of policy makers. The need to reduce large volumes of experimental data to a single comprehensible conclusion is as important when scientists are communicating with each other, as it is when they are communicating with policy makers or the public.

Both government and industry sometimes suggest that "the public is stupid". This is a myth. The public includes a wide range of people with a corresponding range of intelligence, skills and interests. Communication with the public is a crucial component of EIA; and if it is done well, the fundamental aspects of EIA should be comprehensible to almost any member of the electoral public. It has been suggested that the public cannot understand probabilities or confidence levels, but this is simply incorrect: risks and odds are a commonplace feature of, e.g., card games, betting, and insurance.

Industry representatives (e.g. McIntosh 1989) have sometimes asked "why we appoint government agencies at considerable cost to carry out [monitoring] if they are to become merely agents for public opinion". But that is precisely what democratic governments are intended to be – though in practice, history suggests that governments act more as agents of industry than of public opinion. Either way, governments are unreliable unless under scrutiny. They are as subject to incompetence, ineptitude, and corruption as any other institution. Individuals within government may do their best; but are often hampered rather than aided by bureaucratic frameworks. So what is needed is greater accountability of government agencies to the public.

In conclusion:

1. Science and management have different goals, and so do scientists and users of science.
2. Science is central to EIA but not its only component.
3. One of the tasks of environmental consultants is to liaise between scientists and managers, as well as between proponents, governments and the public.
4. EIA is a very valuable process and one of the cornerstones of successful environmental planning and management.

5. The main problems in EIA are institutional rather than technical or economic, and would be overcome if: environmental feasibility studies started sooner; environmental consultants had more time to keep abreast of progress in science; and scientists were more used to expressing expert opinions as well as results. To overcome institutional problems requires public pressure for institutional change. The more the public demands greater accountability from government agencies, and the more weight the electorate places on good resource management decisions by politicians, the greater the commercial incentive for better environmental management by the proponents of development projects, and for better science in EIA.

EIA: Should We Do It Differently?

In most of the developed western nations, environmental impact statements (EIS's) or equivalent documents are generally prepared by consultants who are commissioned by project proponents.

A number of politicians and conservation groups (Sanders 1989; Salmon 1990) have complained that the consultants are not independent: because they are paid by the proponents, expect to get further assignments from the same industry, and in some cases also hope to carry out construction work on the project if it goes ahead.

Such groups therefore argue that EIS's should be prepared by independent consultants; and that to achieve this, the EIA consultants for any project should be selected or nominated by the relevant planning or regulatory authority, and paid by the proponent through that authority.

Alternatively, it has also been suggested (Coombs 1990) that in order to exercise more careful control over the exploitation and export of exhaustible resources, environmental impact assessment should be conducted by public judicial inquiries. It is certainly true that environmental impact predictions have been particularly detailed, quantitative and testable for past development projects which have been the subject of public inquiries (Buckley 1989b).

However, the question as to whether EIS's should be produced entirely by the proponent or independently has interesting implications. Under the system presently used in most western nations, an EIS is a document produced entirely by or on behalf of a project proponent, for assessment by government and public. Public complaints that an EIS cannot be unbiased if it is prepared by consultants who are paid by the proponents may be correct, but they are misguided: an EIS is, and is intended to be, a statement by the proponent. Arguably, the real problem is not that EIS's are produced by the proponent, but that planning authorities and community groups assessing EIS's do not have access to the same time, resources and expertise as the proponents who prepared them (Buckley 1989a, 1990).

There have been a number of moves in recent years for EIS's to be prepared by the government rather than by the proponent. This is commonly the case in New Zealand, for example, and there are moves by some agencies in other countries for EIS's to be prepared by consultants nominated by the planning agency but paid by the proponent. This is already provided for in EIA/planning legislation in at least some countries and states: the relevant minister has the right to have an EIS carried out on his behalf at the proponent's expense. In general, however, this option would not be adopted unless the proponent did not carry out its own EIS; and it is an option which is rarely, if ever, used in practice.

There are also instances where government regulatory agencies employ external professional environmental scientists to review proponent EIS's. One government agency in Australia, for example, uses both consultants and academics as reviewers. This seems to be a valuable strategy and one that is likely to continue and increase. There are, however, still some crucial questions to answer. Firstly, can these reviewers carry out a really critical assessment if they do not have access to the same original data as the proponent's consultants, or the same amount of time to analyse it or predict likely impacts? Secondly, who pays for the reviewers: the proponent or the taxpayer? There is no hard and fast answer to this question: clearly, it is a matter of policy. At present, effectively, the taxpayer pays for assessment. There are very few cases where project proponents have paid for two consultants, one to act on their own behalf and one to act on behalf of the communities concerned.

It is arguable, however, that a corporation, no matter how large, should not enjoy advantages which would not be available to an individual citizen. Increasingly, individual citizens are bing charged for any service provided by public agencies, although those agencies are supported by the taxpayer. If such a "user pays" philosophy is adopted, then clearly project proponents should pay the costs of consultants working on behalf of the government. The logical extension of this policy would be to require proponents to fund two teams of consultants: one to produce an EIS on their behalf, and another to review it on behalf of the government. Funds for the latter would be paid to the government regulatory body concerned, which would have the responsibility of selecting the consultants. Such a strategy would work even if the proponent were a public agency, such as an electricity commission.

This approach would have the advantage of shifting the responsibility for the technical assessment from a government regulatory body to a group of consultants. It would increase the proponents' costs in gaining development approval, and these increases would be passed indirectly to consumers. It would reduce government costs, however, and increase community confidence in our environmental planning systems. It would probably take longer for planning approvals to be granted, but would greatly reduce the likelihood of contentious public debate subsequently. Such debate has been of great concern to the banking and finance industry of late (Davey 1990) and a system which ensures that debate was completed before approvals were given would probably be welcomed by lenders. Without making any judgement, I predict that strategies of this type will increasingly be adopted over the next few years.

There have also been suggestions recently that EIS's should be replaced by EEIS's (economic and environmental impact statements). This also raises some interesting issues. It has always been argued by the private sector that the economic aspects of development are the commercial responsibility of the proponent, and that the purpose of an EIS is simply to demonstrate to the community that the environmental impacts of the proposed development are within acceptable bounds. In practice, of course, there is community concern over economic as well as environmental aspects; especially for large developments. The public wants to be able to make a balanced judgement between economic advantages and environmental disadvantages in the same way as their elected governments are supposed to do on their behalf.

There is therefore considerable merit in requiring the economic aspects of new proposals to be open to public scrutiny, particularly where there is any degree of public sector involvement, or where the development is based on the use of public resources such as forests or minerals. EIA legislation does, of course, already provide for proponents to present economic information in EIS's, since it requires the proponent to show what the benefits of the project would be as well as its environmental impacts. The degree to which this is done in practice depends on the requirements of planning authorities and on the predilections of the proponent concerned. In the past, it is certainly true that economic information provided in EISs has been extremely sketchy. Currently, however, it is interesting to note that government agencies in many countries are placing increasingly greater emphasis on economic analysis of new projects; especially environmental benefit-cost analyses and environmental input-output analyses. In fact, this has created a new demand for consultant expertise in environmental economics.

In conclusion, it seems to me that there is nothing fundamentally wrong with the way we do EIA in theory; but there are two problems with the way we do it in practice. Economic information in EIS's is inadequate and needs to be improved considerably, especially for projects which involve the exploitation of public natural resources. Analyses by competent resource accountants or environmental economists, either as part of or in conjunction with EIS's, need to become a standard tool in development planning and regulation.

The second problem is that much less time and effort and expertise goes into the assessment of an EIS than goes into its preparation. There are at least four different ways this problem could be overcome, not necessarily exclusive. In increasing order of cost and complexity these are: (1) more environmental staff in government planning agencies; (2) external consultants to review EIS's on behalf of planning agencies; (3) EIS consultants commissioned by planning agencies rather than the proponent; or (4) two teams of consultants for each EIS, one to prepare it and the other to assess it.

Ecologists and Private Enterprise

The Industry-Government-Public Triangle

Almost everyone in the "developed" world relies on industry. Industry makes an enormous, sometimes forgotten contribution to our everyday material well-being. However, it would be perfectly feasible for industry to provide us with the same manufactured products at a greatly reduced environmental cost. The same basic raw materials would be required, albeit perhaps in slightly different proportions; the labour inputs would probably be significantly greater.

Private corporations, however, are structured to provide profit to their shareholders; and the level of their investment in environmental protection is determined by that structure. To match competitors, they must always seek to cut costs. They undertake environmental protection measures in response to external commercial constraints, principally government regulation. They will invest in such measures until the costs outweigh the perceived benefits to the corporation: in money, time, or risk avoided.

It is the role of government to provide commercial constraints, in the form of environmental legislation, so that the commercial benefits of investment in environmental protection by private corporations outweigh the commercial costs to those corporations. Since increased environmental regulation effectively increases the labour input required to obtain a given manufactured output – in the sense, at the individual level, that one must work longer to afford to buy the same item – the intensity of environmental regulation imposed by governments reflects their perceptions of the trade-off preferred by their electorate between this increased labour/goods ratio, on the one hand, and a reduced rate of environmental deterioration, on the other. However, the linkages between the preferences of the electorate and the actions of the government are very poor. Governments show considerable inertia in responding to changes in community preferences. Indeed, a cynical observer might suggest that the only times when governments move rapidly is when they are moving to protect the vested interests of powerful individuals, against the interests of the community at large! The net effect is that changes in environmental legislation come about only as the result of sustained and intense pressure from the public.

Ecologists in Management

Why should ecologists work in environmental management? The simple answer is that ecologists ought to be better qualified than anyone else to make decisions about the environment. The current rate of global environmental deterioration is very rapid and still increasing. This means that ecologists must necessarily be conservationists; or they will soon have nothing left to study. Conservation is urgent; so environmental managers must use existing political and socio-economic systems, because there is simply no time to improve them. Practical conservation and environmental protection involve economics, politics and business management as well as the environmental sciences. The aim of environmental management is to use existing systems to improve environmental protection or at least reduce continuing environmental degradation. Decisions relating to environmental management cannot be delayed. There is no time for ecologists to provide training in ecology for others, who will then make the actual decisions: ecologists must be involved in those decisions themselves.

Our existing political and socio-economic systems, which environmental managers must work within, include private corporations and industry. The quality of environmental management by these corporations has a major and significant effect on the rate of global environmental deterioration. Environmental management programmes are far more effective if they are integrated into overall corporate management strategies, rather than being imposed from without. Such integrated environmental management is only possible if competent ecologists are prepared to work in industry, either in individual corporations or through industry associations (see Appendix). If ecologists want industry to do a good job of environmental management, they must be prepared to help. If ecologists refuse to work for private enterprise, how can private enterprise undertake good environmental management?

Ecologists are needed both in operating corporations and in consultancies. Different corporations have widely differing structures for environmental management. Rarely are ecologists employed directly in line management positions. Large corporations, with operations at a number of distinct sites, often employ environmental scientists in their corporate headquarters; either as part of a risk management unit, a government liaison unit, or an environment unit as such. Both these large corporations, and smaller companies operating at only a single site, also employ environmental scientists on site, usually reporting to the site operations manager. Depending on the type and scale of activities involved, operating corporations may employ either a single generalist environmental officer, or specialist staff involved in rehabilitation, chemical and biological monitoring, and so on. In environmental consulting, there are three main employment niches for environmental scientists. The first is in managing the preparation of EIS's and equivalent documents, as an executive in one of the larger environmental or environmental/engineering consultant companies. The second is as a specialist in a particular field of environmental sciences, either in a small specialist company which subcontracts to one of the larger companies, or as a staff member in one of those companies. The third is in environmental troubleshooting, which requires a very broad range of skills in addition to ecology per se. There seems to be few, if any, environmental troubleshooting companies as such; individuals involved in environmental troubleshooting usually work either as freelance consultants or as part of some larger organisation.

Private Sector Pressures

Environmental management needs cash: so environmental scientists in private corporations must constantly remind corporate management that funds committed to environmental protection are insurance premiums, which protect the corporation against the risk of externally imposed closure or curtailment of income generating activities. They must also remind the executive of legal links between authority and responsibility in corporate management structures: are environmental personnel to be in line management or advisory capacity? To maintain their own professional expertise, they must remind the executive that it is cheaper to keep competent staff trained than to keep replacing them with new personnel.

Even if the corporation accepts all of the above, however, there will always be the potential for a conflict between the interest of the company and the professional responsibilities of its environmental scientists. In such cases it is vital that professional responsibility comes first: just as it should, and generally does, in other professions such as medicine, law or engineering. Our society – private enterprise included – expects and accepts that professionals in these disciplines will adhere to their professional codes of conduct, and ignore pressures from vested commercial or private interests. Professional environmental scientists should expect and merit the same treatment.

All of these pressures are slightly less acute for ecologists working in environmental consulting companies than for those working in operating development corporations; but the professional responsibilities are no different. Consultants, ecologists included, are hired guns; but hired guns are expected to shoot straight.

Ecologists working in private enterprise are often accused of compromise. But effective environmental management almost always involves compromise. The aim of the private sector ecologist should be to modify corporate project management so as to reduce environmental damage. In solving environmental problems, economic and political issues are as important as technical ones: solutions do not work unless they are adopted. The means must be constrained to exclude immoral, unethical and (usually!) illegal practices, but within these constraints – and recognising that politics and economics are considered to be legal and moral practices in current social structures – then the success of private sector ecologists should be judged on results rather than methods. Indeed, if all available means to solve a particular environmental management problem are not explored, that in itself represents a compromise of professional responsibility as an environmental scientist. This is not to condone those who abrogate professional responsibility to become corporate apologists. Nor is it to criticise the environmental activists: it is they who attract media attention, which raises public awareness, which produces political pressure, which leads to environmental legislation, which creates commercial constraints on operating corporations, which leads them to employ professional environmental scientists to carry out active environmental management. But unlike academic ecologists, who are judged on their ability to identify critical problems and the methods they use to investigate them, ecologists in private enterprise are judged by their ability to find practical and immediate solutions to real problems created by others.

Environmental management is a continuing process, in private enterprise as elsewhere. One of the major tasks faced by ecologists in private enterprise, however, is the prediction of environmental impacts associated with major development projects in various sectors of primary and secondary industry. Corporate environmental monitoring programmes provide the data to test these predictions. Such systematic environmental audit provides a measure of our performance in understanding natural ecosystems and their response to anthropogenic disturbances. Of course, this is not the measure of performance that a private sector employer would use; nor is there an equivalent measure of performance for ecologists in government or tertiary education! The recently completed national environmental audit for Australia (Buckley 1989b; see Chap. 6) has shown that the accuracy of past environmental impact predictions has varied enormously, through several orders of magnitude. Contrary to expectation, there appear to be no consistent patterns in the level of precision achieved for predictions relating to different environmental parameters and different types of development.

Acknowledgements. Previous versions of the first two of these three essays were published in *Search* and *EIA Newsletter* respectively, both in 1990. A previous version of the third essay was first presented to the Australian Institute of Biology in 1989 and published by AIB in an edited conference volume entitled *Ecology 2000.* The generic environmental policy for industry institutes and associations was first prepared for the Australian Institute of Mining and Metallurgy, and published in its generic form in *Australian Biologist* and the *Bulletin of the Ecological Society of Australia.*

References

Buckley RC (1989a). Precision in environmental impact prediction: first national environmental audit, Australia. CRES, ANU, Canberra

Buckley RC (1989b) What's wrong with EIA? Search 20:146–147

Buckley RC (1990) Environmental science and environmental management. Search 21:14–16

Coombs HC (1990) The return of scarcity. Cambridge University Press, Melbourne, 171 pp

Davey C (1990) Financing in the new environment. In: Building bridges (seminar proceedings, 21.5.90). Business Review Weekly, Australian Consolidated Press, Sydney

Fairweather PG (1989) Where is the science in EIA? Search 20:141–144

McIntosh JL (1989) Successes of EIA should not be forgotten. Search 20.

Odgers B (1989) Commonwealth recognises need for better science. Search 20:145

Ruckelshaus WD (1983) Science, risk and public policy. Science 221:1026–1028

Salmon S (1990) Australian Conservation Foundation priorities. In: Building bridges (seminar proceedings, 21.5.90). Business Review Weekly, Australian Consolidated Press, Sydney

Sanders N (1989) Speech to Royal Australian Institute of Public Administration, 6.2.90, Canberra.

Schindler DW (1976) The impact statement boondoggle. Science 192:509

Appendix: A Generic Environmental Policy for Industry Institutes and Associations

The Institute/Association:

1. Recognises the need to extract and use such resources wisely and carefully, to minimise associated environmental degradation, and to balance the costs and benefits of such use in a socially equitable manner.
2. Endorses the concept of sustainable development at all spatial scales.
3. Recognises and supports international and community concern about global environmental issues.
4. Endorses the rational consideration of environmental planning and management issues in domestic and foreign policy at a national level in Australia, and in legislative and administrative frameworks at the federal, state and local government level.
5. Endorses the use of regional environmental planning techniques, including total catchment management, multiple-use strategies, environmental benefit-cost analysis and resource accounting techniques, to evaluate the capability and suitability of land and water resources for different alternative purposes.
6. Rncourages industry associations, the Institute included, to sponsor research in fields relevant to environmental planning and management, and to promote responsible environmental planning and management in industry.
7. Encourages research into, and adoption of, products and processes which can reduce pollution.
8. Encourages individual corporations to formulate and adopt environmental management policies; set up and undertake regular audits of their environmental management programmes; make public such information as is required to demonstrate competence in environmental management; employ professional and technical staff with appropriate skills in the environmental sciences; and train personnel in appropriate environmental management techniques.
9. Encourages individual members to be aware of environmental issues, to conduct their professional work in an environmentally responsible manner, and to educate others in these areas as appropriate

Chapter 11

Environmental Research by the Private Sector

Abstract

This review summarises environmental research by the private sector in the developed western nations, with particular reference to: organisation, institutional structures and funding; users and applications; training; relevance to national policy, effectiveness of information; and deficiencies and strategies to overcome them.

The principal conclusions are as follows. Most private-sector environmental research is in four main categories:

1. Design of new processes and equipment with reduced emissions or energy consumption; carried out by equipment manufacturers or engineering arms of major corporations; and not generally available to the public.
2. Research required for preparation of documents to comply with planning, development approval and EIA legislation; chiefly carried out by environmental consulting firms; available at least in summary form to government and public, in EIA documents; but relatively difficult to locate and examine once the development has received approval.
3. Environmental monitoring to comply with pollution control standards, and commitments made in EIA documents or imposed as conditions of development consents; chiefly carried out by operation corporations or their consultants; generally available to government regulatory agencies but not to the public.
4. Research on rehabilitation and revegetation; carried out by operating corporations and rehabilitation consultants; sometimes available through publication in conference proceedings and journal articles, but not on a routine basis.

This research is driven principally by requirements to meet environmental legislation of various types.

Reasons for Research: Environmental Law

The activities of individuals and corporations are constrained by a range of laws and regulations relating to environmental protection. To comply with such environmental legislation, private sector organisations must develop capabilities in environmental management, either in-house, or through external consultants. It is to meet the information needs of their environmental management programmes that private corporations carry out environmental research. The type and level of detail of such research reflect differences in environmental legislation between countries and jurisdiction, and changes over time, as well as characteristics of the corporations and their operations. It is therefore useful to review existing environmental legislation in the developed western nations.

Environmental legislation can usefully be considered in three main categories, concerned respectively with land and water resources planning, pollution control, and environmental impact assessment (EIA). Each of these can involve both local and national governments; but for major resource developments, national or state governments generally have the primary responsibility. Local governments generally have the main responsibility for smaller-scale planning.

Planning law encompasses an enormous and diverse body of legislation, but three aspects are particularly relevant here: development approval, resource use, and land use and management.

Any form of private sector activity involving building, engineering construction or localised resource exploitation generally requires specific development approval, including appropriate zoning. Depending on the location, scale and type of development, such approvals may be granted by local government agencies or may be referred to state planning agencies. The amount of environmental information needed to support a development application varies enormously: from little or none, to full EIS's or more. There are significant discrepancies between the requirements for different industry sectors, *de facto* if not *de jure*. Tourist developments, for example, even if quite large, are generally handled by local government, whilst mineral developments are more likely to be referred to national or state agencies.

In addition to development consents, some countries and states have legislation requiring approval for the use of particular resources. Water is the prime example, but there are also ordinances in relation to harvesting particular plant and animal species, for example.

Particular forms of land use are also controlled by law in some areas. Examples include regulations controlling vegetation clearance, use of fire, stocking rates, weed control, and use of pesticides.

EIA legislation in most countries is embedded in or coupled with planning legislation, and under the administration of the same agency. The precise requirements, and the formal titles of the documents involved, differ between jurisdictions; and the corresponding requirements for environmental research differ accordingly.

Pollution control legislation is largely the responsibility of national or state government agencies. Local governments, however, are generally responsible for managing municipal and domestic refuse, odours from particular industries such as abattoirs and tanneries, discharge of wastes from moored boats, and so on.

Organisations Performing Research

Overview

Large resource development corporations and other operating corporations need environmental information for environmental management. They obtain this information from a range of sources:

- published scientific literature
- unpublished reports and data from government agencies, higher education institutions, and other companies
- research by industry associations
- direct research by corporation personnel
- contract research by consultants

In addition, resource development corporations buy pollution control and monitoring equipment of various types, and the manufacturers of such equipment must carry out research during its design and development. Finally, resource extraction and process technologies differ greatly in their environmental impacts. Environmental factors may be involved in designing processes and equipment. This may also be classed as environmental research.

Environmental research by the private sector is thus performed by:

- resource development corporations
- industry associations

- equipment manufacturers
- consultants
- private sector research and training institutions

Operating Corporations and Industry Associations

In general, only the largest resource development corporations – both private and public sector – have their own environmental research staff. Most companies either rely entirely on consultants, or employ a small number of staff for day-to-day environmental management, and use consultants for specific research assignments. Where operating corporations do carry out their own research in-house, it is generally specific to the corporation's own projects and processes, though it may incidentally have wider application.

Some examples of such in-house environmental research include:

1. Environmental monitoring programmes covering, e.g.
   - air and water quality;
   - fauna and flora;
   - noise.
2. Reclamation and revegetation research by a number of mining (and to a lesser extent forestry) corporations, including:
   - germination requirements of native species;
   - trials of seeding, planting and establishment techniques, including:
     - soil preparation (e.g. topsoil replacement):
     - fertilisation and watering regimes.
3. Development of atmospheric and oceanographic dispersion models for particular applications.
4. Development of recycling and recovery processes; note, However, that these are currently driven principally by economic incentives rather than environmental legislation:
   - sulphur recovery in coal gasification;
   - re-refining of waste oil;
   - reprocessing mineral tailings.
5. Development of more energy-efficient technologies in various industry sectors (again, driven by energy costs).

Most major industry sectors have industry associations of various types, some of which carry out or sponsor environmental research.

Equipment Manufacturers

Equipment manufacturers who carry out environmental research fall into four main categories, namely those manufacturing:

1. Major process technologies, where environmental legislation provides a significant commercial constraint on operating corporations using the processes concerned.
2. Recycling and recovery equipment.
3. Emission control equipment, e.g.
   - electrostatic precipitators;
   - flue gas desulphurisation units;
   - catalytic crackers;
   - wet scrubbers;
   - flocculation and neutralisation equipment;
   - waste encapsulation.
4. Pollution monitoring equipment.

Consultants and Private Sector Research Institutions

Most environmental research by the private sector, especially project-specific field research, is carried out by environmental consultants. These may be considered in four main categories:

1. Large EIA and environmental planning firms.
2. Small firms or individuals specialising in particular disciplines.
3. Environmental economists, resource accountants and lawyers.
4. High-level consultants (individuals or small groups) involved in troubleshooting, audit and evaluation.

The larger EIA consultancies have staff sizes of up to thousands and are often part of, associated with or derived from consultant engineering firms. There is a relatively high "differentiation of expertise" within their staff. Generally speaking, a small number of senior executives act as salesmen, who obtain EIA contracts from client companies, and then divide the technical work between other staff who specialise in particular disciplines or environmental components. These specialist staff will thus carry out similar kinds of work repeatedly, for different EIA projects. Typical specialisations include:

- baseline geology, sedimentology, soils, hydrology
- meteorology and atmospheric dispersion modelling

- riverine, lacustrine and marine dispersion modelling
- groundwater hydrology and contaminant transport
- water quality: baseline and monitoring
- air quality: baseline and monitoring
- waste management
- baseline flora and fauna survey: terrestrial and marine
- cultural impact assessment, archaeology and anthropology
- civil engineering and infrastructure development
- urban and regional planning

Specialist consultancies cover these same fields, but act on contract to the EIA consultancies or directly to primary clients for specific assignments. A large proportion employ fewer than ten trained professional staff, though there are some (e.g. in hydrology) which employ over 100.

Environmental economists, resource accountants and lawyers are often based in academia or government agencies, but there are also many working in private practice in some countries.

In addition, there is a relatively small category of environmental consultants who have professional experience in a range of disciplines, problems and projects, and who have elected to remain as professional environmental scientists rather than become executives in environmental consulting firms. Consultants in this category tend to concentrate in four areas:

1. Troubleshooting.
2. Audit of corporate environmental management programmes.
3. Review and evaluation of other consultants' work.
4. Assignments where a range of environmental expertise is required but logistic considerations restrict the number of environmental staff employed, e.g. in engineering design teams and overseas aid projects.

There are relatively few private sector institutions which carry out research principally to maintain competence in teaching, rather than simply carrying out contract research assignments on a consultant basis. Some, for example, run executive short courses, which require secondary research in their preparation.

Types of Research

Scope

This section concentrates on research carried out by the private sector for its own use. This excludes research carried out by private sector consultants on behalf of government agencies, which is funded by the public sector and treated here as public sector research. The major types of environmental research carried out by industry are as follows:

1. Research required for EIA procedures:
   - baseline survey;
   - impact predictions.
2. Environmental monitoring programmes:
   - for compliance with legislation;
   - for testing EIA predictions;
   - for ongoing management and process control.
3. Reclamation, rehabilitation and revegetation research.

Research associated with EIA

Most industry-sponsored environmental research is associated in some way with EIA legislation and procedures. Typically, corporations planning major new development projects will go through a number of successively more detailed and formal steps, each requiring more detailed environmental information.

- Preliminary environmental assessment (PEA): informal assessment, confidential to the corporation.
- Notice of intent (NOI): first formal notification to government.
- Public environmental report (PER): used in some countries for smaller projects or as a forerunner to an EIS.
- Environmental impact statement (EIS) or equivalent.

All such EIA documents contain at least the first three of the following stages:

- description of existing environment: baseline surveys
- description of proposed development
- prediction of expected impacts

Table 1. Information sources for environmental baseline surveys

Environmental component	Typical information source and research requirements
Physical environment	
Climate	Published literature
Meteorology	At least 1-year on-site monitoring
Air quality	On-site monitoring if air quality already impaired by other developments
Geology and seismology	Previous data, published and unpublished
Geomorphology and sedimentology	Field research for few projects only
Hydrology: surface and underground	Field research often required
Water quality: surface and underground	Baseline monitoring if discharge anticipated
Soils	Field survey usually required: nutrient analysis sometimes
Biological environment	
Terrestrial vegetation and flora	Field survey almost always required
Terrestrial fauna	Field survey almost always required
Marine of aquatic flora and fauna	Field survey if discharge or disturbance to sea, lake or river expected
Human environment	
Land use and tenure	Compilation only
Archeology and material heritage	Field research needed in rural areas
Anthropology and cultural heritage	Field research sometimes needed
Population and demography	Existing data usually available
Infrastructure	Existing data usually available
Noise	Measurement needed for noisy developments

–   proposals for minimising and mitigating impacts
–   proposals for ongoing management and monitoring

Research is typically involved in baseline surveys and some impact predictions. Most commonly, PER's and EIS's are prepared by EIA consultants, who may subcontract specialist consultants if necessary. Some components of the baseline description are commonly derived from published literature; others require project-specific research as summarised in Table 1. Clearly, the particular components requiring field survey in any given project depend on the type, scale and location of the project, and in particular on expected emissions to air and water, groundwater seepages, and solid wastes.

Impact prediction in EIA generally involves comparison with other similar projects; relatively simple calculation (e.g. of dilution or noise attenuation); or straightforward application of existing models (e.g. dispersion models). Rarely is research involved. In some cases, however, predictive models are developed specifically for a particular project. These include atmospheric, oceanographic and groundwater dispersion models, population models for particular plant and animal species, and so on.

Environmental Monitoring Programmes

Environmental monitoring programmes are set up principally to test compliance:

- With standards set in pollution control legislation;
- With environmental protection commitments made by the proponent, or requirements imposed by regulatory agencies during the EIA and planning approval process.

The parameters most commonly monitored include:

- Concentrations of individual pollutants in emissions to air and water;
- ambient concentrations of individual pollutants in air and water on site, at the site boundary, and at predetermined monitoring points, typically up to 10 km from the emission source, but occasionally further (e.g. downstream of a major mining operation or offshore from a major marine discharge)
- noise levels at site boundary.

Parameters less commonly monitored include:

- abundance of particular plant and animal species;
- pollutant concentrations in biological tissues and soils;
- physical and chemical properties of groundwaters.

Measurement techniques range from sophisticated electronic probes to rather crude methods such as visual obscuration estimates for stack particulate emissions. Sampling designs likewise range from carefully designed spatial layouts with continuous or frequent and regular recording, to isolated spot measurements of almost no scientific value. Unfortunately, the latter are more common.

Reclamation, Rehabilitation and Revegetation Research

A common condition attached to development approvals, through the planning and EIA processes, is a requirement to rehabilitate all or part of the site. Such conditions rarely stipulate scientifically verifiable standards or performance criteria for such rehabilitation, but they do sometimes specify a particular end use or capability. Whilst some private sector corporations seem to use delaying tactics and obfuscation to avoid meeting their responsibilities for rehabilitation, others have set up their own research programmes, or contracted research to rehabilitation consultants or university departments, specifically to determine optimal revegetation strategies for particular sites. Much of this research is also relevant in other areas and contexts. Requirements for successful revegetation strategies generally require at least a minimum programme of research. The elements of such a programme are listed in detail by Buckley (1987).

Research Products and Availability

Not all of the environmental research conducted by the private sector reaches the public domain, and much that does is not easy to locate. Environmental impact statements and associated supporting documents are generally made available for public comment for a short period, typically 6 weeks or 2 months. During this period they are commonly sold from a small number of outlets and may be deposited in local libraries. When the period for public comment ends, EIS's – though still public documents – become hard to obtain in practice. Most private companies will continue to sell copies or make them available to the general public as long as stocks remain, but some corporations and agencies seem to deliberately withdraw them from sale and circulation. In such circumstances the only copies may be those held by the relevant State planning agency, and these are only available for inspection in that agency's offices and at its discretion. This is particularly true for supporting documents, which generally contain far more detailed data than the EIS itself.

It is worth noting that whilst EIS's are public documents, the same is not necessarily true for assessments of those EIS's by government planning and regulatory agencies. This is a significant deficiency in current EIA processes in many countries.

In contrast to EIA documents, which are public even though unpublished, data collected during environmental monitoring programmes – even those specified as part of the EIA and planning approval process – are generally not available to the public in many countries. They are submitted to the government agencies responsible, and those agencies are often extremely reluctant to release them. Indeed, some private companies have argued that government agencies are not legally entitled to release their monitoring data. This will differ between individual projects, depending on the jurisdiction and the precise wording of relevant legislation. In many cases, however, private sector environmental monitoring data do not become available to the public unless individual staff members working for the corporations concerned obtain permission for external publications in scientific journals or technical reports, which does not happen very often.

Users of Private Sector Environmental Research

EIA Documents

EIS's and associated supporting documents are used by the government and public during the EIS process. They may also contain original data which can be valuable in a wider sense to governments, the public, and the scientific community.

Baseline data are generally very site-specific, but in little studied rural or wilderness areas such localised information, even though a "spot snapshot", may still be the only data available and are hence useful additions to regional survey information collected by government agencies and research institutions. The main parameters for which original data are commonly collected include:

- flora and fauna: species inventories, occasionally population estimates
- meteorology: wind velocity roses, atmospheric stability classes
- air quality: parameters depending on type of development
- hydrology: stream gauging, water table
- water quality: usually pH, salt composition

Models developed for particular EIA's and detailed in EIA documents may also be applicable more generally, in which case they may be of value to government agencies and research institutions. Dispersion and population models are most common.

Impact predictions made in EIA documents are effectively hypotheses as to the response of given ecosystems to given anthropogenic disturbances. Environmental monitoring data provide the means to test these hypotheses. Testing the accuracy of such predictions provides a measure of our scientific understanding of ecosystem processes, and also provides information needed to refine predictive models. Such systematic comparison of predicted and actual impacts, known as audit, is hence of considerable scientific value (see Chaps. 6 and 7).

Monitoring Data

Environmental monitoring data currently have two users:

- The company concerned, to test compliance with standards and for use in ongoing environmental management.
- Government regulatory agencies, to test compliance.

If publicly available, corporate environmental monitoring data are also of great value to:

- the public, to check that developers are meeting environmental protection commitments and that government agencies are acting effectively and without negligence;
- environmental scientists,
  - to refine predictive models (audit, as above);
  - to examine patterns of variation through time of particular environmental parameters.

Rehabilitation and Revegetation Research

The results of revegetation research, though relatively site-specific, are often applicable in comparable operations elsewhere. Private sector revegetation and rehabilitation research may therefore be used by scientists in government agencies and research institutions and by personnel responsible for revegetation in other operating corporations, in both the public and private sectors.

Control of Private Sector Environmental Research

Funding is controlled directly by the companies concerned, and except in the largest companies with operations at many sites, is generally limited to research needed for immediate application in ongoing environmental management, as dictated by legislation, government requirements or commitments made in EIA documents.

It is rare for corporate environmental research staff to control their own budgets. More commonly, expenditure is controlled by executives in line management (e.g. site operations manager or corporate technical services manager), to whom environmental research staff must submit funding requests.

Very little substantiated information is available regarding actual expenditure by private corporations on environmental research. Some companies and industry associations have released estimates, but not the basis on which they are made or the records needed to substantiate them.

Training

Most training carried out by the private sector is on-the-job. "You don't get trained here, you get here trained". Experience gained by environmental staff in private corporations *is* valuable training, however – particularly where junior appointees are given the opportunity to work with experienced environmental managers. Many companies also send their environmental staff to conferences and short courses. These tend to be industry rather than professional conferences, and professional rather than scientific. Consultant firms send senior ("sales") staff to industry conferences, principally as a marketing tactic; and specialist staff to specialist conferences (planning, law, marine science, hydrology, etc.). A wide range of short courses in various aspects of environmental science and management have been offered in recent years: by tertiary education institutions, professional associations, and commercial organisations. Companies will send their staff to these if they perceive that the benefit to the company, in dollar value of increased staff expertise, will outweigh the cost of the course.

Use of Environmental Research by the Private Sector

This review is concerned principally with research performed by the private sector. It is worth noting, however, that the private sector also uses environmental research performed by scientists in government agencies and research institutions, and published in scientific journals, textbooks, conference proceedings and government reports. Environmental scientists in private corporations often do not have access to the same library facilities as those in academic institutions, though some consultant firms routinely use computerised literature searching and document retrieval systems in a way which academics can often no longer afford. Any consultant preparing EIA documents, for example, will naturally compile information already available before planning to collect original data – and in most cases, such existing data have been produced by public sector research. Despite this, however, there is a noticeable tendency for reports produced by the private sector to cite other private sector documents (e.g. previous EIS's) in preference to the scientific journal articles or books: there is much less research integration between the private sector and the public than there is within each.

Deficiencies

Regulatory Frameworks

Current regulatory frameworks for environmental planning and management in the developed western nations suffer from a number of limitations. These affect both the performance of environmental research by the private sector, and the ability of government to resolve competing needs for resource development and conservation. Deficiencies of current frameworks have been reviewed by Buckley (1989). Perhaps the main deficiency is lack of integration in many senses:

- Spatial: need for regional rather than project-centred planning so as to incorporate cumulative synergistic and cross-project impacts;
- Temporal: need for better audit and operational feedback mechanisms so that both the public and private sectors can learn from past experience.

-   Economic: need for improvement and wider application of environmental benefit-cost analysis and other environmental economic techniques.
-   Administrative: very severe need for co-ordination of government agencies responsible for different sectors, and at different levels; need for greater consistency between different government areas, to prevent them competing for business by lowering environmental standards.

At present, there are no incentives for environmental research by private corporations except:

-   in developing new equipment or processes with economic advantages;
-   to fulfil the requirements of EIA and planning legislation;
-   to comply with pollution control legislation at minimum cost;
-   to comply with environmental protection commitments at minimum cost (e.g. revegetation research).

Information Access and Retrieval

At present most nations do not have any single repository of EIS's, let alone other private sector environmental documents, in the entire country. Government environmental agencies generally hold most or all EIS's for their area of jurisdiction, but not necessarily all supporting documents. Even where they do hold such documents, they are often unavailable for consultation by the public except on the premises.

To overcome this problem it would be very useful to have central repositories of EIA and related documents with computerised indexing and searching capability and national access and delivery systems, so that any consultant or government assessment agency, for example, could readily search for analogues and past case histories for any specific environmental management problem.

References

Buckley RC (1987) Revegetation strategy, Nabarlek uranium mine, NT. Amdel Report 1656. Amdel, Canberra
Buckley RC (1989) What's wrong with EIA? Search 20:146–147

Chapter 12

Environmental Planning and Policy for Green Tourism

Abstract

With good environmental planning and management, natural-areas tourism can make a major contribution to conservation; but if poorly managed, the tourist industry will damage precisely those areas with the greatest conservation value. In particular, the only forms of tourist development which should be permitted inside conservation areas are those whose primary purpose is based on wilderness recreation or enjoyment of conservation values. Facilities for other forms of recreation should be constructed outside conservation areas. Sound policy and planning tools are required to achieve these aims. Whilst the tourist industry as a whole has an incentive to protect its environmental resource base, this does not necessarily apply to individual tourist developers and operators in the short term. There is an immediate analogy to the pastoral industry, where environmental degradation is now widespread.

Information needs include: environmental baseline data; environmental sensitivities to tourist-related impacts; indicators of environmental change as a result of tourist impacts; and audit of actual impacts. All these need to be related to the type, timing, intensity and location of tourist activities. Economic information is also required: both on the economics of the tourist industry, and on conservation values and option costs of environmental damage.

Standard environmental impact assessment, though a valuable tool, is not particularly well suited to environmental planning for the tourist industry. Tourist developments tend to occur in particular types of environment, and to be small in individual impact but large in number. Cumulative impacts are therefore of particular concern. Social impacts are also particularly important for many tourist developments. EIA therefore needs to be coupled with other environmental planning tools, notably environmental benefit-cost analysis, environmental sensitivity mapping, and regional environmental planning.

Environmental policy instruments and management tools for the tourist industry must cover three main aspects: zoning, intensity, and multiple use strategies. They fall into five main categories: regulation and surveillance; incentives and disincentives; physical protection and hardening; education; and information collection and dissemination. Environmental planning and policy for tourist industries needs to take a broad perspective covering international as well as domestic tourists, destinations, costs and competition. Attempts to produce national environmental guidelines for tourist development are commendable, but need to be integrated into more comprehensive national tourist strategies. Such strategies also need to consider controls on foreign investment in land and tourist development, to counter the increasing vertical integration in foreign-owned tourist operations. They need to include mechanisms for generating a financial return from public environmental capital used by private sector tourist operators. However, such mechanisms must be careful to avoid placing managers of conservation areas in a conflict of interests between short-term economic imperatives, and the primary goal of environmental protection for these areas. Strategies should specifically consider social equity aspects; and finally, they might consider the use of tax instruments to control tourist development by overseas interests.

In conclusion, there is an urgent global need to conserve the world's remaining natural areas; not least, because they contain resource capital in the form of irreplaceable genetic diversity. Economic returns on this genetic capital, however, would be long-term, so a mechanism to generate short-term cash flow from these natural areas is needed urgently. Tourism provides the only option currently available; and it can also increase public awareness of environmental issues. It is, however, crucial that it be well managed, or its environmental costs could greatly outweigh its environmental benefits. Careful use of environmental planning and policy tools is therefore particularly crucial in the tourist industry.

Scope and Context

The tourism industry can usefully be considered in two major components: natural-areas tourism and city-based tourism. Here, I am concerned only with the former, also known as green tourism. City-based tourism includes, e.g., visits to city landmarks, buildings, entertainment and cultural attractions, shopping, casinos, etc. Natural-areas tourism includes both resort-based and safari-type tourism, at all economic levels from luxury travel to backpacking, which occurs in and relies on relatively undisturbed features of the natural environment as the primary drawcard. Both natural-areas and city-based tourism have an international as well as a domestic component; and many package tours incorporate both types of tourist activity. Previous reviews of environmental management in the tourist industry include El-Hinnawi and Hashmi (1982), Holdgate et al. (1982) and Duffield and Walker (1984).

Tourism in most countries cannot be analysed accurately from a domestic perspective alone. It must be seen in a much wider context, covering at least the major originating countries for inbound tourists and the main competing destinations for these tourists. The number of tourists visiting any country also depends on the costs of international air travel, foreign exchange rates, and economic growth and income distribution in the countries from which these tourists originate. For example, the number of Japanese tourists visiting Australia has risen because of growth in the Japanese economy, the increasing relative value of the Japanese yen, and the decreasing real costs of international air travel between Japan and Australia, as well as the Japanese perception that Australia is a safe and interesting destination to visit.

Issues

Well-planned and managed, natural-areas tourism is potentially an industry with a high and indefinitely sustainable economic return. If poorly planned and run, however, economic returns will be very short-lived. Continuing economic returns from natural-areas tourism depend on maintaining the environmental quality of the natural areas concerned; i.e., minimising the environmental impacts and degradation associated with their use for recreation and tourist development. Adequate environmental and economic planning and management is hence particularly critical in this sector of the tourist industry. A poorly run industry will rapidly destroy its own resource base, namely the natural environments which tourists come to see and enjoy. Management is needed to prevent damage to the natural environment; to tourist experiences; and to the social environment for local residents.

It is thus in the interests of the natural-areas tourist industry in any country to maintain environmental quality of that country's natural areas. This does not, however, mean that individual tourist operators and developers have an incentive to preserve the natural areas on which they rely for their immediate income. Individual operators and development corporations can maximise their dollar return on capital investment by exploitative development which yields a high income for a short period of time, at the cost of environmental deterioration. When income starts to decrease as a result of environmental damage, the corporations concerned can either convert from natural areas to resort or city-based tourism; or they can simply sell out and invest their capital in a completely different industry. Tourist development corporations can hence exploit natural environments for their own short-term gain, passing their costs to the environment, the community as a whole and future tourist operators who will no longer have the same resource base.

There is a direct analogy to the pastoral industry in many countries. The industry as a whole relies on the maintenance of environmental quality in grazing lands; but individual pastoralists can maximise returns by overstocking and other management practices which produce long-term environmental deterioration. There is no reason to presume that the tourist industry will be any different from the pastoral or forestry industry in this regard. This divergence between optimal strategies for individual tourist operators and developers, the tourist industry as a whole, and the entire community, means that self-regulation is never likely to achieve adequate environmental planning and management in the tourist industry. Externally imposed environmental policy measures, whether regulatory, technical or economic, are needed to provide the incentives for individual tourist operators and development corporations to undertake good environmental planning and management.

Information Needs

Management is only as good as the information on which it is based; the same applies to the design of environmental policy instruments such as regulations and economic incentive schemes. For tourism in natural areas, information is needed in three main categories: on the natural environment, on tourists and the industry, and on economics.

The primary resource for natural-areas tourism is the natural environment; and it is therefore essential to know the state of that resource, and how it changes through time – both independent from recreation and tourism, and as a result of recreation and tourism. We need to know how different components and different types of natural environment are affected by different kinds and intensities of tourism. If possible, this information needs to be expressed in the form of sensitivities and thresholds of environmental change to different levels of tourist activity. Compiling this information requires baseline surveys, regular monitoring and state-of-the-environment reporting, and systematic audit of environmental impact statements associated with tourist developments. Also required are environmental indicators, e.g. easily monitored environmental parameters which can be used to quantify environmental change, at various scales in space and time. These might include parameters such as changes in population size and structure for a range of critical species; proportion of different community types disturbed in different ways (including buffer zones); changes in animal behaviour (territorality, breeding, movement, etc.); visual effects; and physical aspects (such as water quality). Indicators of social change are also needed.

A range of descriptive statistics is also needed to define the state of the tourist industry at any given time. These include past, present and future numbers of tourists in different categories at different destinations, with particular reference to: seasonal variations; their intentions, impressions, expectations, preferences and degrees of satisfaction; their reactions to changes in natural and social environments and visitor experiences; and their activities and behaviour patterns. Information on the corporate structure of the tourist industry, its infrastructure requirements, its investment patterns and its structure and control would also be valuable.

Economic information required for good planning and management includes conservation values of natural areas used for tourism and recreation, monetised as far as possible; option costs of damage to these areas; damage, repair and rehabilitation costs of environmental deterioration; capital and maintenance costs of development infrastructure; financial burdens on local councils and ratepayers; tourist expenditure patterns; values placed by tourists on natural areas used for recreation; estimates of consumer surplus and appropriate resource rents potentially available from these areas; and price elasticities of supply and demand of natural areas for use in recreation.

Environmental Planning Tools

Overview

At present, the same tools are used for environmental planning and management in natural-areas tourism as for any other form of development (Buckley et al. 1989). These fall into three main categories: land use and water resources planning; pollution control; and environmental impact assessment (Buckley 1988). In recent years, a range of new environmental planning techniques has been developed. These could be used much more widely to improve the effectiveness of existing planning tools; to improve integration between the three main areas listed above; and to provide additional information and insight for use in rational decision making.

Conservation Values

In planning an industry based on a careful balance between, and integration of, development and conservation, it is clearly vital to be able to assess and quantify conservation values as well as economic costs and benefits. There are many different types of conservation value and many ways of estimating them (cf. Buckley 1985, 1987). Some of these can be expressed in economic terms: these include non-damaging production, e.g. of water; non-damaging use, e.g. for some types of recreation; and option values, e.g. of gene pools. Other values are fundamentally non-economic, but are no less real for that, as shown by their expression through political processes. These include moral values of various types. If conservation values are to be incorporated into planning processes, they must be quantified in some way (Buckley 1987). This requires a precise definition of the type of value concerned, sources of data, and means of measurement. For values such as those associated with use as a water catchment, such quantification is conceptually straightforward, even though it has rarely been performed in practice. For values held by individuals and expressed only through political processes, quantification is extremely difficult, and requires analysis of political processes rather than economics or planning.

Environmental Sensitivity Mapping

Environmental sensitivity is a term given to the relationship between an external stress applied to a given environment or ecosystem, and the magnitude of the change it produces. It includes aspects such as the reversibility of that change; the cumulative impacts of repeated stresses; and interactions between different types of stress. Maps showing different types of environmental sensitivity can be particularly useful planning tools, especially in relatively pristine natural areas, and in planning for a number of small developments of similar type in a set of similar environments. Both of these criteria apply to natural-areas tourism development in Australia. Techniques and applications of environmental sensitivity mapping have been detailed by Buckley (1982; see also Chap. 2).

Environmental Benefit-Cost Analysis

Techniques for environmental benefit cost analysis (EBCA) have advanced considerably in recent years (e.g. Buckley 1987; Randall 1987; Nash and Bowers 1988; Tietenberg 1988; Common 1988; Folmer and van Ierland 1989). If information on conservation values is available, EBCA can be particularly useful in planning natural-areas tourist development. Potential applications include: comparing different possible land use strategies for different areas; deciding whether to approve particular development proposals; evaluating alternative regional development strategies; assessing possible approaches for resource rent appropriation; and assessing possible fees and charges for tourists or tour and resort operators.

Regional environmental planning

Attempts to integrate environmental considerations into planning at a regional scale – regional environmental planning (REP) – are relatively recent. Several so-called REP's have been produced in Australia to date, for example, but these are either relatively local in scale, or are principally development plans (Buckley 1987, 1988). A regional approach to EPM would be particularly valuable in relation to the tourist industry, since it is more effective than single-project environmental impact assessment (EIA) in considering and incorporating interactive and cumulative effects resulting from the simultaneous development of a large number of individual resorts or other tourist operations. A regional approach to environmental planning and management would also be particularly valuable in large and relatively undisturbed areas. Another prime candidate for a coherent regional approach in many countries is the coast. Coastal zones form rather unusual regions for planning purposes: coherent in terms of landform and use, but not in terms of spatial shape and extent. This presents some special planning problems, e.g. in relation to infrastructure development, which are best tackled from a regional perspective.

Environmental Impact Assessment

Environmental impact assessment in the orthodox sense suffers from a number of limitations (Buckley 1988, 1989a, b; see Chap. 9): it operates at the scale of the individual project; it ignores cumulative and interactive effects; it is often treated as a once-off planning hurdle; and its operational feedback mechanisms are generally weak. Despite these limitations, it is a well-established and valuable procedure and should continue to be used for all new resort and tourist developments. Its limitations can be reduced by using EIA in conjunction with other environmental planning techniques. Tourist developments possess a number of particular features which need to be considered in EIA. These include seasonality, extensive infrastructure requirements, and disproportionately high social impacts. In addition, different types of tourist development have different types of impact: the impacts of resorts are relatively localised, those from tours more diffuse. One useful approach, saving time and costs both for proponents and for planning and regulatory agencies, would be to compile generic EIA documents for similar resort developments and similar safari-type tourist operations. These could then be adopted to individual development applications quickly and cheaply. Such documents could include generic EIA guidelines, generic scoping checklists, and even generic EIS's.

Environmental Audit

If EIA is to be used as an effective management tool, environmental impacts must be monitored and checked back against impact predictions, and ongoing operational procedures modified if need be, if actual impacts do not match predictions. This should be – but often is not – a routine part of the environmental management of any development project. At a slightly broader scale, the systematic review of actual and predicted impacts across a range of projects, e.g. resorts or tour developments, has been called environmental impact audit (Buckley 1990; see Chap. 6). At present, there is no regular program of environmental impact audit for any industry in any country. Such a programme is particularly important for natural-areas tourism, where impacts on the environment have had a direct effect on the industry's resource base as well as on the community's conservation heritage.

Environmental Management Tools

Overview

Environmental policy for the tourist industry needs to cover three closely related issues. The first is zoning: which areas should be used for tourism, which for tourism and other uses contemporaneously, and which solely for conservation or other uses? The second is intensity of use: how many people, engaged in what activities, can be accommodated in a given area without environmental degradation? The third is multiple-use management: how can tourist operations be run so as to maximise net economic return without risking environmental degradation?

Potential government actions to improve environmental planning and management in natural-areas tourism fall into five major categories: (1) direct control by regulation and surveillance; (2) provision of incentives and disincentives, either economic or otherwise; (3) physical protection of specific areas, either by excluding people or by hardening the areas concerned against human impact; (4) education, at a range of scales; and (5) the acquisition, compilation and dissemination of information, by sponsoring research of various types. All three levels of government need to be involved if any of these approaches is to be successful.

Regulation and Surveillance

Governments have various avenues for regulation and surveillance of natural-areas tourism. These include: control over foreign equity; legislation, standards, guidelines and codes of practice; environmental impact assessment, monitoring and audit; financial instruments such as taxes and grants; coordination, facilitation and dispute resolution; and sponsored research.

For most tourist developments, planning, pollution control and environmental impact assessment are actually carried out at the local government level, even if ultimate responsibility is at a national level. In most countries there is a need for much greater coordination at the national level, as opposed to ad hoc and piecemeal development in individual local government areas. Current practices commonly do not allow adequately for assessment of cumulative impacts, which are of particular concern in the tourist industry. Local government processes also tend to escape public scrutiny and are hence particularly subject to abuse.

Regulations have little effect unless enforced; and this requires surveillance. To maintain environmental quality in natural areas used for tourism and recreation requires continued monitoring by ranger staff familiar with local areas. Shortage of funds for ranger salaries and logistic support is of major concern for natural areas worldwide.

At the scale of individual people, regulation can be used to control points and times of access to natural areas; and the number of people engaging in any particular activity in any particular area at any given time. It can also be used to prescribe penalties for breaches.

Incentives

One problem with current environmental planning and management in the tourist industry is that different areas and countries compete for investment by tourist development corporations, by offering incentive packages which may contain direct grants (e.g. in the form of subsidies or preferential interest rates on loans); relief from normal government charges; and exemptions from normal environmental legislation. All these are of concern, the last particularly so.

A second problem is that individual tourist developers, in their attempts to maximise visitor numbers, tend to incorporate drawcards of various types in their developments, as an incentive to visitors; and some of these are inappropriate in natural areas. A prime example is the construction of so-called wilderness resorts which incorporate facilities for non-wilderness sporting recreation, such as tennis courts, golf courses and the like. Tennis, golf and similar sports are certainly legitimate forms of recreation, but not in wilderness areas.

Governments have the option to provide economic incentives for good environmental management by individual tourist operators and developers in the form of performance bonds of various types. These have been canvassed by the tourist industry in some countries (e.g. Feros/ATIA 1989; IAC 1989, p. 103) but are certainly not standard at present.

Physical Protection

Direct physical protection of particular features of natural environments is rarely an option, especially in extensive natural areas. It has the disadvantage that it generally introduces a visual impact; and it also tends to accelerate recreational succession, where visits by those in search of wilderness experience are replaced by those in search of mass social recreation. Common examples of attempts to harden the environment by direct physical protection include made tracks and duckwalks on heavily used paths; boardwalks and viewing platforms at heavily used lookout sites; ropes and chains around fragile sites; and the provision of firewood at heavily used campsites and barbeque sites, to minimise the collection of firewood from surrounding vegetation (e.g. Buckley and Pannell 1990; see Chap. 13).

Education

All of the techniques outlined above are likely to be far more effective if coupled with environmental education. There are many different options for such education, ranging widely in the immediacy of the impact. The most immediate is on-site education in the form of leaflets, posters, displays, video presentations, and signs. There are indications (Gale and Jacobs 1987; Buckley and Pannell 1990) that tourists in natural areas appreciate such information, learn from it, and take greater care to reduce their environmental impacts where it is available. One option for environmental education with an impact lag time of only days or weeks would be to show environmental training videos on inflight programmes of inbound aircraft, targeting foreign tourists while they are a captive audience. Other avenues for environmental education include TV, radio, and printed media; the design and adoption of environmental policies by individual tourist corporations and the tourist industry as a whole; displays at local community centres; and the introduction of environmental education in school and university curricula.

Policy Considerations

National Policies

There is currently a need for coherent and detailed national policies on development and environmental management in the tourist industries. This will require close liaison between government, industry, and the conservation movement. Such policies should identify preferred geographic areas for tourist development of different types, considering potential land-use conflicts with other industry sections; and provide means to integrate overall tourism policy with other sectoral policies, National Conservation Strategies, and so on. They need to consider taxation aspects, as outlined earlier, and other possible economic policy instruments. They need to define the rights of indigenous and aboriginal peoples in relation to tourist development on traditional lands, and the rights of local communities affected by major tourist developments in rural areas. They need to consider arrangements for coordination between the various government agencies concerned; and they finally need to incorporate provisions for regular monitoring, review and revision.

Categories of Foreign Investment

One particular aspect which needs to be considered in any national tourist policy is the role of foreign investment in tourist development. There are two major avenues by which tourism brings overseas funds into any country, and these must be distinguished clearly. The first is simply expenditure on domestic goods and services by overseas visitors; the second is foreign investment as such, namely the inflow of overseas capital to purchase partial or complete equity in tourist resorts and other developments, such as tour companies.

Returns on Public Environmental Capital

The basis of international tourism to any country's natural environments is the use of that nation's environmental capital, a public asset, to generate revenue for the private sector tourist industry. Governments need to act to ensure that in the process, national "environmental capital" is not reduced by the destruction, degradation or alienation of natural environments. Besides requiring good environmental planning and management both at regional and individual project scales, this also requires that environmental costs should be included in economic analyses of proposed tourist developments, in as rigorous and conservative a way as possible.

The most logical institutional structure for use of a common asset to produce private income is of course some form of resource rent, rather than relying on income, payroll and company taxes to capture some public return. Resource-rent taxes are particularly valuable in the case of foreign investment, where domestic tax structures are often ineffective. They can be coupled with rebates from company tax to provide an advantage for domesticallyowned companies and to avoid discrimination against particular industry sectors. It is important to appreciate that irrespective of any resource rent considerations, some form of public return from private sector use of environmental resources is necessary simply to cover the costs of inevitable degradation of these resources associated with such use, no matter how competent the environmental management. It is also important to ensure that funds captured from tourist development in heritage, coastal and other natural environments are used specifically or principally to prevent environmental damage in those areas, rather than simply returned to consolidated government revenue.

Social Equity

Besides overall benefit-cost balances, it is important to consider who receives the benefits and who pays the costs: questions of social equity. The following points are relevant. Environmental resources are owned by the nation; and they are largely in public ownership. Resort development capital may be domestic public, domestic private, overseas private, or some mixture of these. Capital expenditure in construction may go either to domestic or overseas concerns unless legislation requires use of domestic goods, services and contractors; and the same applies to operating expenditure on goods, services and salaries. Operating profits will accrue to shareholders of companies which own resorts, which may be overseas; and expenditure on travel and transport may also end up either in-country or overseas, if domestic sectors are purchased through overseas carriers at discount rates. The costs of environmental degradation and social disruption, however, are borne solely by the country where they are located. For that country to benefit from the use of its common-owned environmental resources by private companies, either domestic or overseas-owned, it therefore needs some or all of the following: legal requirements to use domestic labour, goods and services in construction and operation; or a tax on foreign products and services used in substitution; or a requirement for high domestic equity; some form of environmental performance bond to guard against degradation of environmental resource capital; and/or some form of direct or indirect tax or rent on the use of common-owned environmental resource capital to produce income for private corporations.

Taxation Incentives

Most national governments have substantial powers, often little exercised, through their control of domestic taxation. They can, for example, set differential tax rates for domestic and foreign-owned corporations; they can institute resource rent taxes for the use of domestic natural resources by overseas investors; or they can institute new taxes such as bed taxes for tourist accommodation facilities. Each of these would produce changes in current markets for tourists and tourism corporations, and these effects would need careful examination before deciding whether any such taxes should be introduced.

Conclusion

Tourism is a two-edged sword as far as the environment is concerned. Poorly managed tourist development can irreversibly degrade precisely those natural areas which are of the greatest conservation value; as has indeed happened in many parts of the world. Well-run tourism, on the other hand, potentially provides the lowest impact option for generating an immediate financial return from these areas; and without such an immediate economic incentive to conserve them, these areas will continue to be affected by other land uses less compatible with conservation. I conclude that we should welcome the growing worldwide enthusiasm for natural-areas tourism, but that the use of such public environmental capital should be permitted only under careful control and open public scrutiny. We should make full use of the best available environmental planning and policy instruments, at all scales from local to national, to create a framework which encourages responsible environmental management by the industry. With such a framework in place, it will be in the interests of the industry's most reputable operators, and those with the longest investment time horizon, to monitor and control the potentially less responsible activities of speculative developers and their ephemeral corporations. Let us hope that environmental policy and law are developed in such a way as to maximise the beneficial effects of natural-areas tourism and minimise its environmental costs.

Acknowledgements. This essay arose from a submission to a Senate Inquiry into tourism. It was written at the Centre for Resource and Environmental Studies, Australian National University. Other parts of the submission were written by Dr. John Dargaval and Dr. Helen Ross, also of CRES. A previous version was first delivered to a conference run by the National Environmental Law Association in Adelaide in November 1989.

Example: Coastal Environments

The considerations outlined above apply to all forms of tourist development in relatively undisturbed natural environments. They are, however, particularly critical in those areas with highest conservation values; highest fragility or sensitivity to environmental impact; and highest development pressure. National heritage areas generally have high conservation values, and many are highly sensitive to environmental impacts. Some are currently under development pressure, others less so. Coastal regions worldwide are also coming under increasing pressure for tourist development; not only in the more populated areas but also in much more remote areas. Coastal environments differ greatly in their conservation values and their sensitivity to different types of environmental impact, both of which are strongly dependent on the degree of development in the past (cf. e.g. Beekhuis 1981; Lal 1984). Environmental management is particularly critical in the more remote and pristine regions.

   Coastal environments have a number of special features which must be considered in planning, whether for environmental management, tourist development or both. On areas with sandy beaches and coastal foredunes, these include physical hazards such as floods, storm waves, and king tides; biological problems such as noxious weeds and fragile dune vegetation; and particular management issues such as dune stability, trampling and off-road vehicles (ORV's), land tenure and public access; and buffer zones against coastal erosion and cutback. Coastal wetlands, which include mangroves, saltmarshes, estuaries, and brackish-water coastal swamps, are important for fisheries and conservation as well as recreation. Many national governments also have specific obligations regarding wetlands, in relation to international conventions on migratory wildfowl and endangered species. On rocky shorelines, the principal issues are increasing residential development pressures, as the number of remaining residential sites on coastal headlands diminishes; and the conservation of rocky-shore plant communities, many of which contain plant species which occur only in this type of habitat, and sometimes only in very limited geographic areas. Tropical reefs are subject to a range of impacts, including physical and biological stresses such as cyclone damage and crown-of-thorns starfish, as well as those associated with fisheries and tourism. The last may include trampling damage to corals, shell collecting, spearfishing, and pollution from boats and resorts. Marine parks and island resorts have a range of specific management problems, not least being the interdigitation of terrestrial and marine zones of jurisdiction.

References

Beekhuis JV (1981) Tourism in the Caribbean: impacts on the economic, social and natural environments. Ambio 10:325-331

Buckley RC (1982) Environmental sensitivity mapping: what, why and how. Miner Environ 4:151-155

Buckley RC (1985) Determining conservation priorities. Environ Geochem Health 7:116-119

Buckley RC (1987) Environmental planning techniques. SADME, Adelaide

Buckley RC (1988) Critical problems in environmental planning and management. Environ Plan Law J 5:206-225

Buckley RC (1989a) What's wrong with EIA? Search 20:146-147

Buckley RC (1989b) Precision in environmental impact prediction: first national environmental audit, Australia. CRES/ANU, Canberra

Buckley RC (1990) Environmental audit: review and guidelines. Environ Plan Law J 7:142-146

Buckley RC, Pannell J (1990) Environmental impacts of tourism and recreation in national parks and conservation reserves. J Tour Stud 1:24-32

Buckley RC, Ross H, Dargavel J (1989) Environmental planning and management, social impacts and interstate coordination in the Australian tourist industry. Report to Senate Standing Committee on Environment, Recreation and The Arts, Canberra

Common M (1988) Environmental and resource economics: an introduction. Longmans, London

Duffield BS, Walker SE (1984) The assessment of tourism impacts. Perspectives on environmental impact assessment. In: Bisset R, Tomlinson P (eds) WHO/Reidel, Dordrecht, pp 479-515

El-Hinnawi E, Hashmi M (1982) Tourism and the environment. UNEP Nat Resour Environ Ser 7:221-232

Feros V, for the Australian Tourism Industry Association (ATIA) (1988) Statement. In: Industries Assistance Commission, Proc Sem Environmental Impacts of Travel and Tourism, B, 68. IAC, Canberra

Folmer H, van Ierland E (eds) (1989) Valuation methods and policy making in environmental economics. Stud Environ Sci 36 Elsevier, Amsterdam

Gale F, Jacobs J (1987) Tourists and the national estate. Australian Heritage Commission, Spec Aust Heritage Pub Ser 6. AGPS, Canberra

Holdgate M, Kassas M, White G (1982) Tourism. UNEP Nat Resour Environ Ser 8:544-560

Industries Assistance Commission (IAC) 1989 Draft report on travel and tourism. IAC, Canberra

Lal PM (1984) Environmental implications of coastal development in Fiji. Ambio 13:316-321

Nash C, Bowers J (1988) Alternative approaches to the valuation of environmental resources. In: Turner RK (ed) Sustainable environmental management, principles and practice. Westview, Boulder, Colerado, pp 118-144

Randall A (1987) Resource economics (2nd edn) Wiley, New York

Tietenberg T (1988) Environmental and natural resource economics (2nd edn) Scott Foresman, Boston

Chapter 13
Environmental Impacts of Recreation
in Parks and Reserves

Abstract

National parks and conservation reserves are subject to increasing levels of recreation and tourist pressure. These produce environmental impacts associated with travel, accommodation and recreational activities. Typical impacts in parks and reserves include soil erosion and compaction, damage to vegetation, disturbance to wildlife, water pollution, increased fire frequency, vandalism and noise. To minimise the environmental degradation associated with tourism and recreation may require: appropriate land-use zoning; regulation and surveillance of access and activities; direct physical protection of particular areas; and education both on-site and elsewhere. In addition, it is important to provide incentives to encourage low-impact types of recreation, such as contemplative, naturalist and wilderness travel activities; and discourage high-impact types such as sporting and social activities, use of motorised vehicles, and accommodation involving building and engineering construction.

Introduction

Tourism is now a major international industry. One sector of the industry which is growing particularly fast is tourism and recreation in natural areas, where the tourist attraction is provided by relatively undisturbed natural environments. National parks and conservation reserves are subject to increasing levels of tourism and recreation, firstly because recreation in natural areas is becoming ever more popular, and secondly because real funding for the management and maintenance of conservation reserves has fallen so that reserve managers have been forced to seek alternative sources of funds.

Good environmental planning and management is particularly crucial in natural-areas tourism because environmental impacts are not external to the industry, as they are in the case of most primary production and secondary manufacturing industries; but internal and indeed central to the economic base of the industry itself. If well planned and managed, natural-areas tourism is potentially an industry with extremely low environmental impact, and high and indefinitely sustainable economic return. If poorly planned and run, however, the reverse will be true: high environmental impact, low and short-term economic return. Whilst individual corporations can certainly extract large profits from short-term non-sustainable tourist development in natural areas, such an approach will rapidly destroy the resource base for the green tourist industry as a whole, to say nothing of its impacts on domestic recreation and on cultural and environmental heritage.

Management of tourism and recreation in natural areas must consider three main issues, as follows:

1. Zoning: which areas should be used solely for tourism, which for tourism and other uses contemporaneously, and which solely for conservation and other uses?
2. Intensity of use: how many people, engaged in what activities, can be accommodated in a given area without environmental degradation?
3. Multiple-use management: how can reserve areas be managed so as to generate a net economic return from tourism and recreation without compromising their primary use for conservation?

Planning in any of these areas needs information on the relationship between the numbers, activities and behaviour of visitors, and the environmental impacts they produce; questions of response sensitivity and thresholds. The most reliable way to obtain such information is to examine what impacts have actually occurred in the past.

Previous reviews by El-Hinnawi and Hashmi (1982), Holdgate et al. (1982) and Duffield and Walker (1984) identified broad areas of potential concern but found few specific examples to report. Tourism has still not received a great deal of attention from academic ecologists, but a substantial body of information is now available from scientists and managers responsible for parks and reserve areas.

Impacts on the Natural Environment

Impacts on the natural environment may usefully be considered in three main categories: those associated with transport and travel; those associated with accommodation or shelter; and those associated with recreational activities per se. Major impacts on the physical and biological environment in each of these categories are summarised in Tables 1–3.

In addition to these primary impacts, a wide range of secondary impacts can also occur. As one common example, many conservation areas are traversed by tracks, which may provide service access for fire fighting, garbage removal, provision of firewood etc.; or which may predate the declaration of the reserve. These tracks, even if not formally open to the public, provide access to vehicles and people. Such uncontrolled access is particularly significant in large remote areas which typically have too few rangers for adequate surveillance. Continued use of these tracks by vehicles causes soil erosion and compaction, prevents the regrowth of vegetation, introduces weeds and fungal pathogens, and increases fire risks. In some cases, erosion as a result of uncontrolled vehicle access may eventually render the tracks impassable for service vehicles, so that, for example, the tracks are no longer serviceable for fire fighting. Besides the direct impacts of vehicles, people using these tracks may light fires, intentionally or unintentionally; shoot wildlife; damage vegetation at casual campsites; and collect firewood: which in turn can lead to a decline in vegetation productivity and soil nutrient status, changes in the vegetation both as a floristic assemblage and as fauna habitat, and damage to plants both directly and by increased suscepti-bility to pests and pathogens (Huxtable 1987).

Secondary impacts can also arise from attempts to mitigate primary impacts. For example, heavily used walking trails commonly suffer erosion and downcutting. They are then widened into multiple trails as pedestrians avoid the eroded areas. To prevent further erosion, managers may "harden" the track by installing paving, duckboarding, or similarly made paths. In addition to the visual impacts of such paths on visitor experience, track construction may also produce additional impacts on the natural environment. For example a heavily used walking track in an alpine park in Australia was recently paved and gravelled. Besides forming a conspicuous and intrusive visual scar, the track is now flanked by introduced weeds. Presumably, those responsible for providing the gravel had omitted to sterilise it, so that it still contained weed seeds; and

Table 1. Environmental impacts of transport and travel[a]

Means of transport/ travel	Vegetation clearance or damage[1]	Soil erosion or compaction[1]	Wildlife disturbance, shooting or habitat destruction[6]	Solid wastes
Light planes, helicopters	Airstrips only	Airstrips only	Depends on speed, altitude, frequency of flights	Empty fuel drums at remote strips
Bus or car on road	Roads and verges cleared	Compaction and erosion on unsealed roads	Noise depends on traffic density; roads can act as barriers; road kills	Litter
Car or 4-wheel drive on tracks	Tracks cleared; tend to be widened and new tracks out	Dust, gully erosion and compaction widespread	Road kills, noise shooting	Litter
Off-road vehicles off track[2]	Severe and extensive vegetation damage	Erosion widespread, depends on terrain and soil type	Widespread noise disturbance; ORV's used for shooting	Litter, human wastes
Mountain bikes	Less severe than ORV's	Localised in heavily use areas	Distrubance in heavily use areas	Litter, human wastes
Horses[3]	Trampling on horse trails	Localised, trails and holding paddocks	Minimal, unless riders rowdy or shooters	Horse manure
Hiking[4]	Trampling on heavily used trails	Localised on heavily used areas	Generally minimal	Human wastes
Power boats[5]	Campsites, shoreline and aquatic vegetation	Not applicable	Noise, fishing and shooting	Garbage at campsites, jetsam
Unpowered watercraft	Generally none	Not applicable	Fishing only	Garbage and jetsam

[a] Numbers in parentheses indicate the following references:
(1) Ovington et al. (1973); Liddle (1975); Edwards (1977); Keane et al. (1979); Ingram 1980; Calais (1981); Calais (1982); Pitts (1982); Upitis (1982); Mackay (1983); Chape and Chalmers (1984); Gibson (1984); Ringewaldt (1984); Bayley-Stark (1985); Brandis and

Table 1 (*continued*)

Water pollution[7]	Air pollution	Noise[8]	Increased fire risk	Weeds and fungi[9]
–	–	Loud, but intermittent	Little or none	Airstrips only
Petroleum residues in runoff from roads	Exhaust fumes	Line source, volume depends on traffic density	Sparks, cigarette butts	Along road verges
Turbid runoff	Exhaust fumes	As above	Sparks, cigarette butts	Along track verges
Campsites only: bacteria, soap	Exhaust fumes	Major impact, since ORV's can enter otherwise quiet areas	Sparks, butts, campfires	Spread on tyres
Campsites only: bacteria, soap	None	Voices only	Butts, campfires	Spread on tyres
Nutrients, bacteria, downstream of holding paddocks	None unless very crowded	Voices only	Butts, campfires	Spread in fodder if carried
Campsites only: bacteria, soap	None	Voices only	Butts, campfires	Minimal, on boots and socks
Fuel residues, nutrients, bacteria, antifouling paints	Exhaust fumes	Engine noise	Campsites only	Campsites only
Bacteria, soap	None	Voices only	Campsites only	Campsites only

Batini (1985); Cook (1985); Calais and Kirkpatrick (1986); Kuss (1986); Liddle and Thyer (1986); Neyland (1986); O'Loughlin (1988); Brown (1988); Gillen (1989), Snelson (undated); Gillieson et al. (undated). (2) Alexander (1981); Kay (1981); Pech and Graetz (1982); SADEP (1984); Sanpws (1983); Brown (1988); TDLPW (1979); (3) Snelson

Table 2. Environmental impacts of accommodation and shelter[a]

Type of accommodation or shelter	Vegetation clearance or damage[1]	Soil erosion and/or compaction[1]	Wildlife disturbance or habitat destruction[6]	Firewood collection and campfires[10]
Resorts, hotels				
Construction	Site clearance	Short term, during construction	Habitat cleared, noise	
Continuing	Tracks, etc.	Unsealed tracks, etc.	Shyer species leave area	Collected elsewhere, if used
Fixed car or caravan camps[11]	Site clearance initially and continuing, tracks, etc.	If ungrassed and increasing with use	Habitat clearance, shyer species leave area	Large area often denuded
Overnight car/4WD camps[11]	Increasing with use	Increasing with use	Depends on frequence of use	Large campfires common
Horse/hiker huts	Local site clearance, trampling	Localised, depends on soil type, etc.	Minor, localised	Large area often affected, regular large campfires
Boat-access shore sites	Increasing with use	Bank erosion	Minor, localised	Large area often affected, regular large campfires
Often-used bush camps[11]	Localised, new tent sites	Localised, depends on soil type, etc.	Minor, localised	Depends on vegetation type: large area may be affected
Single-use camps and bivouacs	Minimal or none	Generally none	Temporary or none	Minimal or none

[a] Numbers in parentheses indicate references, see Footnote to Table 1. Additional observations by RB.

(undated). (4) Helgath (1975); Leonard and Plumley (1979); Kay and Liddle (1984); SANPWS (1984); NSWNPWS (1985); ANPWS (1986a). (5) SADEP (1984); Bayly-Stark (1985); Cook (1985); ANPWS (1986b), Nichols (1988). (6) Busack and Bury 1974; Barnett et al. (1978). (7) Pitts (1982); Brown (1988); O'Loughlin (1988); TDLPW (1988); Gillen (1989), Snelson (undated); Peerless (undated). (8) SADEP (1984); VNPWS (1987);

Table 2 (*continued*)

Solid wastes[12]	Water pollution[7]	Noise[8]	Visual[13]
Construction rubbish, builders' rubble;	Sediments	Construction plant	Construction site and plant
Garbage treated sewage	Sullage, increased nutrients	Machinery and motors	Conspicuous buildings and infrastructure, large vehicles
Garbage, litter, toilets	Sullage, increased nutrients, bacterial	Generators, car engines, chainsaws, radios, voices	Vehicles, caravans, large tents, equipment, campfires
Litter, human wastes	Bacterial, soap	Car engines, chainsaws, radios, voices	Cars, large tents, campfires
Litter, horse dung, human wastes	Bacterial	Saws, voices	Huts, cleared paddocks, campfires
Litter, fish guts, human wastes	Petroleum residues	Outboard motors, voices	Boats, large tents, fires, clearance
Some paper, human wastes	Bacterial, soap	Voices	Small tents, fires
Generally none	Generally none	Minimal or none	Minimal and temporary

Williams (1988); Gillen (1989); Peerless (undated); Snelson (undated). (9) Brandis and Battini (1985); Neyland (1986). (10) Lewis (1978); SANPWS (1983); SADEP (1984); NSWNPWS (1985); Huxtable (1987); VNPWS (1987); TDLPW (1988); Gillen (1989). (11) Leeson (1979); Cole (1981); Pitts (1982); ANPWS (1986a, b); Brown (1988); O'Loughlin (1988). (12) NSWNPWS (1985); Brown (1988); TDLPW (1988); Gillen (1989). (13) ANPWS 1986a; Williams (1988).

Table 3. Environmental impacts of recreational activities in natural areas

Type of activity	Accommodation or shelter	Travel and transport in recreation area	Additional impacts
Principally sporting "excitement" activities			
Downhill skiing	Resorts or lodges	Skis	Ski lifts
Kayaking	Tents	Kayaks	–
Sailing	Yachts	Yachts	–
Biking	Tents or lodges	Cars, bikes	–
Climbing	Tents or huts	Cars, feet	–
Caving	CAves or camps	Cars, feet	Cave fauna
Hunting (game)	Hotels or huts	ORV's or feet	Loss of wildlife
Shooting (birds)	Hotels or camps	Cars, boats	Loss of wildlife
ORV's	Hotels or camps	ORV's	
Principally naturalist "contemplation" activities			
Resort stays	Resorts, hotels	Cars, coaches	Ill-informed
Plane safaris	Resorts, hotels	Planes	sightseers;
Coach tours	Resorts, hotels	Coaches	Vandalism to
4WD safaris	Tents, camps	4WD vehicles	archaelogical,
Horse safaris	Tents	Horses	cultural and natural
Canoe safaris	Tents or huts	Canoes	heritage areas
Ski touring	Tents or huts	Skis	
Bushwalking	Tents or huts	Feet	
Birdwatching, etc.	Various	Feet	
Fishing	Various	Boats, powered or otherwise	

the disturbance to the track margins provided a suitable habitat and
opportunity for these seeds to germinate and establish. The secondary
impact, namely introduction of weeds, is arguably much more severe than
the primary impact, namely downcutting of pedestrian tracks. As another
example, Hamilton-Smith (1987) reported that a moisture-proof door
installed at a cave reserve in Australia to minimise damage to the cave
walls and aboriginal paintings, caused the local extinction of a relatively
uncommon cave insect.

The precise impacts of different types of travel and recreational activity also depend on local environmental parameters such as aspect, steepness, soil type and vegetation. Trampling causes more erosion on some soils than others, for example. Human wastes are more likely to create problems in areas with thin soils; and pollution from human wastes is more likely to be significant in highly oligotrophic waters such as those of montane or sandy freshwater streams.

Besides impacts on the biological and physical environment, recreational activities may also produce detrimental impacts on the human environment. Such impacts fall in to three main categories. The first includes damage to archaeological sites and materials such as cave walls, rock art and carvings (Pitts 1982; ANPWS 1986a; Gale and Jacobs 1987; Kiernan 1987); and souveniring and vandalism (Gale and Jacobs 1987; Gillen 1989). The second major category of impacts is cultural, and includes breaking cultural rules, e.g. by trespassing on sites or photographing paintings of special significance, or engaging in culturally offensive behaviour of various types (Pitts 1982; ANPWS 1986a; Gale and Jacobs 1987; Gale et al. 1988; Gillen 1989, Snelson undated). Such impacts may be deliberate, or more often, occur through ignorance. The third category is of impacts on local residents, generally through heavy use of infrastructure.

Impacts on Visitor Experience

Surveys of visitors to natural areas show that they expect and want such areas to have little or no development (Downing and Clarke 1979; Buckley and Pannell 1990). Visual impacts, noise and crowding are common sources of complaint, and environmental damage even more so (Frissel and Duncan 1965; Stankey 1973; Badger 1975; Lee 1975; Clarke and Stankey 1979; Lucas 1979; Vaske et al. 1982; Buckley and Pannell 1990). Many of these complaints reflect conflicts between different groups of visitors, notably the asymmetrical conflicts between those who use mechanised means of transport and those who do not (Lucas 1964; Jacob and Schreyer 1980; Adelman et al. 1982; Dellora et al. 1984). These concerns, however, are often disguised by recreational succession (Ovington et al. 1973; Pitts 1982; Prosser 1986; VNPWS 1987): as the number and density of visitors at a particular site increase, and the characteristics of that area change in consequence, the type of people visiting the area, and their expectations, enjoyment and requirements, change over time.

Those who have come to the area to enjoy wilderness pursuits based on the enjoyment of undisturbed natural environments are replaced by those who have come to enjoy sports or outdoor social activities. Visitor surveys may thus still indicate that visitors to the area are content with current conditions; but they are not the same visitors. Those who visited the area in its earlier, more pristine state, dissatisfied with changing conditions, simply no longer go there. This makes it extremely difficult to monitor deterioration in the quality of visitor experience in any given area.

Management

Requirements for improving management of tourism and recreation in national parks and conservation reserves fall into two main categories: information and action. The first requirement is baseline information and resource inventory, not only in the reserve areas themselves, but for other natural areas within the region or country as a whole. This is necessary to assess the significance of potential environmental degradation within particular areas. The second requirement is to monitor environmental change, both that due to natural causes such as fires and rainfall variations, and that due to anthropogenic factors such as visitor pressure, feral animals and weeds, and land use in neighbouring areas. Linked with such monitoring of environmental changes, we need to monitor the numbers, types and behaviours of visitors to different parts of each reserve area, taking account of seasonal variations. From these types of information, reserve managers can identify specific management problems and issues which require action.

Management action can be considered in four main categories: regulation and surveillance, incentives, protection and education. Different types and levels of regulation are required at different scales in space and time. At national and regional scales, this approach can involve overall land-use planning for conservation, tourism and recreation, and other land uses. At the scale of individual reserves for natural areas, it can include tools such as general guidelines for tourist development in natural areas, and zoning for different uses in different parts of a reserve area. In the case of zoning, it is important to ensure that activities in one zone do not impinge on the planned functions of another. As a common example, tourist development and recreation in the upstream part of a catchment may adversely affect water quality in the downstream region; so if the latter has been zoned purely for conservation, it may suffer water quality deterioration even though there are no recreational activities in the conservation zone itself. Regulations can also be used to control the numbers of visitors entering a particular area in any given time period, their access points, and the types of activities they may undertake. To ensure that such regulations are actually effective, however, requires some form of deterrent if they are breached, such as a fine or other penalty; it also requires surveillance to detect such breaches. Surveillance – typically by rangers – requires time, personnel and resources which can eat heavily into the reserve manager's limited budget.

The activities of visitors, and the resulting impacts on the natural and human environment, can often be controlled more effectively by incentive systems than by regulation. As one very obvious example, if a given area is intended for conservation and low-impact wilderness recreation, then it is important to avoid any form of development which encourages non-wilderness recreation. Facilities for non-wilderness recreation and sports, such as, e.g., tennis courts, barbeques, golf courses, trail bike areas and ski lifts, should be placed outside wilderness areas.

Where high visitor numbers are perceived as desirable or inevitable, one management option is to protect or harden the areas concerned so as to minimise the impacts produced. Common examples might include paving of roads and tracks, installation of duckboarding along heavily used pedestrian routes and walking tracks, and provision of firewood, fireplaces and toilet facilities at heavily used campsites. Such hardening, however, tends to accelerate recreational succession.

The fourth major management option is education (Busher 1979; Geist 1979; O'Loughlin 1988). In wilderness areas this may be the only option; and it can be very effective (O'Loughlin 1988). Often the public does not appreciate the environmental impacts it may be causing in conservation areas (Huxtable 1987). In general, visitors to conservation areas react positively to the provision of on-site information, modifying their behaviour to reduce environmental impacts (Gale et al. 1988); though there will always be exceptions. There are many different avenues for environmental education associated with tourism and recreation. The most immediate is on-site: in the form of leaflets, posters, displays and signs. Other avenues include in-flight videos on inbound aircraft; TV, radio and printed media; the design and adoption of environmental policies by individual tourist corporations and the tourist industry as a whole; displays at local community centres; and the introduction of environmental education in school and university curricula.

Discussion and Conclusions

There is very little published information on the environmental impacts of natural-areas tourism and recreation, even in designated national parks and conservation reserves. The expert knowledge of reserve managers, gained through experience with the reserves concerned over a substantial period of time, would perhaps remedy this deficiency. It would not be easy to compile, however, and it is unlikely to be quantitative.

Since the demand for natural-areas recreation and tourism is increasing, and the supply of natural areas is not, it is realistic to assume that levels of tourism and recreation in parks and reserves will continue to increase in the immediate future. Informed management to minimise the impacts of such tourist pressure is therefore particularly important; and this requires information on the relationship between visitor numbers and activities, and their impacts on particular types of environment. Research in this field will therefore be critical to the successful management of our parks and reserves.

Meanwhile, some general principles may be stated as follows. Multiple-use management in parks and reserves should be restricted to uses which do not compromise the primary objective of conservation. Use of reserve areas as water catchments is one possibility, as long as dams and other storage systems are downstream of the reserve area. Some types of tourism and recreation are also acceptable, but others are not; and those which are, need to be confined to particular zones of the reserve areas, so that their impacts do not spill into zones intended for conservation per se. To minimise environmental impacts of tourism and recreation requires a combination of planning and regulation, incentives to encourage particular activities and discourage others, physical hardening of areas receiving highest visitor pressure, and education both on-site and elsewhere. The question of incentives is of particular concern in a number of current tourist development proposals. Parks and reserves are suitable only for low-impact recreation, such as those based on wilderness travel and natural history tours, etc. High-impact recreation such as sporting and social activities, the use of motorised vehicles and large-scale engineering and building construction should be discouraged in parks and reserves. It is thus inappropriate for tourist developments in park and reserve areas to include facilities such as large hotels, conspicuous cable cars and ski lifts, tennis courts and golf courses, or marinas or water ski areas.

It should not be necessary to argue these points in relation to every tourist development proposal in park and reserve areas. Generic guidelines for natural-areas tourist development, adopted and adhered to by national governments and promulgated to all local government authorities, could overcome problems associated with the current piecemeal and ad hoc approach to natural-areas tourist development in most of the world.

Acknowledgements. This essay arose from a review carried out on my behalf by Mr. John Pannell at the Centre for Resource and Environmental Studies, Australian National University. A previous version was published jointly in the *Journal of Tourism Studies* in 1990.

References

Adelman BJ, Heberlein TA, Bonnicksen TM (1982) Social psychological explanations for the persistence of a conflict between paddling canoeists and motorcraft users in the Boundary Waters canoe area. Leisure Sci 5:45–62

Alexander L (1981) Conservation and exploration: a case study of the Simpson Desert Conservation Park. M Env Stud Thesis, Centre for Environmental Studies, University of Adelaide, Adelaide, Australia

ANPWS (1986a) Uluru (Ayers Rock-Mount Olga) National Park management plan. Australian National Parks and Wildlife Service, Canberra

ANPWS (1986b) Kakadu National Park management plan. Australian National Parks and Wildlife Service, Canberra

Badger TJ, (1975) Rawah wilderness crowding tolerances and some management techniques: an aspect of social carrying capacity. MSc Thesis, Colorado State University, Fort Collins

Barnett JL, How RA, Humphreys WF (1978) The use of habitat components by small mammals in eastern Australia. Aust J Ecol 3:277–285

Bayley-Stark J (1985) Wave action and bank erosion. Aust Ranger Bull 3(3):27

Brandis T, Batini F (1985) Dieback on the south coast. Landscape 1(2)

Brown ID (1988) Managing vehicular recreation in the national parks of the Blue Mountains. Aust Ranger Bull 5(1):17–19

Buckley RC, Pannell J (1990) Environmental impacts of tourism and recreation in national park and conservation reserves. J Tour Stud 1:24–32

Busack SD, Bury RB (1974) Some effects of off-road vehicles and sheep grazing on lizard populations in the Majave Desert. Biol Conserv 6:179–183

Busher RF (1979) Wildland recreational impact from the US forest manager's perspective. Proc Conf, Recreational Impact on Wildlands. US Forest Service, Seattle, pp 11–13

Calais SS (1981) Analysis of visitor impact on the environments of the Cradle Mountain-Lake St. Clair National Park and implications for recreational management. Unpubl MSc thesis, Department of Geography, University of Tasmania

Calais SS (1982) Management of tracks in the Cradle Mountain-Lake St. Clair National Park. Proc Natural Area Management National Workshop, Tasmania. Tasmania National Parks and Wildlife Service, and Royal Australian Institute of Parks and Recreation. TNPWS, Hobart

Calais SS, Kirkpatrick JB (1986) Impact of trampling on natural ecosystems in the Cradle Mountain-Lake St. Clair National Park. Aust Geog 17:6–15

Chape S, Chalmers C (1984) Tourism and the role of coastal management planning in Western Australia. Aust Ranger Bull 2(4):5–6

Clarke RN, Stankey GH (1979) Determining the acceptability of recreational impacts: an application of the outdoor recreation opportunity spectrum. Proc Conf, Recreational Impact on Wildlands. US Forest Service, Seattle, pp 32–42

Cole DN (1981) Managing ecological impacts at wilderness camp-sites: an evaluation of techniques. J For 79:86–89

Cook C (1985) Tourist boats erode banks of Gordon River. Aust Ranger Bull 3(3):26–27

Dellora G, Martin B, Saunders R (1984) Motorised recreational vehicles: perception and recreational conflict. Grad Sch Environ Sci, Monash Univ, Environ Rep 17. Monash University, Melbourne

Downing K, Clark RM (1979) Users' and managers' perceptions of dispersed recreation impacts: a focus on roaded forest lands. Proc Conf, Recreational Impact on Wildlands. US Forest Service, Seattle, pp 18–23

Duffield BS, Walker SE (1984) The assessment of tourism impacts. In: Bissett R, Tomlinson P (eds) Perspectives on environmental impact assessment. WHO/Reidel, Dordrecht, pp 479–515

Edwards IJ (1977) The ecological impact of pedestrian traffic on alpine vegetation in Kosciusko National Park. Aust For 40:108–120

El-Hinnawi E, Hashmi M (1982) Tourism and the environment. UNEP Nat Resour Environ Ser 7:221–232

Frissell SS Jr, Duncan DP (1965) Campsite preference and deterioration in the Quetico-Superior canoe country. J For 63:256–260

Gale F, Jacobs J (1987) Tourists and the national estate. Australian Heritage Commission, Special Aust Heritage Publications Series, No 6 AGPS, Canberra

Gale F, Gillen J, Scott K (1988) Tourist impact on aboriginal cultural sites in the Flinders Ranges in South Australia. Report to Michael Williams and Assoc and Roger Luebbers, Dept of Geography, University of Adelaide, Adeleide, Australia

Geist V (1979) A philosophical look at recreational impact on wildlands. In: Conference Proc Conf, Recreational Impact on Wildlands. US Forest Service, Seattle, pp 1–7

Gibson N (1984) Impact of trampling on bolster heath communities of Mount Field National Park, Tasmania. Proc R Soc Tas 118:47–52

Gillen JS (1989) Coongie Lakes study: visitor studies – full report. Report to South Australia Department of Environment and Planning, Adelaide

Gillieson D, Davies J, Hardey P (undated) Gurragorambla Creek horse track monitoring; Kosciusko National Park. Department of Geography and Oceanography, Australian Defence Force Academy, and NSW National Parks and Wildlife Service, Canberra

Hamilton-Smith E (1987) "Karst Kreatures": the fauna of the Australian karst. Aust Ranger Bull 4(3): 9–10

Helgath SF (1975) Trail deterioration in the Selway-Bitterroot wilderness. USDA For Ser Res Pap Note INT – 193

Holdgate M, Kassas M, White G (1982) Tourism. In: Holdgate M, Kassas M, White G (eds) The world environment 1972–1982. Nat Resour Environ Ser 8:544–560, UNEP/ Tycooly, Dublin

Huxtable D (1987) The environmental impact of firewood collection for campfires, and appropriate management strategies. South Australian College of Advanced Education, Salisbury

Ingram C (1980) United Nations list of national parks and equivalent reserves. International Union for Conservation of Nature and Natural Resources Committee on National Parks and Protected Areas. UNEP/UNESCO, Paris

Jacob GR, Schreyer R (1980) Conflict in outdoor recreation: a theoretical perspective. J Leisure Res 12:368–380

Kay AM, Liddle MJ (1984) Tourist impact on reef corals. Report to Great Barrier Reef Marine Park Authority. GBRMPA, Townsville

Kay J (1981) Evaluating environmental impacts of off-road vehicles. J Geogr 80:10–18

Keane PA, Wild AER, Rogers JH (1979) Trampling and erosion in alpine country. J Soil Conserv Serv NSW 35:7–12

Kiernan K (1987) Soils and cave management. Aust Ranger Bull 4(3):6–7

Kuss FR (1986) A review of major factors influencing plant responses to recreation impacts. Environ Manage 19:637–650

Lee RG (1975) The management of human components in the Yosemite National Park ecosystem. The Yosemite Institute, Yosemite, California

Leeson BF (1979) Research on wildland recreation impact in the Canadian Rockies. Proc Conf Recreational Impact on Wildlands. US Forest Service, Seattle

Leonard RE, Plumley HJ (1979) Information for dispersal recreation planning. Proc Conf, Recreational Impact on Wildlands. US Forest Service, Seattle, pp 50–63

Lewis MM (1978) Quantitative studies of arid zone recreational impacts. M Env Stud Thesis, University of Adelaide, Adelaide, Australia

Liddle MJ (1975) A selective review of the ecological effects of human trampling on natural ecosystems. Biol Conserv 7:17–35

Liddle MJ, Thyer NC (1986) Trampling and fire in subtropical dry sclerophyll forest. Environ Conserv 13:33–39

Lucas RC (1964) The recreational capacity of the Questico-Superior area. USDA For Serv ResPap LS15. Lake States Forest Experiment Station, St. Paul, Minnesota

Lucas RC (1979) Perceptions of non-motorized recreational impacts: a review of research findings. Proc Conf, Recreational Impact on Wildlands. US Forest Service, Seattle, pp 24–31

Mackay J (1983) Summit walking track investigations. NSW National Parks and Wildlife Service, Kosciusko District

Marion JL (1987) Environmental impact management in the boundary waters canoe area wilderness. North J Appl Forest 4:7–11

Neyland M (1986) Tasmanian world heritage area and *Phytophthora cinnamomi*. Aust Ranger Bull 3(4):6

Nichols Jean A (1988) Antifouling paints: use on boats in San Diego Bay and a way to minimise adverse impacts. Environ Manage 12:243–246

NSW National Parks and Wildlife Service (NSWNPWS) (1985) Mount warning national park plan of management. NSWNPWS, Sydney

OECD (1980) The impact of tourism on the environment. OECD, Washington

O'Loughlin T (1988) Wilderness education project report. Report to Tasmania Department of Lands, Parks and Wildlife and the Australian National Parks and Wildlife Service. TDLPW, Hobart

Ovington JD, Groves KW, Stevens PR, Tanton MT (1973) A study of the impact of tourism at Ayers Rock – Mount Olga National Park. AGPS, Canberra

Pech RP, Graetz RD (1982) Use and management of the land resources of the southern Simpson Desert; issues and options. CSIRO Rangelands Res Cent Tech Mem 82/1.CSIRO, Deniliquin

Peerless H (undated) Tourism and the natural environment: analysis of the conflict; with special reference to Cape Range National Park and Ningaloo Marine Park. Western Australia Department of Conservation and Land Management, Perth

Pitts DJ (1982) Carnarvon National Park: a case study of management response to changing use pressures. Proc Natural Area Management National Workshop, Tasmania (unnumbered). Tasmania National Parks and Wildlife Service, and Royal Australian Institute of Parks and Recreation. TNPWS, Hobart

Prosser G (1986) The limits of acceptable change: an introduction to a framework for natural area planning. Aust Parks Recr 22(2):5–10

Ringewaldt D (1984) Firewood usage in Parks. Aust Ranger Bull 3(1):11

South Australia, Department of Environment and Planning (SADEP) (1984) Coorong National Park and Game Reserve Plan of Management. SADEP, Adelaide

Snelson D (undated) Horse-riding management in Ku-ring-gai Chase National Park (pamphlet). NSW National Parks and Wildlife Service, Sydney

South Australia, National Parks and Wildlife Service (SANPWS) (1983) Flinders Ranges National Park Management Plan. SANPWS, Adelaide

Stankey GH (1973) Visitor perceptions of wilderness recreation carrying capacity. USDA For Serv Res Pap INT-142. Ogden, Utah

Tasmania, Department of Lands, Parks and Wildlife, (TDLPW) (1988) Cradle Mountain – Lake St. Clair National Park management plan. TDLPW, Hobart

Upitis A (1982) Track management in national parks. A case study: Ku-ring-gai Chase National Park. Proc Natural Area Management National Workshop, Tasmania (unnumbered). Tasmania National Parks and Wildlife Service, and Royal Australian Institute of Parks and Recreation. TNPWS, Hobart

Vaske JJ, Graefe AR, Dempster AB (1982) Social and environmental influences on perceived crowding. Proc Wilderness Psychology Group Conf Morgantown, West Virginia

Victoria, National Parks and Wildlife Service, (VNPWS) (1987) Wilson's promotory national park management plan. VNPWS, Melbourne

Williams M (1988) Proposed Wilpena Station Resort, Flinders Ranges National Park: draft amendment to the Flinders Ranges National Park management plan and draft environmental impact statement. South Australia, National Parks and Wildlife Service, Adelaide

Yuskavitch J (1984) Sands of contention. Amer For 90:17–23

Zaslowsky D (1981) Looking into soles and other weighty matters. Audubon 83(3):60–63

Chapter 14
Environmental Implications of Development Aid

Abstract

We in the developed western nations need to conserve the world's biological resources for our own sake, and yet these resources are mostly in the Third World. As one of the few tools we have is development aid, I argue that a large proportion of development aid should go to projects whose principal aim is environmental protection in developing countries. Our aid budgets are for billion of dollars, or their equivalent, every year; contributed directly by taxpayers. So we should have some say in how aid funds are spent.

Pressures on Biological Resources

Most of the world's remaining biological resources are in less developed countries; in tropical rain-forests and rivers and so on. We in the developed world need those species for their genetic diversity, for breeding pest resistance in crops, for pharmaceuticals, for foods and textiles and so on. We also value them for reasons beyond our immediate needs. People in less developed countries also need them, for their immediate and future livelihood: food, water, clothing, fuel and shelter.

These biological resources, however, are being consumed and degraded at an ever increasing rate. There are three separate sets of pressures, and we need to distinguish them. The first is from subsistence farmers – poor locals, to be blunt. Their first concern is day-to-day survival, and if that means clearing forests for small holdings and stock, or cutting down every available stick for fuelwood, then so be it. These are the people that aid is supposed to benefit, if it ever gets to them.

The second pressure is from Third World businessmen and politicians: rich locals. Powerful and often unscrupulous people, who use their nations' resources to enrich their own pockets. These include government ministers, for example, who grant logging concessions to companies in which they themselves have a large stake, forcing poor and less sophisticated indigenous peoples out of the forests to become "internal refugees".

The third pressure is from the so-called multi-nationals: companies owned by interests in the developed nations, which extract resources from less developed countries and sell them in the developed world. Whatever the resource – animal, vegetable, or mineral – it is almost always treated as a single hit exploitation, rather than managed for a sustained yield. Dug, cut, shot and sold. Even cattle farming, for example, which in developed nations is ostensibly managed for sustained yield, is a much shorter term proposition in the so-called hamburger pastures of the tropics.

The Development Aid Game

Let us turn to aid. Aid is not just rich people in rich countries giving a handout to poor people in poor countries. It is a highly complex political and economic game. While the humanitarian element is there, it is certainly not the only only motive of all the players.

There are two kinds of aid: relief aid and development aid. Relief aid is when we rush food and medicines to scenes of famine or flood. It is true that it does not always work very well in practice. There is a tendency for officials in the recipient nations to appropriate the supplies and sell them at scalper's prices. And by reducing deaths from so-called natural disasters, relief aid seems to produce countries with ever larger populations, still starving, and ever more dependent on yet more relief aid. But at least the intent is humanitarian.

Development aid is different. It is supposed to help developing countries develop – like us. We contrast "developing" economies, based on primary industry and export of raw materials, with "developed" economies such as our own, which have much larger manufacturing and tertiary sectors, and harder currencies. So development aid in nations such as India or China is generally aimed at increasing production and manufacturing.

In many less developed countries, however, only a relatively small elite has access to the cash economy: the bulk of the population relies on an entirely separate subsistence economy. In these countries, development aid is aimed at converting the subsistence economy to a cash one. Planting cash crops instead of subsistence food crops, for example, or logging forests rather than living in them. Power-brokers in less developed countries like this because most of the cash finds its way to them.

So it could well be said that development aid is a process by which poor people in rich countries make compulsory donations to rich people in poor countries. But aid is also used as a political and economic tool by government and industry in both developed and less developed countries. Both the USA and USSR effectively rent land for their military bases with aid, for example. Pacific Island nations have found that a simple way to get more aid money from the West is to hold "trade" talks with the USSR.

A less direct but far more widespread linkage is between aid and trade. For example, the developed western nations often provide aid to start or expand production of a particular commodity, which they then buy. But it is governments which give aid, while private companies buy commodities; the aid game involves political and economic lobbying as well as humanitarian motives.

It is more complicated than that, however. Most of the "development" money flowing into the less developed countries is not aid at all. It is loans: either from commercial banks, or from multi-lateral lending agencies (MLA's) such as the World Bank. In order to repay these loans, or even the interest, the less developed countries need cash; so they will clamour for aid to help develop primary industries which yield short-term cash returns.

This means that development aid does not necessarily help subsistence farmers. In fact, it may leave them worse off, if they are displaced by big new development projects. Development aid helps rich locals more than poor locals. These national get-rich-quick schemes often have very serious environmental costs: denuded landscapes, eroded soils, polluted air and water, extinct species. In the short term these environmental costs are borne by the poor rural population, not the rich, urban elite.

In countries such as India, Korea and China, for example, where recent development has taken the form of break-neck industrialisation, there has been massive and widespread air and water pollution. "Industrialise now, clean up later" was the policy. But these countries are now realising too late – just as we have done – that "cleaning up" is expensive, difficult or impossible. Again, it is the poor – in this case the urban poor – who bear the main brunt of this pollution. But in the long-term, these environmental costs are borne by the whole world – including we taxpayers in the developed nations who provide aid and loan funding.

To summarise: taxpayers in the developed Western nations pay for development aid, which helps rich officials in less developed countries sell their countries' natural resources cheaply to multi-national corporations, so they can pay off loans from multi-lateral lending agencies: and in the process rich Third World power brokers and corporation shareholders get richer, the Third World poor end up little better or even worse off, staff in aid organisations and MLA's get promoted, and the world's remaining biological resources get degraded and depleted at ever-increasing rates.

Aid for Environmental Protection

What can we do about it? Third World governments argue that it is their sovereign right to exploit their countries' natural resources. But that does not mean we should abet them with aid. Clearly, the first thing we can do is to stop giving aid for environmentally damaging projects.

We can do more – but it means playing politics and economics, which are pretty much inseparable at a global scale. All suggestions will fail unless we can convince the governments concerned, through their political and economic power bases, that change is in their interests. In aid-recipient nations, these power bases vary widely – the military, big industries, international financial institutions – rarely the electorate. We cannot expect to influence them much.

We also have to bear in mind that Third World politicians do not like to be told what to do or what is good for them, and they especially do not like to be patronised. And we have to appreciate that most Third World governments do not really know what is happening in their own countries, particularly in terms of land use.

Where we can have some useful influence is in our own countries, the aid donor nations. Short-term exploitation of Third World biological resources does nothing for us, or indeed for our politicians, so they have nothing to lose by changing the aid policy in this regard. On the other hand, we in the developed nations will bear the cost of environmental degradation in the Third World. The warning signs are there, and we ignore them at our peril: pollution, soil erosion, forest clearance, species extinction and so on. We have to make environmental management in overseas aid into a hot political issue here at home.

That does not mean being anti-development or anti-industry. We all want economic prosperity and material well-being. But it means that we want environmental costs and benefits made explicit, and taken properly into account in development planning and management. And that means that we want our aid and trade policies, and government organisations which administer them, to use our tax dollars to help conserve those resources in the Third World – for our benefit – not to squander them for short-term gains by others.

We need better environmental assessment, planning and management of all our bilateral aid projects – the ones we fund directly. We need environmental accountability on the part of all the multi-lateral aid and lending agencies to which we contribute funds. Aid funds should be spent principally for environmental protection in recipient nations. That means aid with environmental strings.

We want our governments to tell politicians in less developed countries that they need to conserve their biological resources, and we need them to conserve their resources too. We know that they cannot always afford to protect them, and in fact they are under many pressures to exploit them. So we should give them aid specifically for environmental protection.

Pollution control equipment for power stations is one example; consultant expertise to help in regional environmental planning is another. Further examples include: scientific expertise to help define the country's best conservation areas and national parks; funds to train and pay staff to manage those parks, to guard them against degradation, and to help earn foreign exchange from tourism, and perhaps from sustained-yield harvesting of valuable plants and animals; funds to help control soil erosion, and so on.

One consideration here is that a lot of bilateral aid is "tied", meaning that the country which receives it has to spend it on goods and services from the country which provides it. Many companies in the aid-donor nations have a vested interest in continuing aid projects. All that needs to change is the purpose of those goods and services, or the type of project. There is no need for concern on the part of industry.

Of course, Third World politicians may not like aid for environmental protection. They would rather have cash. But we should make it clear – diplomatically, of course – that it is that or nothing. If they want our money, they should have it under our conditions. And I bet they will still take it. After all, it does not cost them anything.

There are also strategic considerations, as the less developed countries will turn to other countries for aid. Yet, I feel that taxpayers in most Western nations are tired of seeing their money spent on massive white elephant development projects that favour the rich over the poor, cause enormous environmental damage, rarely reap economic returns, and do absolutely no good to those taxpayers who gave up their hard-earned cash in the first place. It only needs one or two examples for most western nations to adopt a policy of aid for environmental protection.

Environmental Management in Aid Agencies

Now some practical details. The first thing is that all aid agency staff – not just the lower echelons of the aid bureaucracies, but the senior executives, too – need some training in why good environmental management is so important and how to incorporate it into their everyday operations. This has already begun in a small way, but must be expanded. The second thing is that every aid agency needs professional environmental scientists on its staff. Not just a token one or two, but a significant contingent. Preferably, they should form a distinct environmental unit responsible through a chief environmental scientist to the chief executive officer.

These environmental professionals should have three functions. First, they should be available to troubleshoot environmental problems on existing projects and future ones. Second, they should have routine inputs to all new aid projects and programme – from the earliest project concept, throughout the operational phases, to final monitoring and audit. And third and perhaps most important, they should be responsible for designing aid projects and programme whose primary purpose is environmental protection in the recipient nation.

That requires a major shift in policy, but a necessary one, because we should be directing most of our overseas aid to conservation of biological resources in less developed countries – for our own sake.

Acknowledgements. A previous version of this essay was broadcast by the Australian Broadcasting Commission on the programme "*Ockham's Razor*" in 1989. An edited transcript was printed in the Bulletin of the Centre for Resource and Environmental Studies, Australian National University.

Chapter 15
Trends in the 1990's

Public Environmental Awareness

Increasing public concern over global, national and local environmental management issues has produced a strong and growing contingent of green voters, green consumers and green investors. There is a growing public demand for active involvement in development decisions, and for individual personnel in industry and regulatory bodies to be held publicly accountable for their decisions and the consequences of their actions. There is also a trend towards direct action by community groups who feel that they have been unjustly overridden by development interests. This has happened recently in Japan, the USA, Canada and Australia, for example.

International Issues

An increasing number of environmental management problems are recognised as transnational or global in scope, requiring the exercise of international environmental diplomacy and the broadening and strengthening of international legal instruments of various types. These may affect domestic environmental legislation, and international trade. They include:

1. Atmospheric pollution problems such as the enhanced greenhouse effect, ozone hole and acid rain.
2. Pollution of the oceans, transnational lakes, and the icecaps.
3. Reduction of biodiversity through tropical deforestation and through overfishing.

Regional Emphasis

There is an increasing emphasis on regional environmental planning and total catchment management to overcome problems associated with ad hoc decisions, cross-project impacts, and cumulative impacts caused by a number of similar small developments in one area. Regional environmental planning approaches are also needed where parcels of similar land within a region are held under different types of tenure and land-use constraint. A number of states and nations are now adopting legislation which embodies these approaches.

Impacts on Industry

There is no sector of industry or commerce which is entirely insulated from these changes. Some sectors and companies are responding by lobbying against green trends; others are seizing new market opportunities.

For the mining, process and chemical industries, the immediate pressure is to reduce wastes: through process design, recycling and emission control. In engineering, the focus is on environmental design and technology. In the energy sector, there is a new emphasis on energy efficiency rather than energy generation. In infrastructure development, there is a similar emphasis on efficient use of resources, such as water. In agriculture, pastoralism, forestry and fisheries, there is increasing concern over management for sustainable yield. In the hospitality industry, the growth market is green tourism. In manufacturing and retail, products and packaging are shaped strongly by green consumers.

The finance sector is involved in several different ways. The first through changes in share prices: rising share prices for companies which successfully manufacture or retail either green consumer products, or recycling or pollution control technologies or processes; and falling share prices for resource development companies which fail to gain environmental planning approvals, or gain them only under stringent conditions. The second is through risks associated with lending to or insuring companies or projects with potential environmental liabilities: either because cash flows are delayed and no longer cover interest repayments, or because assets and securities lose value; or by direct transfer of statutory penalties or other liabilities to financiers or insurers. Thirdly, there is currently rapid growth in so-called green investment. And finally, the finance sector is increasingly involved in brokering environmental rights and credits of various kinds.

Opportunities for Business

In manufacturing and technology, there are new opportunities for business in designing energy-efficient and resource-efficient processes and plants; and in pollution control, waste treatment and recycling technology.

In the service sectors, there are increased environmental consulting opportunities for engineers, accountants, lawyers, economists and ecologists; in environmental design, audit, insurance and accounting.

Even in the finance sector, opportunities are likely to be created through domestic and international trading in resource and environmental credits of various kinds, as well as through green investment.

Commercial Risks

The legal and financial risks which industry and commerce face from poor environmental management have increased greatly and are continuing to do so (Chap. 8). They include penalties, asset forfeits, cleanup costs, compensation claims, forced closure, and compulsory plant upgrades; and lost market share, lower share prices, higher finance costs, reduced credit and higher insurance premiums.

Liability for environmental damages and degradation is being applied more and more widely and strictly. The trend is for liability to be applied:

1. Strictly: to all consequences of an action, even if it was neither illegal, deliberate, negligent nor reckless.
2. Jointly and severally: to all past and present owners and operators for the site(s) concerned, whether or not they actually caused environmental damage.
3. To individual directors and staff, as well as to corporations.

Owing to the increased financial risks and stricter application of liability, there is currently a very rapid growth in corporate environmental audit

(Chap. 7) and insurance (Chap. 8). These trends are likely to continue through the 1990's.

Economic Instruments

There is increasing emphasis on the use of market-based measures for environmental protection. These include taxes, charges, levies, bonds, tradeable or bankable permits and rights, and modifications to property rights (Chap. 5). Coupled with these are a variety of environmental accounting techniques (Chaps. 3, 4). Economic instruments of environmental policy can in theory be both efficient and equitable. They provide incentives for particular actions without removing individual freedom of choice. They generally need to be coupled with or supported by regulatory and technological instruments. From a policy viewpoint they can be used to deter environmentally damaging activities, improve social equity, raise revenue or recover public sector costs.

Property Rights

It has been suggested that if property rights in the environment were clearly defined, market processes would protect it. Briefly, there are two main conceptual approaches, which we may distinguish as public and private ownership respectively. The former is being used increasingly; the latter is advocated by some private sector economists, but has several serious difficulties.

The underlying philosophy for the public ownership approach is that a country's natural resources are owned jointly and equally by its citizens; and that democratic governments should ensure a reasonable return from any private use of those resources (Chap. 4). In calculating the expected return, all social costs and benefits must be taken into account, including environmental ones. Charges for the right to use public natural resources, either for consumption or for waste disposal, are justified by this approach; and are in fact becoming more and more widespread. The choice between economic instruments such as charges and tradeable rights, and purely regulatory "command and control" measures specifying standards and practices of various types, is seen purely as a question of efficiency and effectiveness rather than philosophy. An emission right gives its owner the right to pollute; but equally, so does an emission standard which does not need to be purchased.

The private ownership approach derives from economic theorists. They have considered examples such as water quality in a lake or river which is used both as a resource, whether for consumption or recreational enjoyment, and as a receptacle for effluents. In theory, as long as someone owns the water and can charge others to use it, then market processes should lead to a level of pollution with greatest aggregate benefit to all users, irrespective of which party is the owner. Unfortunately, this does not work in practice, since it ignores:

1. Benefits where the links between water quality and individual welfare are not understood: e.g., those associated with the maintenance of intact aquatic ecosystems.
2. Benefits for which there is non-rival consumption: e.g., good health due to the absence of disease-producing microorganisms.
3. Social equity and ability to pay.

Most importantly, it does not work for property rights which can be converted entirely to cash by destroying the resource concerned. Someone who owned a tract of forest, for example, would have no incentive to manage it for sustainable yield if it would be more profitable to clear-fell it, sell the timber and residual land for cash, and use the cash to buy another asset with high, short-term yield.

So assigning private property rights to components of the environment would not necessarily lead to improved environmental management, and should not be advocated except for specific tradeable rights and quotas.

Tax Reform

There is an urgent need for review and reform of national tax regimes in the context of environmental policy. Such reform should concentrate on three main issues:

1. New taxes which act as incentives for good environmental management.
2. Abolition of special grants and tax concessions encouraging poor environmental management.

3. Deductibility of expenditures on improved environmental management; perhaps coupled with concessional deductibility or rebatability in the short term.

With appropriate design and rates, such reform could be revenue-neutral for government and cost-neutral for industry, whilst encouraging investment and improving environmental management.

Conclusions

As the natural environment becomes steadily less green through human activity, the business environment is greener than ever before. Environmental issues are of major community and electoral concern worldwide. In consequence, environmental management is now a major component of any corporation's overall management, environmental markets, a significant component of its overall markets, and environmental strategy, an essential component of its overall strategy.

Acknowledgements. A previous version of this essay was presented to the Bureau of Industry Economics *Manufacturing Outlook Conference* and published as a guest editional in *Environmental and Planning Law Journal* in 1990.

Afterword

Environmental management is an extremely broad and dynamic field, involving a wide range of professions in science and engineering, humanities and social sciences, law and business. It is hard to predict how it is likely to change in the next few years. But what is clear is that it will become more and more important, as the planet's natural resources are stretched further and further by an ever-growing and demanding human population.

Many of the most pressing environmental management issues are now global in scale and immediate in urgency. Some were first identified by environmental scientists, others by members of conservation groups. Some may have technological solutions, and industry is good at finding these if the financial incentives are sufficient. Others, however, can only be solved by reducing consumption of natural resources. And financial incentives depend on regulation and market pressures, which are ultimately driven by individual citizens: e.g. green voters, green consumers, green investors.

Yet people are also the cause of the problems; and though our ever-increasing population and wasteful consumption is widely recognised as folly, people still have two, three, or more children, and still strive for greater industrialisation and economic growth. Everyone wants increased material well-being; everyone depends on a functioning global environment, but we can only have both if we limit our population. Without that, the best efforts of environmental planners and managers will ultimately be fruitless.

On a more optimistic note, however, I hope that in the meantime these essays may interest and inform both those currently working in environmental management, and those training to do so in future.

Index